# Those Early Days...
## A Pioneer History of Sedona and Vicinity

## *SEDONA – OAK CREEK*
and the
## *VERDE VALLEY REGION*
of
## *NORTHERN ARIZONA*

SEDONA WESTERNERS CO

Copyright © 1968, 1975, 2008 Sedona Westerners

All rights reserved. No part of this publication may be reproduced, stored in a retrieval system or transmitted in any form or by any means, electronic, mechanical, photocopying, recording or otherwise, without the prior written permission of the publisher.

Layout by William Levengood

Cover Design by Courtney Amato

Printed in the United States of America

Those Early Days.....

## ART

The next few pages are reproductions of the original Cowboy Artist of America drawings that graced the covers of the first two editions of "Those Early Days". In keeping with the traditions of the first two editions, where each had different cover art, so do we now continue with that tradition with new art. However, the art from the past editions are included for your continued enjoyment.

Those Early Days…..

Those Early Days…..

## ACKNOWLEDGMENTS

This book has been made possible only as a result of the efforts of many individuals. Those efforts, channeled through the organization, known as Sedona Westerners, were directed under "Trail Bosses" Tex Dallas, Allen Bristow, and Ollie Simon, who in succession provided leadership and persistence.

The book committee wishes to call particular attention to the invaluable historical detailed accuracy provided by Albert "Ab" Thompson. In addition to his own contributions, it was through the wide acquaintance of his continuous residence that many others were persuaded to submit their own material. Mr. Rollie Houck, of the Sedona Camera Shop, not only taped the stories of a number of old-timers, but reproduced the old photos used in illustrating the book. He also succeeded in securing from the distinguished local Western Artist, Charles Dye, a contribution of the drawing "Over the Rim", appearing on the front cover, and from another local resident, Joe Beeler, also a prominent western painter, his drawing "Old Brind", used on the back cover. These renowned artists are charter members of the Cowboy Artists of America, Inc., devoted to depicting life in the Old West.

The committee gratefully acknowledges the help of Wilma Dallas, Gladys Allen, Evelyn Wright, and June Dieckmann in typing and transcribing stories. The professional and technical experience of Ruth Coleman, together with her enthusiasm have been of major importance and cannot be overlooked. It must be noted that valuable assistance was rendered by Elizabeth Rigby in publicizing information through the press.

Not least, we wish to thank all those contributors, whose names, of course, are indicated in connection with their stories. Nor do we forget the help and encouragement of many others.

## 2008

This is the third reprint of this book. The Sedona Westerners offered the printing rights to the Sedona Historical Society/Sedona Heritage Museum for a period of time. The Society is happy to be responsible for making this wonderful reference book available again for all those interested in Sedona history.

The original art for the cover of this edition was created by Courtney Amato, and donated to the Society for this reprint. Courtney is currently and aspiring artist attending the New York School of Visual

Arts. As this is printed, modern printing options allow for a full color cover and we are fortunate that Courtney's art graces the new cover.

The Sedona Historical Society/Sedona Heritage Museum gratefully acknowledge the exhaustive work of Bill Levengood for preparing this book for the modern printing process, and along with his wife Francine for their work to correct the index. There are also thanks to Janeen Trevillyan for facilitating a variety of aspects of this project, and to the Society's Board for their commitment to the project.

Those Early Days.....

## PREFACE

The committee that has undertaken selection and compiling of material for this book feels it necessary to explain certain factors governing its decisions.

First, it must be noted that there will be apparent omissions of some individuals whose stories should be included. This was not necessarily by intent, but rather by our lack of success in getting contributions of the necessary material. We regret this and trust there will be no misunderstanding.

Second, it will seem that though many stories include events occurring outside the Oak Creek and Verde Valley area, such material is essentially a related part of the lives of those settlers who lived here in early days. Also, it seemed obvious that there has to be a general regional focus on Oak Creek and the Verde Valley as a whole, since there were so many family connections and the shared activities and experiences of friends and neighbors. We felt that in a few cases it was hard to decide if some very interesting material came close enough to be of local significance. It seemed that we must keep to the central theme of conveying to our readers the picture of WHO the first settlers were and depicting the way they lived.

Appreciation must be expressed to those who have helped by offering their stories.

**SOME TRAIL BOSSES OF THE Sedona Westerners:**

| | |
|---|---|
| Dean Gregory (deceased) | 1964-1965 (Circa) |
| Tex Dallas | 1965-1966 |
| Allen Bristow | 1966-1967 |
| Ollie Simon | 1967-1968 |
| Ellsworth Schnebly | 1968-1969 |
| Don Willard & Mike Wright | 1969-1970 |
| Charles Knaus | 1970-1971 |
| Dr. Ed Long | 1971-1972 |
| Lew Goddard | 1972-1973 |
| Dixon Fagerberg, Jr. | 1973-1974 |
| Vic Sterzing | 1974-1975 |

Book Committee
Allen L. Bristow, Lewis H. Goddard, Ellsworth M. Schnebly, and Albert E. Thompson

## 2008

With the printing of this third edition, we have recreated this book in a digitized format. Every effort has been made to correct any imperfections that may have existed in the first two printings. However, being human, there may be a few we haven't found.

One of the advantages of having the book in digitized format is that we can print in small quantities and make additional corrections as we go. Should you find any errors, we would appreciate it if you would contact us at sedonamuseum@esedona.net

THE SEDONA HISTORICAL SOCIETY

Those Early Days.....

## INTRODUCTION

While we do not claim any literary honors for this little volume, we do feel that it will fill a long felt need.

There is practically no published information about pioneer times in this locality.

Prior to World War II there was not much interest shown in the early day happenings of the area. There has been a great influx of new people in the past 25 years. There are people in the Chamber of Commerce office and the Sedona public library, almost every day asking for printed matter about Sedona, Oak Creek and the Verde Valley area but it is almost nonexistent.

Some few of the old timers have wished that something could be done to preserve the early day history before the old timers are all gone and it is too late to collect any of it. To many of the new comers, Sedona is like Topsy, it "just growed up", and they are unable to get any information about what it was like in the past.

The Sedona Westerners' group had no intention of compiling a book when they started out to put up signs on some of the nearby hiking trails. They soon found that there was confusion about place names of some of the nearby landmarks.

They called on the old timers of the area for help. All of the old timers who answered the call were given honorary lifetime memberships in the organization. In the course of authenticating place names, much pioneer history was uncovered. In order to take the evidence down, a tape recorder was brought to the meetings and the talks were recorded.

More and more interest was shown in the pioneer stories and old timers from the surrounding areas were invited to the meetings and their talks were recorded or else they later wrote their stories and sent them in to the Sedona Westerners group.

The Sedona library called on the Westerners group for a pamphlet of early day history to lend to the many patrons who were constantly asking for something of that sort.

A committee was appointed to prepare such a pamphlet. In the meantime so much material came in, it was decided to try for a book; and the library is still waiting for the pamphlet.

Ever since the big migration to this part of the country started at the close of World War II there has been a small percent of them who thought they were Columbus. Without asking if certain landmarks of the area had a name already, they gave names to them. If they stayed long in the area they were the first ones to inform later arrivals of the names they had given to the places.

Ever since the first Forest Reserves were set aside in the West in the 1890s, under the Department of Interior and the General Land Office, the officials have tried to retain the pioneer place names. The General Land Office made the first official surveys before the Forest Reserves were set up and they made the first official maps. Almost all of those early maps are quite accurate in giving pioneer place names.

Sometime after the Forest Reserves became National Forests and were under the jurisdiction of the Department of Agriculture, we had some few Forest officials who were not so careful to keep their maps correct. Some few of the old landmarks that had one name on the old General Land Office maps had a different name on Forest Service maps.

The Sedona Westerners committee that was appointed to work with the Forest Service officials of the present time, trying to clear up some of the confusion has found our District Rangers and other Forest officials very cooperative and helpful. It will take time but we feel that eventually all confusion about place names will be cleared up.

Although the old timers agree pretty much on the pioneer names of places they do not always agree about why they were named as they were. At the present time there is almost no one living who has personal remembrance of the 1870s when many of these places were named. We have to depend on stories told to us by the ones who were living here at that time.

If, in reading some of these stories you find some discrepancies in the different stories that could be the reason. In passing information down from one generation to another it is only natural that it is some different in different families.

A few of the old place names were changed even as far back as 70 years ago. Some of them had two names almost from the start. As it was not considered important enough to argue about, one of the names became better known and the other was dropped. Also some few of the old campgrounds have been entirely washed away by big floods, or acquired by private interests and the names have been changed.

A book reviewer could no doubt take our little book and pick it to pieces and find all kinds of flaws in it. But just remember that there is not a professional writer among its contributors. Furthermore, some of them never had very much formal education.

We Sedona Westerners are proud of the literary efforts of our

Those Early Days…..

members.

## 2008

The Westerner hiking club is entrenched with tradition. It is a mutual appreciation for the history of this majestic area that has led to the partnership between the Sedona Westerners and the Sedona Historical Society for the purpose of reprinting Those Early Days. The Westerners wish to thank the Historical Society and their historian, Janeen Trevillyan for bringing the reprinting of Those Early Days to fruition. And most of all, the Westerners are most grateful to those early settlers whose adventures live on through this book and on the very trails that take us to the magical places of Sedona.

A club goal "to authenticate, record and perpetuate the original historical names of places in the Sedona area" was actually listed in the 1965 version of the club's Constitution and By-laws. Originally a social club for the purpose of providing entertainment for members and visitors, hiking was soon introduced as the activity, which would eventually consume Westerner attention. With almost 300 miles in the Red Rock Ranger trail system today, it is hard to imagine a time when there were no marked trails, no trailheads, no signs and no trail maps. In 1965, the Westerner hikers, with Forest Service approval, marked ten trails with wooden signs and created a trail map for distribution to visitors. Unfortunately, the wooden signs became collectors' items and disappeared as fast as they were installed. Meanwhile, as the Westerners were installing signs at hiking trails, they soon discovered that there was much confusion about the names of some of the Sedona landmarks located near the trails. Cathedral Rock was sometimes called Court House Rock, Courthouse was called Church Rock and Capitol Butte was called Gray Mountain.

Along with their new hiking obsession, Westerners determined to accurately identify Sedona landmarks. To accomplish this, the newly formed, Sedona Westerner Historical Committee, scheduled meetings for early settlers, descendants and any other "old-timers" currently living in the area. These old-timer memories resulted in about 8000 feet of audiotape. Although there were "heated discussions" concerning some of the names of landmarks, consensus was finally achieved. Forest Service maps were corrected and Westerner maps used the newly "authenticated" names. The compilation of the stories and memories of these early pioneers led to the publication of the book, Those Early Days. In 1985, even though it was a break from tradition, the wooden trail signs were replaced with the present vandal-resistant metal signs, using residual funds from the sale of this book. Today the original 45 metal signs are still present and serve as a visual testament to earlier contributions by the Westerners to Sedona. As the Forest Service identifies need, the Sedona Westerner tradition continues with the installation of more metal trail signs, perhaps with residual funds from the reprinting of this very book.

SEDONA WESTERNERS

Those Early Days.....

## TABLE OF CONTENTS

Preface .................................................................................... ix

Introduction ............................................................................ xi

This Is Red Rock Country - Don Willard ............................... 1

The Story of Sedona - Albert E. Thompson ........................... 3

History of Homesteads of Upper
    Oak Creek - Albert E. Thompson .................................... 8

A Bit of Arizona Postal History - Harold H. Longfellow ........... 21

The First White Child Born in Sedona - Margaret J. Stilson ...... 37

The First Family to Patent Land in Sedona Village
    Roy Owenby As Told to Albert E. Thompson .............. 41

Early Roads of Sedona Area - Albert E. Thompson ................ 47

Roundup of 1896 - M.O. Dumas ............................................ 58

Roundup of 1896, Poem - M.O. Dumas ................................. 64

Earmarks - Albert E. Thompson ............................................. 65

Place Names in Sedona Area - Albert E. Thompson ............... 67

How Sedona Was Named - Ellsworth M. Schnebly ................ 72

Ramblings of Clara Purtymun - Clara Purtymun .................... 79

An Indian Scare - Albert E. Thompson .................................. 88

Gail Gardner Talks to Sedona Westerners - Taped ................. 89

Gail Gardner Sings a Song to Sedona Westerners - Taped ....... 93

Don Bell Tells His Story to Sedona Westerners - Taped ......... 95

A Follow-Up Talk by Don Bell - Taped .................................. 99

Howard Wingfield Talks to Sedona Westerners - Taped ......... 100

Fletcher Fairchild Makes a
    Talk to Sedona Westerners - Taped ............................ 102

A Taped Interview With Dan Purtymun - Laura McBride ........ 108

A Tragedy - Albert E. Thompson ............................................. 114

One Old Timer's Re-View - Don Willard .................................. 115

The Old Corral (Poem) ............................................................. 122

More About Cowboys - M.O. Dumas ........................................ 125

A Cowboy's Prayer, In commemoration of
 "Rimmy" Jim Giddings - M.O. Dumas ............................... 127

The Last Long Trail Drive - M.O. Dumas ................................. 128

Howard Wingfield Makes Another Talk - Taped ....................... 137

"Bear Tree" Jimmy - Albert E. Thompson ................................. 139

How To Dismount From a Horse - Albert E. Thompson ............ 141

The Munds Family, the family that has so many landmarks named for them - Sedona Westerners Book Committee, from information supplied by Inez Loy Lay, Jennie Munds Wingfield and Sally Munds Williams ................ 142

A Bear Hunter Who Lost - Albert E. Thompson ....................... 146

The First Sheriff of Coconino County
 and some poems - Lenore Francis Dumas ......................... 150

Dutch Oven Poem - R.W. McNeill ........................................... 153

An Old Time Doctor, Dr. M.A. Carrier - Inez Lay .................... 156

They Were Afraid of Each Other - Albert E. Thompson ........... 160

The Loy Family, another family with many Landmarks
 named for them - Inez Lay ................................................. 161

Pioneers of The Red Rock Precinct - Frieda Schuerman Loy .... 164

Mysterious Graves - Albert E. Thompson ................................. 169

A Forest Ranger's Experience in Sedona
 - Fred W. Croxen, 1st .... ................................................. 170

The Winter of The Deep Snow,
Or The Schoolmarm's Dilemma - Edith Lamport Croxen...........177

More About The Big Snow Storm - Albert E. Thompson............180

Early Builders of Sedona - Inez Lay .............................................185

They Were Tough in Those Days - Albert E. Thompson...........188

Another Oak Creek Old Timer
Ambrosio Chavez - As told to Albert E. Thompson....................189

A Taped Interview - Albert Thompson and Laura McBride .....192

From Trail Dust to Jet Trails - Allen L. Bristow........................198

You Don't Need a Saddle - Albert E. Thompson........................207

A Remarkable Woman of The Early West - Lenore Dumas.......208

How To Slaughter a Beef - Albert E. Thompson........................212

How Carl Richards Came to Sedona -
As told to Sedona Westerners Book Committee .......................213

A Loaf of Bread For a Nickel - M.O. Dumas ...............................219

Some Memories in Pictures - Don Willard .................................222

Beaver Head Stage Station - Albert E. Thompson .....................226

A Rolling Stone - Charles Smith ..................................................229

A False Alarm - Albert E. Thompson...........................................235

A Lost Retreat, Poem - Dr. Lee B. Woodcock,
Introduction - By Mildred Johnson ............................................236

An Old Time Sedona Family - Minnie Farley Steele .................237

Early Sedona Fruit Growers - Helen Jordan..............................240

The Torture Rod - Fletch Fairchild ..............................................244

From Kerosene to Kilowatts - Wilma Dallas...............................251

The Narrow Gauge - Don Willard ...............................................254

As Time Draws On - Wilma Dallas ............................................. 256

Old Roads - Virginia Finnie Webb ............................................ 258

How The Sedona Country Hooked Me - Dixon Fagerberg, Jr ..... 269

The Old Adobe ........................................................................ 274

Aunt Dit, The Pioneer School Teacher - Allen L. Bristow ......... 275

The Loner - Don Willard .......................................................... 278

A Brief History of the Schnebly Hill Road
   - by Ellsworth Schnebly ....................................................... 281

The Prospector and His Three Burros - Donald B. Willard ......... 286

Those Early Days.....

**This was one of the first efforts to eliminate the hazards of travel through Oak Creek Canyon. Blasted from the white cliff just couth of Encinoso Camp Grounds in 1924**

Those Early Days…..

## THIS IS RED ROCK COUNTRY
*by Don Willard*

If the above sounds like a certain television commercial, be assured it has had years of priority. There is another familiar expression we often hear, "It is sure easy to look at". This is truly an indication that the viewer enjoys the scenic outlook. There is something about it; however, that is certainly not so easy, and that is to define or describe the Red Rock Country. This is not to say that it is merely a matter of finding adequate words for the purpose, although that in it self is a task not lightly undertaken. Certainly there is more to it than staying overnight in a motel room, riding along the highway, or one or two interviews, before one can acquire a more than casual feeling or understanding of the really vast splendor and variety, or the geology and history of the region.

Volcanic rimrock, stratified sandstone and boulder-strewn creek bottoms; the stream with its sycamores, alders and oaks; the seeming mystery of deeply hidden canyons; the mighty work of erosion on every hand producing fantastic carvings to delight the eye; greenery of juniper and manzanita softening the lavish coloration of rock formations; hiking trails to landmarks and historic sites. What else shall we add?

Oh yes, here and there a squirrel or blue jay to scold the intruder, or a fiery penstemon or Indian paint brush; then for the artist the challenge of changing tints and lighting and the struggle to express them.

To see the sun's first rays touching the top of a mountain promontory; to see the moon rise between sharp projections of the jagged skyline on a starry evening; or to explore some canyon where there is no sound or sight of the handiwork of man. These are real experiences of the Red Rock country. For sheer emotional impact, consider the glorious once-in-a-life-time sunset, lighting the rocky cliffs eastward after a summer storm with a soft firelight glow, and all of this framed with a perfect double rainbow arching against rain clouds overhead. This visual counterpart of the words and melody known as "The Lost Chord", has been for some a stirring memory.

The real expanse and perspective of the Red Rock country can be grasped in some degree, especially when viewed from certain vantage points accessible to those who will take the time and make the effort. Many years ago when the narrow gauge railroad into Jerome was the main entrance route to the Verde, there was a certain point where passengers got their first glimpse of the red rocks. It came to be known as "First View". From there on into Jerome they could observe the distant color panorama extending from Sycamore Canyon to the Mogollon rim of Oak Creek. To residents of Jerome, the view was and still is spectacular. Another superb vista from the summit of Mingus Mountain shows the entire valley with a border of scenic grandeur to the east. From the top of Schnebly Hill there is still another thrill waiting in a setting never to be forgotten, and from the air a new and different way to see and enjoy an area second only to the Grand Canyon in awesome magnificence is now available.

The usual and accepted feeling is that the Red Rock country is identified with Sedona and Oak Creek. While this is certainly correct, yet it is easily seen to include a section of the Upper Verde extending from Perkinsville on the Williams to Jerome road, to Sycamore Canyon and thence to Oak Creek and even Beaver Creek above Montezuma Well. All of these are interesting and colorful with individual features of attractions. Rock forms and shapes often suggest names of objects to which they seem to bear a certain resemblance. This has been particularly true in the Sedona and Oak Creek area; for instance, we have Bell Rock, Steamboat Rock, the Coffee Pot, House Mountain, and others. These were mentioned to illustrate the richness of material to excite the imagination and provide pleasure to nature lovers and even ordinary sightseers.

Some particular scenes now acquiring nationwide fame in color photography and art are: Red Rock Crossing, Bell Rock, Wilson Mountain, Slide Rock and the falls, Midgley Bridge, and many, many others. But these are only introductory to endless adventure and enjoyment for those who are willing to leave the highway to find the whole true story of the Red Rock Country.

Those Early Days…..

## THE STORY OF SEDONA
*by Albert E. Thompson*

When entering Sedona from either direction on U.S. Highway 89A one sees a State Highway Department sign that says, "Sedona, Founded 1902", and gives the elevation.

In one sense that is absolutely correct. The Sedona post office was established June 26, 1902, and named for Mrs. Sedona Schnebly.

However that sign might give the impression that no one had lived there prior to that date. Not long ago someone asked me what the place was called before the post office was established. For a bit I was at loss for an answer.

After doing a little thinking, I remembered that I had heard old timers speak of the place as Camp Garden, and a very pretty name it is too.

The place has been continuously occupied since 1879, and John J. Thompson took squatters rights to the Indian Gardens ranch in 1876. Before there was a post office, folks generally called the name of the family who were living there at that time.

In the early 1880s the officers of the army camp of Camp Verde had a summer camp about where the present Nelson Shopping Center is in Sedona. They called their camp, Camp Garden. I have no way of knowing whether or not the garden part of the name was taken from the name of Indian Gardens. That is something to speculate about.

The first family to take up residence in Sedona was the Abraham James family, who moved there from the present Page Springs fishponds, in the spring of 1879. Mr. James only lived two years after he made his home there, but his widow and son stayed on there until 1895. There were others who came and went in the meantime, some who made some improvements, such as cabins and ditches. None of the land was surveyed in the early days, so squatters rights was all they could take.

In 1895, the year the James family moved away, Frank Owenby Sr. filed on 80 acres and stayed until he patented the land. His homestead was what was known in more recent years as the George Black ranch. The James place was the present Fred Hart ranch until recently when it was subdivided.

The first road to the area was from Beaver Head Flats, by the way of Big Park. It is often spoken of now as the Rim Rock road. That name is rather misleading, because the road is many years older than the name of Rim Rock.

All of the old timers called the road the beaver creek road or Big Park road. In my opinion either name is more fitting, than the name Rim Rock, because the Rim Rock post office was not inexistence before the late 1920s. If one who lived on Beaver Creek mentioned the road, it might be fittingly called the Sedona road, because it was first built to the present Sedona. The first wagon was taken over the road from Sedona to Cottonwood in the early 1880s, and the Schnebly Hill road was opened for wagon travel in 1902. The wagon road to Indian Gardens was finished in late 1901, but was not opened through Oak Creek Canyon until 1914.

The village of Sedona never had a school until 1910. There was a school started in Oak Creek Canyon in 1899, with D.E. Schnebly as teacher. It was located at what is now called Lower Manzanita Camp, which is half way between the Thompson ranch and the Purtymun ranch. All of the first pupils were either Thompson or Purtymun, except one, Bessie Thomas. It was a summer school only.

The Purtymun family moved away in late 1901 and the school was moved to Indian Gardens in 1902. There was school there most of the time until 1906, but attendance dropped so low that year that the school was discontinued.

For a few years the younger Thompson children attended school at Red Rock, where there had been a school since 1891. The Thompson family moved to Red Rock each fall, and the children had a few months of school. In 1908 three more families move to Sedona and took homesteads. There were children in all of the families. By 1910 there was a forest ranger named Claude Thompson stationed at Sedona, who had two school age boys. The Lee Van Deren family lived at Clay Park, the present Tacaloma Lodge, and had been moving to Camp Verde in winter to a school. Van Deren told the Sedona families who were trying to get a school that he would move to Sedona and put his children in school if they succeeded. With the Farley, Owenby, and Lay families, together with the Loy family, who were living there at that time, Coconino County allotted enough money to build a small schoolhouse. It was a one-room house about 12 by 16 feet in size. I think the first teacher was the ranger's wife, Mrs. Claude Thompson.

The new school was so handy for all of the mountain farmers and cattlemen, that more and more of them built winter homes in Sedona and sent their children to school there. By 1914 the little school became so badly crowded that the county built a new schoolhouse that was used with add on rooms, until it burned down in the summer of 1948, and the present building was put up.

Those Early Days.....

Soon after the Schnebly family bought the Frank Owenby ranch in Sedona they built a two-story resort hotel. They kept a small country store in the hotel. When the last of the Schnebly family moved away, Elijah Lay kept a store at his ranch house for a while. J.A. Fenstermaker had a store for a while when he lived at the Farley ranch. Later Frank Thompson had a store, when he lived at the present Walter Jordan place. After Frank Thompson, Frank Owenby Jr. had a store where the later Harts Store was in Sedona. When he moved away Morgan Thompson kept a store in the same place. Morgan was the first one to sell gasoline in Sedona, though he did not have a gas pump. The gas was hauled in drums and drawn out in a measuring can. That was about 1923.

About 1925, L.E. Hart bought the Van Deren ranch in Sedona and built a more modern country store on the site where Morgan Thompson's store had been and put in gas pumps. He ran that store until the highway was built through, about 1940, and he was no longer on the road. He put a more modern store yet, where the Nelson Shopping Center is now. After his death, the store burned down and the present store was built.

After World War 11 and the boom started for Sedona, new stores have gone up at the rate of at least one a year.

Sedona has had a ranger station since soon after it had a post office. When the first National Forests were established the rangers were called line riders and they did not have stations. The National Forests were called Forest Reserves at first. Two of our first line riders locally were John L. Thomas and Jerry Fisher. By the time they got to be rangers, Bill Wallace of Mormon Lake, who was a ranger for years, built a two-room log cabin for a ranger station in Sedona.

I understand that the first forest ranger to be stationed in Sedona was a man named McLean. About 1905, James D. Baily, a former Arizona Ranger was stationed in Sedona in winter and at Munds Park in summer. He was ranger there until 1909, when M. O. Dumas, later Dr. M. O. Dumas, took over. He was only there one year when he was relieved by Claude Thompson. Fred W. Coxen took over from Thompson in 1912 and stayed until 1915, when he was replaced by Jesse Bushnell. Bushnell was there until 1928, when his older children reached high school age and he was transferred. That brings up to what I call modern times, though Sedona was not a very big town then.

The first bridge across Oak Creek was the bridge at Oak Creek Falls that opened the canyon road in 1914. In the fall of 1915 Coconino County started work on the first Sedona bridge. George Black was the

*Hart's first store in Sedona. The store was located at Soldiers' Wash bridge on the present Brewer Road - built in the late 1920's and used until the early 1940's.*

*Hart's second store in Sedona, built by L.E. (Dad) Hart about 1939 at present Nelson's hopping center. Store burned after Mr. Hart's death.*

Those Early Days.....

foreman of the job. The steel was hauled over from Clarkdale by horses and wagons, before the winter snows came.

Between Christmas and New Year, three feet of snow fell over all of the Sedona country. That delayed the bridge work for a few weeks, but the excavation work for the west end abutment was only slowed down. By the last of January the snow was all gone, but through March the creek was so high all of the school children on the east side of the creek had to cross the creek on a cable. It was the middle of the next summer before the concrete was cured enough so that the steel could be put up and the bridge was finished.

After World War I people started moving west. At first it was farming folks looking for land and all of the open flats for miles around Sedona were homesteaded. During the depression years of the 1930s, and the dry years in Oklahoma and Texas people flocked into Sedona by the hundreds.

Those were the years of the CCC camps and WPA work. A lot of roads and trails were built in the area during those years. By the late 1930s a few people with money began to buy property in Sedona. By the end of World War II the migration started that has made the present Sedona.

## HISTORY OF HOMESTEADS OF UPPER OAK CREEK
by Albert E. Thompson

(Taken from Verde Independent serial, 1963) There have been some changes in ownership since the author compiled this material.

The homestead farthest up toward the head of Oak Creek is known as Chipmunk and Troutdale. Both are part of the old Harding place.

I believe the first person to live there was J.R. (Jack) Robinson. He built a cabin there and a trail up to the rim in the early 1880' s.

The next was the Dave Hart family. They moved there about 1883. They cleared some land and did a little farming but moved away after about 10 years. The Hart boys were Will, Les, Elmer and Lute. They were cattlemen in Northern Arizona later.

Next came Col. O.P. Harding. He filed intention to make a homestead and lived there the rest of his life, but never did make final proof. He died in 1915 or thereabout. He was a member of the Mason Lodge, and after his death the lodge assisted his widow and she made final proof on the homestead. After the death of Mrs. Harding the Masons acquired the place and sold it to George Babbitt Sr. It is owned now by the George Babbitt family.

The next place down the creek is known by old-timers as the Thomas place. The first person to live there was, to the best of my knowledge, C. S. (Bear) Howard. He came there in the early 1880's. He built a cabin and planted a few fruit trees. His cabin was at the site of the present Oak Creek Lodge.

In the late 1880's he sold his rights and improvements to John L.V. Thomas, and his son John L. Old Grandpa Thomas wrote to his son, Louis H., who was in Colorado to come to Oak Creek. When Lou and his wife Rosa arrived, the place was divided. Lou homesteaded the part from West Fork, up the creek, including the present Call of the Canyon resort. John, his brother, took from West Fork down the creek.

J.L.V. lived with Lou and his wife for a while but later moved down with John who was a bachelor. About 10 years before he died, the old man homesteaded a small place farther down the creek. It is the present Don Hoel's Cabins resort.

Before Lou Thomas died (about 1920) he sold all of his land on the east side of Oak Creek. After the death of Lou's widow, James A. Lamport Sr. bought all of the land on the west side. Lamport sold to the Mayhews in 1925 and it is still owned by the Mayhew family.

Those Early Days.....

After John Thomas died, his property went to his sister and another brother. The part east of Oak Creek has all been sold to sub dividers, but some of the Thomas heirs still own all on the west side of the creek.

The J.L.V. Thomas place was sold by his heirs to B.V. Davis in the mid 1920's, and Davis started a resort there and called it Glenwood. It was bought by Don Hoel the present owner, in the late 1940's.

The next place down the creek, Junipine, has had several owners. A man named Bill Dwyer first squatted there in the 1880's. He was a banjo player and got the nickname of Banjo Bill. He lived in a kind of dugout hut and did a little gardening. He also started to build a fishpond at Banjo Bill Springs. The springs were named for him after he moved on in a few years.

In the late 1890's Steven Purtymun and family moved there. They built an irrigation ditch and cleared land and put out an orchard. They also built a nice large log house. Remember, there was no road through the canyon then and everything had to be brought in on packhorses.

In the early 1900's the family broke up and most of them moved away. In the next few years Jess, Dan and Albert Purtymun lived there at different times. Albert Purtymun moved his family there in 1906 and filed on the land. He intended to make it his home. He built a wagon road from the Thomas place down to there. Times were hard for a few years after the financial panic of 1907. Albert had to leave home in 1909 to make a living for his family. Soon after then he relinquished his rights and sold his improvements to Andrew Shumway. In a few years Shumway in turn sold his rights to Charles R. Allen.

Allen was a photographer who had a winter home in Needles, CA, but had spent his summer months on Oak Creek for many years. He made final proof and spent the rest of his life there. He died in the early 1920's and the property was bought by F.M. Gold of Flagstaff. Mrs. Gold gave it the name of Junipine, and it is still owned by the Golds.

Joining Junipine on the south, but all on the west side of the creek, is the present Todd's Lodge. I have heard that the first man to live there was known only by the nickname of Crookneck. He camped there for a short time but did not make any improvements. After he left there the place was known locally as Crookneck Flat.

In 1908, Jesse J. Howard, son of Bear Howard, homesteaded the place. 1908 saw a big increase in the population of Upper Oak Creek, as we will see as we go along.

Jess Howard proved up on the place and lived there the rest of his life. After he died in 1923 his sister, Martha Cook, sold the place to James Lamport Sr. Lamport sold to Bob Roscoe and Ed Thompson. Before they had the place paid out they sold to F. A. Todd. It is still owned by the Todd family.

The next ranch down the creek is the Pendley ranch. I believe the first ones to live there was the J. O. (Jack) Harrington family although there was a man named Warner who had camped there before them. Harrington was later a cattleman in the Flagstaff area and the sheriff of Coconino County at one time.

He built a cabin and a trail to the top of the rim. The place was a very hard one to build an irrigation ditch onto and Harrington moved away in the late 1890's for that reason.

The next one to try it was D. E. Schnebly. He taught the first school on Upper Oak Creek from 1899 till mid-term 1900. He lived in the Harrington cabin for a while when he was teaching school but gave it up for the same reason that Harrington had.

About 1903 the Dave James family lived there for a while. They did not make any improvements but had a baby girl born there.

In the summer of 1907 Frank L. Pendley first came to Oak Creek. He made application for the place the fall of that year. He built a new log cabin in 1908. (The former one had burned down).

For the first few years he worked on the place through the warm months and went to the desert in winter and trapped bobcats near the sheep herds. The territory paid a $5 bounty on bobcats and he could make more money trapping than he could working for wages.

As soon as he got some land cleared he planted fruit trees and dry farmed till he got his ditch finished. He made two tunnels through solid sandstone cliffs. One was 60 feet long and the other was 120 feet long. He swung a flume on a cable between the two tunnels. All of the rockwork was done by hand drilling and dynamite. He got water in the ditch in 1914.

Frank Pendley lived there the rest of his life. He died in the mid-1950's, but most of the ranch is still owned by the Pendley family.

The next ranch down the creek is the present Mission Rancho. Albert Purtymun and his wife spent the winter of 1903-04 there in a tent house. He started work on a ditch and cleared a little land but left in the spring to hunt a job and never came back there.

In 1908 Jess Purtymun filed on the land and lived there long enough to get a patent to it. In 1923 he traded the place to Frank Thompson for the present Walter Jordan ranch in Sedona. Frank sold to the Link Smith family about 1925. Ira Smith got title to the place and

Those Early Days.....

sold it to George Baes who in turn sold to Mrs. Mae Murray and the Lemieux family in the early 1940's. They are the present owners.

There is one small place between there and the Pendley place but it was never a homestead. It was first taken as a mining claim and later as a forest lease.

This being the only mining claim that I ever heard of on Upper Oak Creek, I will tell a little more about it.

Jess Purtymun and Frank Derrick first located it in 1913. The Derrick family lived there in the summer time for a year or two. Jess and Frank did a little digging each year, enough to hold it, until 1917. They let their assessment work lapse that year and it was re-located by Tom Quick and Gus Carlson. Tom and Gus ran a tunnel back into the mountainside for about 100 feet. They struck a little low grade copper but not enough to patent the claim. Tom Quick lived there in a tent part of the time until 1921 and gave it up and left.

In 1925 Albert Purtymun took the place as an agricultural forest lease. He built a house there and put out fruit trees and planted a garden. He lived there until the spring of 1938. That was the year of the big flood in Oak Creek. The flood washed away part of the buildings and a big part of his farming land. He sold his rights and improvements to the Boutwell family. Some of the Boutwells still live there.

There were other forest leases in the canyon and some in the Sedona area. Some of them were later acquired by trade or purchase, but I do not know enough about them to try to write the history of them. The next homestead down the canyon was my dad's homestead at Indian Gardens. J. J. or Jim Thompson first took squatters' rights to the place in 1876 when the Apache Indians' crops were still growing there. That is how it got the name of Indian Gardens.

His original homestead was for only 80 acres. For many years after first settlers came to Oak Creek Canyon none of the land was surveyed. Dad first filed on a piece of land that he thought was where he was living. When the land was surveyed, about 1900, by the General Land Office, he found that he had filed on a piece of land on top of Wilson Mountain. He had to relinquish his filings and file again on land where he was living.

In 1912 he took additional homestead of some 56 acres joining on the up-creek side. He died in 1917, before he proved up on the land. Mother proved up on that part after his death. She sold about seven acres of the up-creek addition but kept the rest of the land as long as she lived. After her death in 1936 the heirs sold all of the remaining

**Jim Thompson and wife Margaret at Indian Gardens in 1905.**

land over a period of years.

The next place down the creek is the Charles S. Thompson place. Jim Thompson, instead of taking the 80 acres down the creek, saved it for his oldest son Frank. Frank filed on the place and farmed it for a few years but got restless and moved on before he patented the land.

Dad then sent for his daughter and her husband, Frank Nail. Nail filed on it in 1909 but only got to stay there a few years. He was killed in a railroad accident at the old Jerome Junction in 1911 where he was working at the time.

His widow lived on the place the required number of years to prove up, but she had married in the meantime and the local U.S. land commissioner would not allow her to make final proof.

Rather than go to court to settle the matter she relinquished her rights to her brother Charles who had become of legal age in the meantime.

Charles filed on the place in 1914. He got patent to the place and still lives there. He is one of the few who homesteaded and still lives on

Those Early Days.....

his homestead. He has sold all of the land on the west side of the creek and some on the east side but still owns several acres including his house.

All of the first homesteaders were required to live on the land and farm part of it for five years before they could get patent to it. Later that law was changed so that a homesteader either prove up at the end of three years or continue on for the full five years before making final proof.

The only other homestead in the canyon proper is my own place at the mouth of Munds Canyon. It joins Dad's homestead on its west boundary. It is the last homestead allowed in Oak Creek Canyon. I still live here and have never sold any part of it. I think it is the only place left intact and still owned by the homesteader in the whole area.

Now we will go to the Sedona area. The oldest patented land there is what is known as the George Black place.

There were various squatters who stopped there for a while from the early 1880's on. Bill James had got a ditch on part of the land and farmed a little but all had moved on.

In 1895 Frank Owenby Sr. moved there and stayed until he patented the land. He sold to Carl Schnebly in 1902. When Carl Schnebly moved back to Missouri in 1905, after the death of their little girl, his brother Ellsworth, or D.E., took the place by himself.

The joining place up the creek, known more recently as the L.E. Hart place, was under the same ditch and was farmed as part of the Schnebly place but was public land. D.E. Schnebly built a house there and applied under the Homestead Act for the land. In the meantime he sold the home place to Charles C. Stemmer and his mother.

Stemmer bought about 1909 or 10 and kept the place until 1916 when he sold to George W. Black. I believe that George Black's widow still owns most of the land.

I had always believed that D.E. Schnebly made final proof on the land and sold it to Johnny and Dave Lay in 1908. I have been told more recently that he only sold his rights and improvements and that Dave Lay made final proof. I do not know which is correct.

Anyway the Lays sold to Lee Van Deren in 1915. Van Deren sold to L.E. Hart and wife Delia in the mid 1920's. The place has been cut up in small parcels and practically all sold in recent years.

The next place up the creek from there, known in recent years as the George Jordan place, was homesteaded by Frank Owenby in 1908. He had only taken 80 acres in the place he sold to the Schneblys so he later took the remaining 80 acres allowed him farther up the creek.

That place was another one that was hard to build a ditch onto. My dad had built a cabin there in the early 1880's so mother and the small children could be near her parents when he was gone from home. B.F. Copple also had a cabin there. After both families moved away the cabins burned down leaving only the stone chimneys standing there. It was known as Chimney Flat when Owenbys moved there.

*Frank Owenby and his wife Nancy -*
*the first family to patent a homestead in Sedona proper*

Owenby got the difficult ditch built and patented the land. About 1918 he sold to J.M. Cook and Frank Spear. Cook did not stay long until he turned the place over to Frank Spear alone. Spear still did not have it paid out when he sold to Claude Black in the early 1920's. Claude only lived there a few years until he sold to the Jordan family in the mid-1920's,

On the east side of the creek, above the bridge, is the place known now as the Steele place. Joseph T. Farley homesteaded there in

Those Early Days.....

1908. The only other person that I ever heard tell of to live there before Farley was a man named Eiberger. I hope I have the name spelled right. Eiberger camped there in the winter and spring of 1901. He fenced a little plot and planted a garden but moved on before it matured. He had no irrigation ditch but apparently the rains came early that year. I can remember my older brothers and sisters bringing watermelons from there up to the old home place at Indian Gardens.

Farley built a ditch and put the land in cultivation. He farmed there until 1915 when he sold to J.A.Fenstermaker and moved to Texas. In the early 1920's, Farley and his newly acquired son-in-law, the late W.C. Steele, came back and bought the place again from Fenstermaker. Later Steele got all of the land on the east side of the creek, and Farley took the small piece on the west side.

The place on the east side of the creek, below the bridge, is known now as the Fred Hart place. It was the first land to be settled and improved in the Sedona area. Abraham James moved there in 1879.

He intended to make the place his home. He built a ditch and cabins and corrals there and put the land in cultivation. He died at his summer cattle quarters at James Canyon on the mountain in 1881. His widow and son continued to live there until 1895 when they traded cattle to John H. Lee for the present Crescent Moon Ranch in Red Rock.

The place was vacant and deserted most of the time from then until 1908 when Elijah Lay and family moved there. He built a house on the upper end of the place and his son Joe built on the lower end. They rebuilt the ditch and improved the land.

Elijah patented the land and lived there until about 1913 or 1914 when he sold to the L. E. Hart family. Ed Hart lived there until 1920 and Fred Hart took the place then. Fred Hart lived there the rest of his life. He died in the late 1950's. They sold most of the land before he died but his widow still owns a small part where the ranch house is.

The L. E. Hart family was no relation to the Dave Hart family mentioned in the first part of this series.

The only other homestead in Sedona proper was taken up as a dry farm by Frank Thompson about 1914. I will not try to cover all of the dry farms in the area because I do not know enough about them.

This one, however, was later irrigated by Walter Jordan and a big part of it is now included in the village of Sedona. It included all of the land on the west side of Jordan Lane, from the post office north, and about 15 acres on the east side at the north end.

Soon after Frank Thompson got patent to the land, he sold 40 acres on the south end to Lee Van Deren. He later sold the 15 acres on the east side and traded his remaining acres to Jess Purtymun, as mentioned before, for the present Mission Rancho. Purtymun traded the place to the Jordan family for a few acres of irrigated land on the north end of the place they had bought from Claude Black.

The next place down the creek from Sedona is what is known now as the Doodlebug Ranch. Several people had lived there in earlier years. It was known as the Bill James place in 1908 when Ira Owenby homesteaded it. Ira got patent to the land although he never did get a ditch on it.

In 1917 he sold it to Tom Bristow, one of the pioneer Bristows of the Verde Valley. Bristow put up a ditch on the place and sold it to George Black a few years later. Black sold to Ralph and Doodie Thomas in the 1930's. Doodie gave it the present name of Doodlebug.

*The James Homestead – home of Sedona's first settlers in about 1890*

In a few years she sold it to the present owners, the Staudes.

The place down, across the county line in Yavapai County, is the Chavez Ranch. Ambrosio Chavez's parents first moved there in 1902. About 1909, when Ambrosio was of legal age, he filed on the place.

There had been other squatters there before them. One, Johnny Robinson, no relation to Jack Robinson mentioned earlier, put a ditch on the place. Dave James also lived there for a while. He traded his rights to Chavez for an old wagon and a set of chain harness. It is the only other place that I know of in the area where the homesteader still lives.

Chavez has sold most of his land but still owns the part where the ranch house is.

Next down the creek is the present Crescent Moon Ranch. It was

Those Early Days.....

homesteaded by John H. Lee - I think in the late 1880's. Lee was a cattleman and used the OK brand at that time. He always spoke of the place as the OK Ranch. As stated before, he traded it to Mrs. James for cattle in 1895.

Mrs. James sold to D.E. Schnebly in 1902. Schnebly only kept the place a short time until he sold to a man named Palmer from Michigan. He was related to the late Dr. E. Payne Palmer, the well-known surgeon of Phoenix.

In 1905 Palmer sold to Henry Schuerman Sr. and D.E. Dumas. The Dumas family lived there until Mr. Dumas died in 1920. Mr. Schuerman died about the same time and the place was rented out most of the time until 1936. Dr. M.O. Dumas and the Schuerman heirs sold it to Andrew E. Baldwin that year. Baldwin died in 1943 and a few years later his widow sold to the Nick Duncans.

The Fred E. Schuerman place comes next. Erwin Schuerman, Fred's father and son of Henry Schuerman Sr., homesteaded there in 1908. There had been several people before him who had lived there for a while and moved on. Different ones of the Huckaby families had lived there at one time or another. They had built log cabins and farmed a little on the low land but had not tried to put water on the high land.

Another squatter, Ben Clay, had a cabin near the creek and farmed the sandy bottom. Also, Juan Armijo farmed the lowland a while. A family by the name of Castillo lived in the Huckaby cabins and had range cattle for a while.

At the time Erwin Schuerman homesteaded, the Pedro Martinez family was living in the old cabins and had a garden under the hill. Martinez worked for the Schuermans. Erwin built a ditch onto the high ground and put most of the land in cultivation. He got patent to the land and lived there the rest of his life. He died in 1929.

His son, Fred, took the place over as soon as he was old enough. Fred has sold a small part of the land but still owns most of the farming land.

Joining Fred Schuerman on the down-creek side is the original Henry Schuerman place. It was never homesteaded.

The Carrol family lived there in the early 1880's. They borrowed some money from Henry Schuerman, who at that time was a baker in Prescott. The Carrols eventually let Mr. Schuerman have the place in payment of the debt. Schuerman moved there to improve the place and sell it to get his money back. He found out soon that it was railroad land and that the Carrols had never owned it.

He bought it again and planted orchards and vineyards and lived there the rest of his life. It included the ranch on the east side of the creek now owned by Carl E. Brown. Henry Schuerman Jr., of F.H., lives at the old family home.

The next place down is now divided into three places. Mr. Schuerman had put the joining land into cultivation and farmed it for years as part of the home place. He had never used his homestead rights so in 1910 he applied for the land as a homestead. He built a house there and he and his wife lived there long enough to patent the land.

Myron Loy, who married the youngest Schuerman girl, now lives in the homestead house.

After Mr. Schuerman died the family sold the south part of the ranch to Jim Black, a cattleman. Black sold to Cecil White and a partner by the time of Cole. In a few years they sold to O.P. Hallermund. Hallermund sold the east part of his land to a man named Seaman and built a house on the west end, which he still owned. I think Sally Hallermund still lives there.

The creek makes a big U bend at the Schuerman Ranch. Where it runs most due west, there is another ranch east of the Schuerman homestead, was homesteaded by a schoolteacher by the name of Jerry Franks about 1890.

I do not know the exact history of the place but Frank Owenby bought about the time he sold his Sedona ranch to the Schneblys. He lived there until 1908 when he sold to Charles T. Hawkins.

In the meantime, the part east or south of the creek was acquired by Roy Owenby and was not sold to Hawkins. Hawkins sold to Haydee Lane ho in turn sold to Ira Hart.

The place was the winter quarters for the XL cattle and was known as the XL Ranch. Harts sold to Charles B. Gaddis about 1925. The Gaddis family lived there until about 1945 when they sold to Karl A. Dietrich, Dietrich sold to L.K. Lindahl who in turn recently sold to A.V. Wetmore, the present owner.

Roy Owenby sold his part of the place to Jose Chavez and his son, Tony, about 1916. The Chavez family did not farm there very long. They had it rented out most of the time they owned it. They were on a deal to sell two or three times but I think they still owned it up to the time it was brought by Mrs. M.P. Wentworth in 1935. Wentworth died in a few years and do not know who owns it now.

The next place down is owned now by Helen Varner Frye. I understand the place was patented by Rich Huckaby.

The Huckaby family lived around the Red Rock area for nearly 20 years. Someone or another lived at one time or another on most

Those Early Days.....

every place there but Rich was the only one who stayed long enough on one place to patent the land. They left the area about 1901.

Henry Schuerman Sr. bought the place when Huckabys left for California. It was rented out to Alejandro Martinez most of the time until after Mr. Schuerman died. When the Schuerman estate was divided, the ranch went to Fritz Schuerman.

Fritz told me that after he moved there he had the place surveyed and found that only a small corner of the farming ground was on the homestead. He made application for the rest of the land. The land office and the Forest Service admitted that a mistake had been made and allowed his entry without delay.

About 1940, Fritz sold to Jack and Helen Frye.

The next place down the creek was homesteaded as two separate homesteads by Juan Armijo and his son, Ambrosio. They had lived part time in the area before they took homesteads.

I do not know the exact date they took the places but it must have been in the late 1890's. They were cattlemen as well as farmers while they lived there.

When L.E. Hart and sons came to Oak Creek, about 1913, they bought Armijo's cattle. The Armijo's rented the place out and moved to the Holbrook area and went into the sheep business. After Juan died, I think in the 1930's, Ambrosio came back and lived there a while. He sold both homesteads, 320 acres, to Andrew Blackmore, a Los Angeles banker, in 1939.

A few years later Blackmore sold to Jack and Helen Frye. Helen Frye soon sold most of the place to a man named Burhop. Burhop did not stay long until he sold to the present owner, Willis Leenhouts, about 1949.

There is only one more place down the creek that is in what is known as Upper Oak Creek. It is the present Bullard Ranch.

I have heard that a man named Juan Nunez or Nuanez first tried to take the place in the 1890's. There was some question as to whether or not Nunez was an American citizen. To get around that difficulty he sent for his father-in-law to come and take the place for him. His father-in-law was Manuel Chavez, father of Ambrosio Chavez.

I do not know all the facts about that but Chavez lived there for quite a while and then it was Nunez's place.

When Harts bought the Armijo cattle they bought the Nunez Ranch at the same time.

Different ones of the Hart boys lived there at times. In the early 1920's they sold to Lee Kellam. Kellam farmed there until about 1940 when he sold to a man named Dayton. The place has changed hands in recent times and I have not kept up on all of the owners, but it is the Bullard Ranch now.

There is one more, small homestead up near the Ambrosio Chavez ranch. If there was any question about Juan Nunez's citizenship, it was cleared up later.

About 1908, he took a 20-acre homestead joining Chavez on the south, but all of the east side of the creek. After his death, his son, L.G. Nuanez, who still lives in Sedona, acquired the ranch. He sold to Doodie Thomas in the 1940's. Since then it has all been cut up and sold in small parcels. It joins, and I think is a part of, the subdivision known as Back O' Beyond.

Those Early Days.....

## A BIT OF ARIZONA POSTAL HISTORY

*by Harold H. Longfellow*

For thirty odd years I have collected these Arizona Territorial envelopes. We call them "covers". The first three years I worked at it, I managed to get the sum of thirteen covers. But three hundred and fifty of these different Territorial Town Covers have come my way since then. A great many of these Post Offices existed for a short time. Some existed only a few years and sometimes only a few months.

Six of the Covers shown are over one hundred years old and are very hard to obtain. About the only way to obtain them now is from some one who has made a collection. Most all of the Covers known of Arizona have been recorded by a member of the Western Cover Society, so that we know the number of covers that are known from a specific Post Office. An example is Sedona. There is just one known cover in existence.

Last year in May 1966, this collection which I own was entered in the Sixth International Philatelic Exhibition, Washington D.C. and I received a Silver Medal award for the exhibit of Arizona Territorial Postal History.

In picking the Covers that are shown in this book, I have tried to show some of the rarest ones and some of the towns close to Sedona. Try to imagine, if you can, the amount of mail that was sent from Sedona at the time that the Post Office was established. Perhaps there were 25 or 30 envelopes per month from the handful of families that lived here at that time. The Official Register listed compensation of the Sedona Postmaster as $20.07 for the fiscal year ending July 1, 1903 and $30.00 for the fiscal year ending July 1, 1911. Mail was carried by horseback twice a week, I am told, from Sedona to Cornville, then on to Cottonwood and Jerome. Here, it was taken by the narrow gauge train to Junction. The "Pea Vine" was the common name for the Santa Fe Railroad at that time.

The Post Office of Sedona was located very near where the Public School is now located. Later, in 1911, the Post Office was moved to the John J. Thompson home 3 miles North of Sedona near Indian Gardens.

There were four Territorial Postmasters. The first was Theodore C. Schnebly, on the 26th June 1902, when the Sedona Post Office was established. The second was Dorsey E. Schnebly 1905. The third was Mary L. Schnebly 1910 and the fourth was

John J. Thompson 1911 through Statehood date the 14th of February 1912.

Incidentally this Sedona Cover was sent by the father of Ambrosio Chavez to the Tax Collector of Yavapai County. The remuneration from this Post Office in those days was very little and was an accommodation by anyone that would take the Post mastership.

Please note on the Jerome strike that it is marked ARIZONA TER. During the Territorial days there were several of these different Territorial strikes and abbreviations, as some of these Postmasters were great abbreviators.

Here are most of them, which I have, "ARIZONA TERR.", "ARIZ. TY.", "ARIZ. T", "ARIZ.", "A.T.", "ARIZONA TER. 2", "ARIZ. TER.", "ARI.", "ARZ.", "ARIZOA", "ARIZONA". By far the most common was "ARIZ". In the early days "A.T." was used a lot, and there are many manuscript cancellations. This was generally used by a small Post Office until a strike could be sent for and made.

The COTTONWOOD Cover that is illustrated, is one of the first cancelled. It is what we call a Pen cancellation or manuscript. The pen cancellation is the handwriting of George M. Willard, who was the first Postmaster of Cottonwood and the father of our Don Willard who has allowed me to exhibit, with this Cover a receipt of the last quarters business of the Cottonwood Post Office for the year 1885. The amount of this receipt is $67.21. Mr. Willard served as Postmaster of this town from July 9, 1885 until Aug. 31, 1899.

Those Early Days.....

A RESUME OF ARIZONA TERRITORY, PERTAINING TO ITS POSTAL HISTORY.

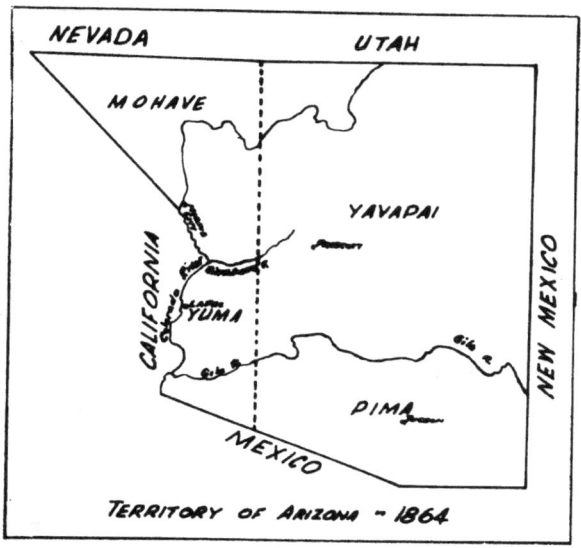

THE MAP SHOWS ITS BOUNDARIES.

THE UNITED STATES ACQUIRED THE LANDS OF THE ARIZONA TERRITORY THROUGH THE TREATY OF GUADALUPE HIDALGO, WITH MEXICO, JULY 4, 1848, AND THE GADSDEN PURCHASE, JUNE 30, 1854, WHICH WERE INCLUDED IN THE NEW MEXICO TERRITORY, SEPTEMBER 9, 1850.

THERE WERE TEN (10) POST OFFICES ESTABLISHED IN THIS SECTION OF WHAT IS NOW ARIZONA. OF THESE TEN (10) POST OFFICES, ONLY TWO (2) CONTINUED THROUGH WHEN ARIZONA TERRITORY WAS CREATED BY THE UNITED STATES CONGRESS, FEBRUARY 24, 1863. THEY WERE:

P I M O   V I L L A G E   AND   T U C S O N.

THERE ARE ONLY FIVE (5) OF THESE PRE-TERRITORIAL POST OFFICES FROM WHICH MARKINGS ARE KNOWN:

F O R T   D E F I A N C E   -   T U C S O N
A R I Z O N A   -   F O R T   B U C H A N A N
T U B A C.

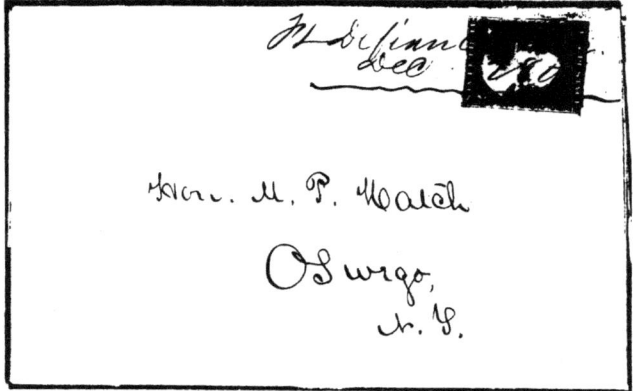

The first Post Office to be established, in what is now Arizona, on April 9, 1856 in Bernalillo County, New Mexico. John E. Webber was its first and only Postmaster, while in New Mexico Territory. This folded cover is dated December 28, 1857 and was written by Captain John Porter Hatch, who gave a most illustrious service to his country, retiring as Brigadier General in 1886. This cover undoubtedly was sent to Albuquerque by Military Express, then on to Santa Fe by stage, and on East.

Those Early Days.....

Fort Defiance, N.M.<br>
Dec. 27, 1857

Dear Father,

     Another mail leaves here to-morrow and I take advantage of it to let you know that I am very well, allthough I cannot say that I am content. We have not received any mail since my last, the last letters from Oswego bore date Sept. 16 & 17. After this we expect our mail with more regularity as Major Brooks has established a Semi-monthly mail to Albuquerque, and has requested that the Express may not be delayed. Our Christmas was a very quiet one, and for me far from a merry one.

     I went last week to the Pueblo of Zuni about 60 miles South of this to buy sheep if possible for the use of the Post. I found the travelling on horseback at this season very cold and camping out at night not as pleasant as in Summer.

     I have been made Quartermaster and Commissary of the Post, adding ten dollars per month to my pay and 20 dollars per month to my duties. It will however relieve me from Company duty when Me Lane arrives. The weather has not been as cold as I had been led to expect, the ground is still covered with snow, but the days are generally quite warm and pleasant. The thermometer has been below zero two or three mornings but rises rapidley with the Sun. To-morrow we commence filling the ice house. Our ice is about 8 inches thick.

     Our garrison is pleasant allthough not lively, Mrs. Major Brooks is a very nice person and quite pretty. The Doctor (a new comer) is a gentlemanly man and is very well informed, one of the young Officers a pleasant man, but like most young graduates imagines he has had considerable more experience than any one else in the Army. The other a young man appointed from civil life very much of a gentleman but entirely unsuited to the profession he has chosen. He is at present confined to his room by rheumatism and home-sickness. He is the only child of his parents and has never before been away from home. We had a death last night among the Soldiers, cause rheumatism. Tis is a terrible disease in this country much worse than at any other place in the United States. A singular thing when the extrem dryness of the atmosphere is considered.

     There has been a very insufficient supply of hay laid in for this Post, and the Major has recommended that the horses be sent to Albuquerque for the Winter. If they are sent down I very much fear that I shall be sent to look after them. I should dislike this very much indeed and hope that some arrangement may be made to prevent it. I like the Post very much and allthough it is pretty much as the Doctor says, that we live the lives of oysters Still I am comfortable here and I do not desire any change. It is so long since I have been comfortably settled that I want to remain.

     There is still no prospect of my getting any leave to go out of the Country, unless you are able to assist me.

     I hope Mac Bronson will be here before the end of the month with Capt. McLane. He was in doubt when he last wrote me what he would determine upon.

     Give my Love to Mother and Elsie.

Truly Yours<br>
Jno. P. Hatch.

Established December 4, 1856 in Dona Ana County, New Mexico. Elias Prevoort, Postmaster. Fr. Marcos visited Tucson in 1539; Kino 1692. In 1848 population of Tucson was 760 persons, whites, Indians and all. Tucson was occupied by U. S. Troops in 1856. August 16, 1856 a convention was held there to organize the Territory of Arizona as a political entity, however it did not succeed until February 24, 1863 when President Abraham Lincoln signed the Arizona Territorial Act.

Those Early Days.....

    Established February 21, 1859 in Dona Ana County, New Mexico. Frederick Hulseman, Postmaster at the time of this manuscript, cancellation which was July 28, 1859 according to all indications. This was the same year that "The Weekly Arizonian", the first newspaper to be published within the area, now known as Arizona, got started in Tubac.

FORT BUCHANAN, N. M.

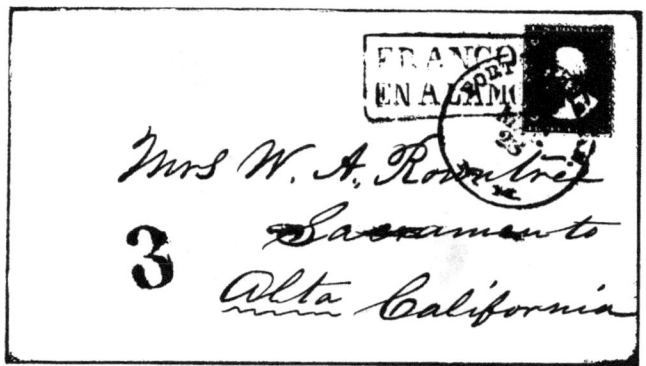

Established June 5, 1857 in Dona Ana County, New Mexico. Elias Prevoort, Postmaster. Location was on Sonoita River, North of present day Patagonia. This famous Fort was destroyed, with all of its supplies, and abandoned July 23, 1861 by the Union Troops when they left for Fort Craig, New Mexico. This cover probably went West on one of the last Butterfield Overland Mail Stages.

Those Early Days…..

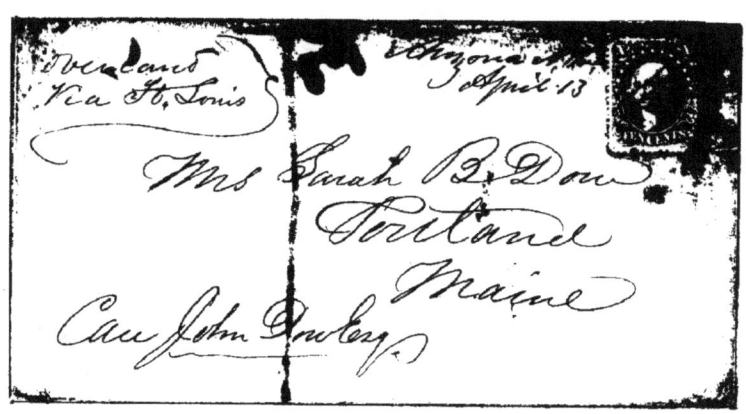

Established March 17, 1858 in Dona Ana County, New Mexico. John Blake Dow was the first Postmaster, however at the time of this pen cancellation, which I believe to be 1859, Lansford Warren Hastings was Postmaster. The manuscript is a different handwriting. This is the second name for this location, the first was Colorado City, the third was Yuma, fourth was Arizona City, and finally by act of Territorial Legislature it was changed to Yuma in 1873.

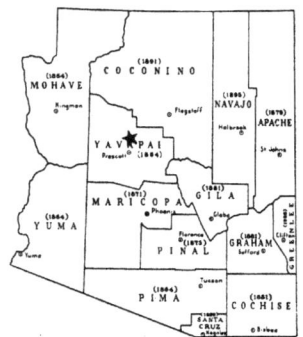

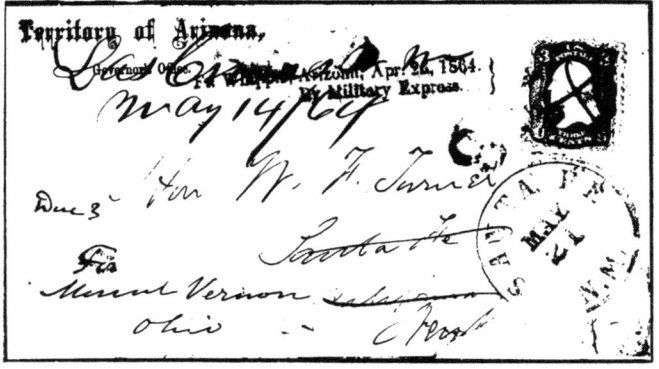

Located twenty (20) miles North of Prescott, at Del Rio Springs, near the headwaters of the Verde River in Little Chino Valley. Arizona's first Territorial Capitol, and while only temporary, it served from January 22, 1864 to May 18, 1864, when the Capitol was moved to Prescott.

This cover was sent by Military Express to Las Cruces, New Mexico Post Office on April 26, 1864, and it reached Santa Fe, New Mexico May 21st, its first destination, then it was forwarded to Mount Vernon, Ohio. The handwriting is Richard C. McCormick's, Secretary of the Territory, and a little later he became our second Territorial Governor and the Honorable W. F. Turner was one of three of our first Chief Justices. At the time this cover was sent, there were just two Post Offices in Arizona Territory, Pimo Village and Tucson. Both were carry-overs from New Mexico Territory. Prescott was our first established Post Office after Arizona was made a Territory, June 10, 1864.

Those Early Days…..

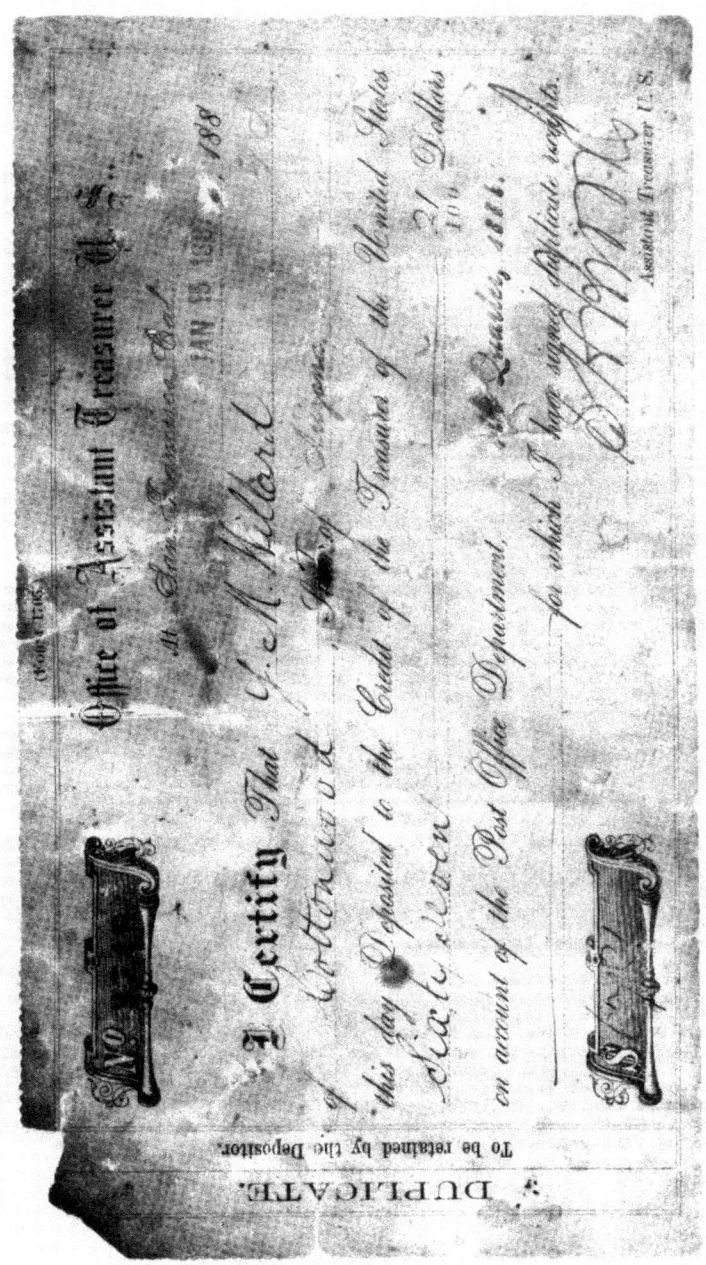

## COTTONWOOD

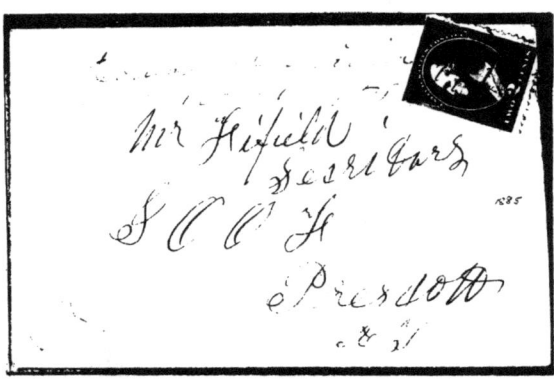

Established July 9, 1885 in Yavapai County. George M. Willard, Postmaster. Located on the West bank of the Verde River, four (4) miles South of Clarkdale. Named for the Cottonwood trees along the river.

Those Early Days.....

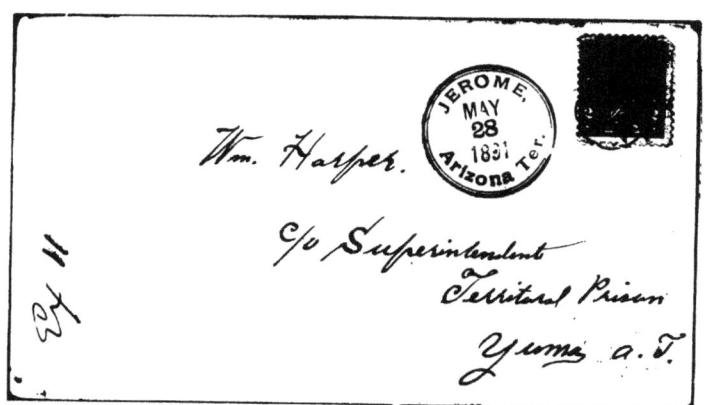

Established September 10, 1883 in Yavapai County. Frederick F. Thomas, Postmaster. Named for Eugene Jerome, mining company official. Located thirty-two (32) miles Northeast of Prescott. Frederick E. Murray, Postmaster at the time of this strike. (Phoenix and Yuma back stamp).

**SEDONA**

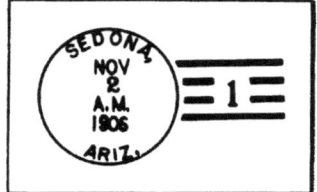

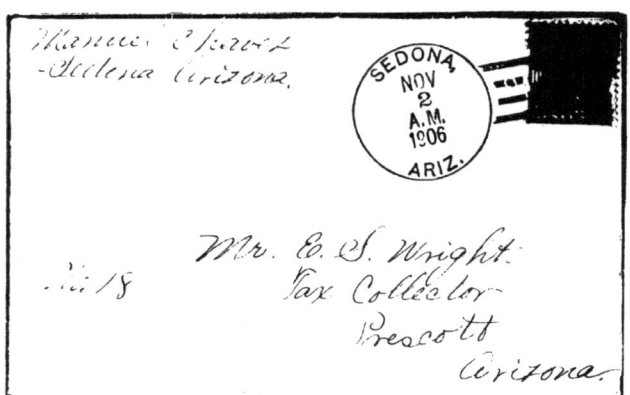

Established June 26, 1902 in Coconino County. Theodore Schnebly was the first Postmaster and at the time of this cover, Dorsey E. Schnebly was Postmaster. Named after Mrs. Carl Schnebly, wife of an early settler, her given name was Sedona. Located thirty (30) miles South of Flagstaff on U. S. Highway 89A. The most beautiful place in this world.

Those Early Days…..

## GRANDVIEW

Established November 27, 1903 in Coconino County. Harry H. Smith, Postmaster. Located thirteen (13) miles East of Grand Canyon, on the rim. A descriptive name. A fine description of accomodations and information on back as well. (Grand Canyon and Williams back stamp).

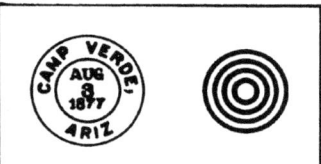

CAMP VERDE

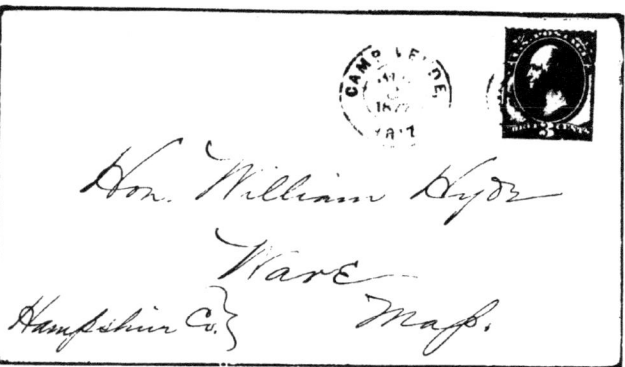

Established March 14, 1873 in Yavapai County. George W. Hance, Postmaster. Named for the Verde River nearby and was descriptive. Location is eighty-seven (87) miles North of Phoenix, just off Highway 69. William S. Head, Postmaster at the time of this strike.

Those Early Days.....

## THE FIRST WHITE CHILD BORN IN SEDONA
*by Margaret J. Stilson*

J.F. (Frank) Thompson was born on the old James homestead in Sedona on April 25, 1882. He was the oldest child of Jim and Maggie Thompson of Indian Gardens and was the first white child born in Sedona. He grew up on the raw frontier where schools were scarce and he had a very sketchy education. What he did learn as a small boy was how to harness freight teams and how to lash a pack on a packhorse. He started driving horse teams at the age when most boys were still playing with toy wagons. He remembered as a boy, and a young man, when all of the Verde Valley ranges were like grain fields.

There was no soil erosion at that time, Big Park and Grasshopper Flat did not have any gullies or washes across them at all. In the spring of the year, open flats looked like flower gardens. Mountain lions and bears were common and grizzly bears were not uncommon. Deer and wild turkeys were plentiful as were antelope. Oak Creek was full of native mountain trout.

He got a little schooling at Red Rock between 1891 and 1899, but it was not much. In 1899 the first school was built in Oak Creek Canyon. Frank was one of the men who helped build the schoolhouse and also one of the pupils when the school opened. The school desks and furnishings were moved from the old San Francisco Peaks District No. 4 near the Pump house, to Oak Creek and became Oak Creek District No. 4. I have heard Dad tell of helping the Purtymun boys bring the desks, blackboard, and tables from the rim straight down to the creek. All country schools had only six-month terms at that time, and although Frank Thompson went to school at times until he was grown, it would total a very short school period. There were thirteen children who attended that last school, which was in 1901. Six of them were Thompsons, six Purtymuns and one, Bessie Thomas.

His father saved 80 acres of land for him at Indian Gardens until he was 21 years old. Frank built a cabin and cleared some land and farmed after he filed on the place. In the money panic and hard times of 1907 and 1908, he left the place to work for wages. He helped build the old County Hospital at Flagstaff in 1907. That is the building, which is now used by the Arizona Historical Society as a Museum. In the fall and winter of that same year he cut and hauled cordwood to Jerome from just off the National Forest boundary near the Windmill Ranch.

In the fall of 1908, Frank went to Gila County near the old

Ellison Post Office on the rim above Pleasant Valley. He worked for Ketcherside's Flying V cattle outfit and he drove freight teams some for Ben Nail.

In the fall of 1909, he came back to Oak Creek and he and a brother started a small cattle outfit. He was too restless to stay in one place for long and he sold out and went back to Young and the Pleasant Valley country in 1911.

He liked to drive freight teams better than anything else so he went to work for Ben Nail again. Soon he bought the complete freight outfit from Ben. There were two wagons and six freight horses.

*J.F. [Frank] Thompson and the ruins of his first cabin in Sedona. This picture was taken about 1960 on the present Walter Jordan Ranch.*

All of the Pleasant Valley area got all of their supplies from Holbrook during the summer months. There was only a pack trail to Globe, 60 miles to the south. Holbrook was about 110 miles to the north and it took about a week to make the trip. Freighting from there was good business except for two things; too much

# Those Early Days.....

competition and the seasons were too short. The road went over such high country, the winter snows did not melt off and the mud dry up before May, and he was lucky if the winter storms did not close the roads before November 1st.

The first winter when the roads became closed, he headed for Miami, AZ where they were building a new copper smelter. He went down over the old so-called road over the Sierra Ancha Mountains to Salt River. He did get work for his teams on the railroad that was being built from Globe to Miami, AZ. After about a month he got sick and had to quit. He moved up to Tonto Basin above Roosevelt and camped and turned his horses loose on the range. When the weather warmed some and he was feeling better he went back to Pleasant Valley. He plowed the Young farm for Miss Ola Young and her sister. Ola Young was postmaster at Young for fifty years. By the time he finished plowing, the roads had dried out and he could start freighting to Pleasant Valley from Holbrook. This was his last year of freighting; he gave it up as a losing game that year when the roads were closed and he went to Phoenix.

By mid-December, he was back on Oak Creek again. He brought all of his freight outfit with him except his trail wagon. He sold most of his horses and went to work on the County road. That was in 1914-the year the first road was opened through Oak Creek Canyon. He worked on the road until spring and then rented a farm and farmed until the next fall.

In the early fall of 1914 he made application for a homestead in what was called at that time, The Knoll Flat in Sedona. He started fencing and plowing land and raised his first crop in 1915.

His place included all of the land on the west side of Jordan Road from about where the First National Bank is now located to Mormon Camp Wash on the north and 15 acres on the east side of the road at the north end. He got patent to the land in 1917 and sold 40 acres on the south end to Lee Van Deren. With more working capital he bought more modern farming equipment and built a better house. He never failed to make a crop while he was dry farming there and he made some bumper crops of dry beans and com. He opened a little store in his new house and was on his way-but by then he was restless and ready to move again. He sold out to Albert Purtymun and bought seven acres of raw land near Indian Gardens. He did some improvements on the place and then sold it and went back to take over the dry farm again from his brother-in-law, Albert Purtymun. The place at Indian Gardens is now the Russell Taylor site. In 1923 he traded the last of his dry farm to Jess Purtymun for the present Mission Rancho in Oak Creek Canyon. He lived there until 1925 when he sold to the parents of Charley and Ira Smith.

He married Hilda Bishop on October 1st, 1925 and for a time he worked for Frank Pendley. For several years then, he followed construction work and lived in tents or rented houses. He acquired a little property at Indian Gardens in 1938 and lived there raising berries and truck garden. He did most of the work on a swinging footbridge so the one neighbor family and his own could get across the creek in winter when the water was high. However, his wife was afraid to cross that bridge but his children were able to get in and out to school.

This was where he was living when the Indian Gardens dance hall was changed to a skating rink. Most of the people of Upper Oak Creek were related to each other in one way or another at that time, but at the present there are only a very few of the old timers left. While Frank and his family were living there, at that time he sold lots of vegetables and berries to tourists, he also gave much of it away to friends. His wife had one of the loveliest flower gardens around there and she helped many people in different ways.

In 1945 he moved his family to East Flagstaff but it was called Sunnyside then. That is where he spent the rest of his life. He passed on April 1st, 1966 from a fractured hip. He had a family of two boys and one girl (myself) and one stepdaughter whom he raised for nine years. She passed away in 1955 in San Diego, California.

My father, Frank Thompson was put to rest only about five miles from where he was born.

Those Early Days…..

## THE FIRST FAMILY TO PATENT LAND IN SEDONA VILLAGE

*by Roy Owenby, as told to Albert E. Thompson*

No historic sketch of Sedona would be complete without some mention being made of the Frank Owenby family. They first moved to what is now Sedona in 1893, and some member of the family has lived not far from Sedona from that time on.

Frank Owenby Sr. and his wife and two small boys left the vicinity of Uvalde, Texas with a pair of little mules and a wagon about 1885. They stopped at Trinidad, Colorado where another son, Roy, was born in 1888. In 1889, the year that Babbitt Brothers of Flagstaff established their mercantile business at that place, the Owenby family arrived in Flagstaff.

One of Mr. Owenby's first jobs in that frontier town was hauling water from the old town spring and delivering it to the houses of the residents of the town. There was no water system of any kind there at that time, so if a resident did not have his own well he bought water from Owenby's water wagon. While he had the water route Frank Owenby got a few cows and started a small dairy. He delivered milk as well as water to his customers. He kept adding more cows to his dairy herd and by the time he left Flagstaff he had a fair sized bunch of cattle. While they lived in Flagstaff a baby girl, Birdie was born in 1890.

Frank Owenby had been a cattleman in Texas and his aim was to get into the cattle business in Arizona. He had scouted the country in various directions from Flagstaff, and Oak Creek in the present Sedona looked good to him.

Roy Owenby the only living one of the immediate family remembers some of the trip by wagon from Flagstaff to Sedona in 1893. Roy said that they traveled the Old Verde road down to Beaver Head station and turned back through Big Park to Sedona. The Old Verde road followed the same general route of the present Black Canyon Highway by the way of Munds Park, Woods Ranch, and Rattlesnake Tanks, but it came down off the rim on the old stage route and immigrant trail to Beaver Head Station.

Roy said that they stopped and visited the James family, the only other residents of the area a short while and drove on across the creek to an old log cabin on the place that Mr. Owenby filed on soon afterward. The James family was living at that time on the land that was patented years later by Elijah Lay. It is just east of the present King's Ransom Motel on the bench nearer the creek. The place where Owenbys located had first been taken by Bill James, son of the first Sedona settler, about 1880. After building a cabin and doing some work on an irrigation ditch, Bill James had given the place up and moved on.

*The Owenby family, moving to the mountain with pack mules, before Schnebly Hill road was built — about 1899. Frank Owenby Sr. is in lead, with Frank Jr. Next is Mrs. Nancy Owenby and daughter Birdie bringing up the rear.*

Although Owenby first filed on the place in 1893, he found out later that the survey was not correct so he relinquished his first filing and filed again in 1895 on the correct place. He brought his little bunch of cattle from Flagstaff to Sedona when he moved there. His brand was, O N B, a phonetic spelling of his name. He kept that brand in use until he sold the last of his cattle in this area to Lee Van Deren in 1915.

Roy said that his father bought a one half interest in a bunch of cattle owned by Dr. Brannen of Flagstaff, branded T V bar, connected. Frank Owenby managed the cattle for several years and eventually bought Dr. Brannen's share. After he became full owner of the T V bar cattle he branded almost all of his increase in that brand and only a small bunch was branded O N B.

At about the same time Mr. Owenby also managed a bunch of cattle branded D C bar that belonged to Dr. M.A. Carrier of Munds Park and Jerome. He later bought the Carrier cattle also.

When the Owenbys lived in Sedona on their first homestead, there was no school closer than Red Rock at the

Those Early Days.....

Schuerman ranch. The family moved to Red Rock to school part of the time and at other times they moved to Cornville to school. Roy clearly remembers being with his father in Barney Pasture in the fall of 1899 to pick up some cattle and drive them around and down the Munds Trail, (present Schnebly Hill). Jim and Ollie Barney and George Purtymun were working on a log fence, the first fence of Barney Pasture. Soon after they got home they moved to Red Rock for the school term. Josie Hance, daughter of Judge George Hance of Camp Verde was the Red Rock schoolteacher that year.

In the late 1890s, Ira, "Tex", and his next younger brother Gail, or Gayley, as he was called, together with Elmer Hart, (brother of Lute Hart), rode to Lower Oak Creek to get some horses. While they were there Gayley was kicked by a horse and died in a short time from the injury.

In 1896, Frank Jr. was born when the family lived at the Sedona place. He was the youngest boy of the family.

About 1900 Mr. Owenby and his son Ira, bought the O K cattle from Les Hart, and ranged them in the Dry Creek area for several years. A few years later Owenby also bought the A J bar cattle except eight cows and calves from Jim Thompson (my dad).

On April 6, 1901, Frank and Nancy Owenby sold their 80-acre homestead in Sedona to D.E. Schnebly and moved to Jerome where they already owned some property in the Gulch, as it was known by all old timers. They kept their cattle however and Mr. Owenby spent a big part of his time on the range looking out for his interests.

In 1903 they bought the Jerry Franks homestead on Oak Creek at Red Rock. The family lived there until 1908. While they were all living there, Ira and Roy bought the X L cattle from Ed Thurston and John Loy and ran them for several years. They also used several other brands at times over the years. Ira branded R I O for a while. That was his initials. Roy used the H slash L brand for a while and also the P bar H brand that he bought from Bill Price.

In 1908, Frank Owenby filed on the remaining 80 acres allowed him under the homestead law. His last homestead was known more recently as the George Jordan ranch in Sedona. He moved there in 1908 and started working on an irrigation ditch. In the same year Ira homesteaded the place known more recently in Sedona as the Doodle Bug ranch. (Present Poco Diablo).

Roy was left at the Red Rock ranch but it was only for a short time. Mrs. Owenby stayed there during school terms and sent young Frank to school before a school was started in Sedona in 1910. Roy married Lena Schuerman in April 1910 and not long afterward the Red Rock ranch and the X L cattle were sold to Charley Hawkins. Roy moved to Flagstaff and worked for the other fellow for a while.

In 1914 he went to Adamana, Arizona and started in the cattle business there. He was there about two years. In 1918 he took a mountain homestead in Fry Park. He planted a crop each spring and worked for wages until time to harvest his crop in the Fall. In the early 1920s he started working in the Clemenceau smelter. He sold his mountain ranch in 1930 to a man named Underwood, who in turn sold to Dr. R.O. Raymond of Flagstaff, and Raymond sold to the Coconino Cattle Company.

In 1911, Frank Owenby bought what Roy called the Long H outfit from Frank Wallace, who lived in Holbrook and ranged cattle from Adamana to Springerville. Owenby moved the cattle to his Sedona Range and branded them over into the T V bar brand, they were all white face cattle and he sold all of his spotted or painted cattle.

He only kept that outfit for about a year though until he sold all of the T V bar cattle to M. O. Dumas, and his cousin Harry Stephens. Mr. Owenby kept his O N B cattle and started building them up, together with a small bunch branded F O that belonged to his youngest son, Frank.

In 1915 Roy was about ready to get out of the cattle business in Adamana, but his father was ready to start over there. Mr. Owenby sold his Sedona cattle to Lee Van Deren in 1915 and sold his ranch to Frank Spear and Jess Purtymun, and moved to Adamana and started in the cattle business with his son Ira. (Ira kept his Sedona Homestead however until 1917, when he sold to Tom Bristow).

Frank Owenby spent the rest of his life in Adamana. He died there in 1937. Mrs. Owenby passed on in 1948 and Ira died soon afterward, and young Frank only lived a few years longer. Birdie, who was a schoolteacher and had never married passed away in the 1920s.

I remember Mr. Owenby as far back as my memory goes. I always spoke of him as Mr. Owenby and still do. He was always good to children. I clearly remember him doing little favors for me when I was only a toddler. One time he came to my rescue when an old turkey gobbler was about to take me down and he was my hero from then on.

He was a rather large rangy built man of a reddish or sandy

Those Early Days.....

complexion. He always wore a big moustache.

After the Clemenceau smelter closed down in the late 1930s, Roy Owenby moved back to Oak Creek at Red Rock, to a ranch his wife had inherited from the Schuerman Estate. He farmed there for a while in the depression years and then started working as manager of the old Jerry Franks homestead where he had lived

*Oak Creek Roundup 1909, Left to right, A.G. (Dutch) Dickinson, Roy Owenby, (Foreman), Joe Lay, Charley Butcher, John Baillie, l.M. Jackson, Bill Smith, (cook), Harvey Thurston, Ed Page (on horse with sack of rope hobbles), Charley Hawkins, George Moore and John Ralston.*

many years before. It had been bought by L.K. Lindahl and Roy became Lindah's manager and cowboy. Lindahl had a small bunch of cattle so Roy was back at his old cow punching job again.

He and Lena sold their Red Rock property to Carl E. Brown Jr. in the 1950s and bought a retirement home from Jay Elmer in Jackass Flat near Dry Creek.

Even after retirement, Roy kept a saddle horse and helped some of the cattlemen, mainly Dale Gardner, when they held their Spring roundup and also when they sold their calves in the Fall and moved their cattle to the Winter range.

Roy started punching cattle about as soon as he was able to sit on a horse by himself. He said his father had to help him on his horse when he first started. By the time he was 12 years old he was a top hand and able to hold a man's job any place around cattle.

Roy has an excellent memory and I have found him to be a very reliable reference of pioneer history of the Sedona area.

Roy has two married daughters. Dorothy, the oldest one, married Willis Edwards and lives in Prescott. Getha, the younger one, married Chester Michael and lives in Phoenix.

In 1960, Roy and Lena celebrated their Golden Wedding anniversary. Lena only lived a few years after that. Roy lives alone in his retirement home now and has lots of time to look back over his many years on the frontier.

He told me recently that they used to hold up cattle and brand calves in the Spring roundup right near his present house. I asked him if he ever dreamed at that time that he would some day have a house and a good well of water in that flat. He said he did not have the slightest idea at that time that there would ever be a water well there. He said he had wrestled and thrown calves down there in hot weather and be so thirsty he could not spit and not a drop of water to be had. After the branding was over they would all get on their horses and race for Oak Creek to get a drink of water.

Times have changed from what they were fifty to seventy-five years ago.

Written by Albert E. Thompson from information supplied by Roy Owenby.

Since this was written, Roy Owenby passed away on August 26, 1967 in a Prescott, Arizona hospital.

Those Early Days.....

## EARLY ROADS OF SEDONA AREA
*by Albert E. Thompson*

According to Thomas Farrish's History of Arizona Vol. 5 page 101, the first expedition to locate a road through Northern Arizona was made by Lt. A.W. Whipple in 1854-55.

In 1858 Lt. E.F. Beal was sent out to make a survey along the same route, the 35th parallel. That would be the route of the present Santa Fe Railroad and Highway 66.

It seems that a branch of that road was laid out soon after from the Valley of The Little Colorado River near the present town of Winslow. It veered southwest over the plateau toward where Prescott was later located and on to the Colorado River at Yuma.

It entered the Verde Valley on Dry Beaver Creek a short distance north of the present McGuireville. In 1876 a stage station was built there and called Beaver Head Station.

After settlements started at Camp Verde in 1865, an army post soon followed. There were some roads built by the army, out from the valley.

One was a road from Camp Verde to the Tonto Rim country east of the valley. Another was the Cherry Creek road. From the best information I can get Cherry Creek road was built to get timbers for the first permanent post buildings at Camp Verde.

As the Verde settlements grew, roads were extended to Upper Verde and to Lower Oak Creek.

When Red Rock and Upper Oak Creek were settled later, the people went up the stage road to the old Beaver Head station and followed up Dry Beaver Creek to Big Park. There the road branched, and one branch went west to Red Rock and the other branch kept on north to the Sedona area. There were no big canyons or bad hills to go over, so a wagon could be driven through without having to do much roadwork.

From here on I am on more familiar ground and can go into more detail in my story.

While there was a road from the Lower Verde to Upper Oak Creek, there was none west across Dry Creek to the Upper Verde.

I believe my Dad, Jim Thompson, was the first, or at least one of the first, to take a wagon across that way from the Sedona area. I have heard him tell of having to use ropes to anchor his wagon to a tree to keep it right side up when he crossed Dry Creek. I believe that was in the early 1880's.

Some of the first settlers at Red Rock had a kind of a "bear slide" road down the steep hillside from the Grasshopper Flat area that connected with the trail from Sedona to Cottonwood.

About 1885 or 1886 Henry Schuerman Sr. moved to Red Rock. Shortly afterward he got a better road out from his place and did not have to go straight up the mountain.

In a few years settlers of both Sedona and Red Rock got fairly passable roads out to the Upper Verde. Most of these first roads were built by the settlers themselves with little if any help from County or Territory.

For several years the only way to get out from the Verde Valley to Flagstaff and the mountain country, was to go to the Beaver Head Station and up the mountain from there. The wagons went up the mountain on the old stage road and turned north from there. They followed a route much the same as the new Black Canyon Highway does now, by Woods Spring and Munds Park to Flagstaff.

That was a long, long, journey for folks of Upper Oak Creek and Upper Verde to take, to get to the mountains. Many of the settlers were cowmen and moved to the mountain each summer and back for the winter. They drove their cattle back and forth by way of one of the many trails leading to the mountain. One of the most popular trails was the Munds Trail.

It came through Sedona and up the mountain much the same way as the present Schnebly Hill Road does.

Jim Munds, one of the sons of William Munds, had a homestead at Munds Park. After his death, John Loy, a brother of Mrs. Jim Munds came to Munds Park to farm the homestead.

From information I have got from old-timers it seems that John Loy was the most industrious worker to have a road built from the old Flagstaff Lower Verde road, by way of the Munds Trail to Oak Creek and the Upper Verde Valley.

I have talked to Roy Owenby several times about the early history of this road. Roy's father, Frank Owenby Sr. came to Sedona in 1893 and homesteaded the ranch that he sold to the Schnebly family in 1901.

Roy told me that he clearly remembered when John Loy hired a man to start work on the road from the Oak Creek end.

I asked him if it could have been as early as 1898. He answered, "It was earlier than that".

From some information I got later I would place the date in 1896.

Roy told me that John Loy hired a man that he remembered only as Jackie, who worked all of one fall on the road. Apparently

Those Early Days.....

it was not much of a road. Roy recalls that Jackie dug a trench along the hillside to make a rut for the uphill wagon wheels to run so the wagon would not upset.

Myron Loy, nephew of John Loy, told me later that Jackie's last name was McDonald. Anyway Jackie got a trail built from the creek up to Bear Wallow Canyon so a wagon could travel it.

Sometime in the winter John Loy came with a wagon and drove up as far as he could and made camp. He brought with him as a crew, Jim Wagner and Ed Thurston. The three of them and Jackie worked the rest of the winter on the road. They got the road built up as far as Bear Wallow Seep.

Apparently Loy was not the only one interested in the road, but he did something more than talk about it. Some money was collected by subscription from both Flagstaff and Valley people. How much money was collected is only a guess now, but was not likely very much.

While trying to get information about this road, I learned that Mr. R.W. Fishback of Sedona had some data on it. He had dug into the roads building on an entirely different matter. Mr. Fishback was kind enough to let me look over his material and use any of it that I wished.

Among other things I found a clipping from "The Arizona Daily Sun" dated September 27, 1951. It is about a faded road petition dated May 12, 1898, found by F.M. Gold, county attorney, and Ralph Barney, county engineer, while searching county records on a modern day road matter.

The petition was signed by 65 Flagstaff citizens. While all of the signers are not listed in the item, those that are listed include some of the most prominent citizens of Flagstaff at that time. Most of the names are very familiar to me.

The petition asks the Board of Supervisors to appoint a viewer to survey the proposed road. The item goes on to say that the petition does not mention the proposed route the road would follow from Flagstaff to Jerome, but that Mr. Gold believes that the petition ante-dated the Schnebly Hill route into the Verde Valley. Mr. Gold gives as his reason for that belief; that a few years previous, he had come across a weathered sign nailed to a tree in the Barney Pasture area, bearing the legend: Jerome and pointing in that general direction, indicating that there had been a road through that area to Verde Valley at one time.

I distinctly remember a sign nailed to a fence post in Fry Park in the early 1920's. It had arrows pointing and was lettered, Flagstaff and Clarkdale. While that may not be the sign that Mr. Gold saw, I am quite sure there was never any such road built or even seriously considered. It is not likely that a sign would remain when there is not the slightest evidence of any such road remaining.

*John Loy, firing a dynamite blast during the building of present Schnebly Hill road. This scene is between Bear Wallow and Merry Go Round about 1901.*

The names given as signers of the petition are as follows: J.W. Francis, Allen Doyel, E.S. Clark, A.T. Cornish, T.E. Pulliam, James Loy, Alex McDermit, T.E. Pollack, B.A. Cameron Sr., George Hoxworth, C.W. VanDeren, H.H. Hoxworth, T.J. Colter, Hugh E. Campbell, John Hennesey, J.T. Daggs, J. Abineau, B. Hock, J.W. Weatherford, G.J. Shultz, J.A. Vail, A.H. Beasly, T.J. Moyer, George H. Coffin, J.E. Jones, C.A. Keller, Harry Kislinbury, and J.W. Power.

I am fully convinced that the petition concerned the Schnebly Hill road, or as it was called at first, The Verde Cutoff Road. My reason is that I never heard a whisper of any other proposed road direct from Flagstaff to Jerome. Furthermore the date coincides almost exactly with the date Roy Owenby believes that John Loy started work on the Verde Cutoff Road.

Those Early Days.....

*Some of the men most responsible for getting a road built down present Schnebly Hill. From left to right: Harry Hibben, Jim James, George Babbitt [County Supervisor at the time], Jim Thompson and John Loy. Jim Thompson took the contract to finish the road. John Loy was responsible for starting on the road.*

    I do not know whether or not any county money was ever put up for the road before 1901, when my dad, J.J. Thompson started work there. I do know that John Loy continued to work there until early 1901. Whether he got any county help or only subscription money is only a guess with me. He got a passable road up to what is called the Merry-Go-Round now. From there on to the top he had, what one of the men who worked finishing up the road called, "A scratched out road". I asked him what he called a scratched out road, and he said, that Loy had the brush cut and some of the easier parts built, but all of the big rock and hard to build parts were left undone. Some of the other men that worked on the last stretch of the road, told me that it appeared that Loy had tried to get a trail finished up the hill that he could get a wagon over, in the hopes that he could get county help. He had got in such a hurry that he had made parts of it impossibly steep. Quite a lot of it had to be changed and located on a better grade. It was all done by hand labor, and the big rocks had to be drilled by hand before they could be dynamited.
    Sometime in 1901 another subscription petition was started. D. E. (Ellsworth)Schnebly, got the promise of $300., and Dad took a small crew and started work late in 1901.

They worked for three weeks, but only one man that had signed up to pay, paid his ten dollars. The crew got nothing for their work.

Apparently the petition of 1896 was turned down by the board of Supervisors, but after a few years, more people got interested in the road, and more pressure was put on the County Board of Supervisors to get the road built.

In the R.W. Fishback data I found notes from the minutes of a meeting of the Board of Supervisors about a new petition. In Vol. B3 page 322. The petition is given as follows: Flagstaff, Arizona February 24, 1902 PETITION FOR THE ESTABLISHMENT OF A COUNTY ROAD

"To the Honorable Board of Supervisors, Coconino County Territory of Arizona."

We, the undersigned, residents of Coconino County Arizona, paying road taxes therein, respectfully petition The Honorable Board of Supervisors of said county to lay out and establish a public road as follows, to wit:

Beginning at a point on the present Flagstaff and Verde Valley Wagon Road about 23 miles south of Flagstaff, extending thence by the most feasible route in a southerly direction across the mesa to a point on the rim near the old Munds Trail, thence down the grade and continuing in a southerly direction to the Yavapai County Line and an intersection with the public road leading to Oak Creek, Upper Verde and Jerome;

(Signed) E.S. Gosney, T.A. Riordan, A.A. Dutton, T.J. Jack, T.J. Colter, T.E. Pollock, CM. Funston, J.C. Milligan, J.H. Murrary, Thomas A. Rickel, Arthur T. Anddres, Robert J. Kidd, W.G. Dickinson, G.W. Black, David Babbitt, L.W. Quinlan.

The clerk is directed to post a notice in three public places in said road district and required by Statute of August 1901, that the Board of Supervisors will act on the above petition on March 17th, 1902.

Another reference to this road is found in the Minutes of The Board Meeting March 17th, 1902. The clerk reported to the Board that the change in the Verde Road had been advertised in accordance with Par. 3972 (Section 3617) Revised Statutes of Arizona.

On motion of Babbitt the following viewers were appointed: John Loy, D.E. Schnebly and W.H. Power.

The clerk is directed to notify the above named persons of their appointment and to request the surveyor to make a plat of said change, and report at next regular meeting.

Those Early Days.....

Minutes of the Board Meeting July 1st, 1902 (page 332) states: The following bills were approved; W.H. Power, surveying and plat Verde Cutoff Road $117.85. From minutes July 25, 1902, George Babbitt, T.E. Pulliam, H.C. Hibben, clerk. J.C. Phelan granted leave of absence from Territory for fifteen days, George Babbitt made acting chairman.

In consideration of the parties having charge of funds for completion of Verde Cut-off Road paying to the County Treasurer the moneys on hand supposed to be about $150, the Board awarded the contract for the completion of said road to J.J. Thompson for the sum of $600. Said road to be completed on or before October 1st, 1902. The said $600 to be paid to said J.J. Thompson when the road is completed and accepted by the Board of Supervisors.

Although I was not very old in 1902, I can remember quite a lot about when Dad was working on that road. Also, I heard my parents and others discuss different things about the road as I grew older.

As the new road was built along the line of the Munds Trail, the road was called the Munds Road by most people. After the Schnebly Family built a resort hotel and kept paying guests at Sedona, some of the guests referred to the mountain the road came down as Schnebly Hill.

As time went on more of the people of Flagstaff spoke of the hill as Schnebly Hill. The last of the Schnebly Family moved away from Sedona by 1910. More new people moved into the area. When an old-timer spoke of the road as the Munds Road, he would have to stop and explain to new comers that it was known to some as the Schnebly Hill Road.

Gradually the name of Munds Road was dropped by most everyone and the name of Schnebly Hill became accepted in general. I have no quarrel with that name for the road, but in writing the story of how the road was built, I wanted to bring out the fact that Schnebly Hill was not the name of the road at the beginning.

For people of Upper Verde and Lower Oak Creek the new cut-off saved about a day's driving time on a trip to Flagstaff. For folks of Upper Oak Creek and Sedona area it saved even more time. From our home place at Indian Gardens it was at least a four-day trip to Flagstaff by way of Beaver Head and Rattlesnake Tanks.

If the weather was wet or the wagons were loaded heavy it took longer. After the new Verde Cut-off Road was finished, the trip to Flagstaff could be made in two days in dry weather. It was also a big time saver for anyone traveling between Jerome and

Flagstaff.

The new road was looked on by everyone in the whole area as a major improvement, and it really was.

Now I will try to tell something of the building of a road through Oak Creek Canyon where the present Highway 89A is located.

Sometime before 1887 Dad built a tolerable fair road right up the creek bottom from Sedona to Indian Gardens. He moved his family up there that year. He only got to use the road a few years until there came a big flood in Oak Creek and washed it away.

Dad said that after the flood he could not find a trace of his road left. Next he started a road away high above the creek. The road started out from Sedona much the same way that Jordan Lane does now. It continued on up the hill to the foot of Steamboat Rock and around Steamboat to Wilson Canyon. It crossed the canyon above the present Midgley Bridge, went over the next high ridge and down to the creek not far below Indian Gardens.

Dad and my older brothers were several years getting the road built, because they only had time to work on it a short time each year. Before that road was built, the only way to get in and out of the canyon was by horse back and with packhorses.

All of the settlers in the canyon had a trail up to the rim near their place. They kept a wagon on the rim. When they wanted to go to Flagstaff they packed their horses with bed and camp outfit, and walked to the top of the mountain. There they hitched their horses to the wagon and drove to town. When they returned they loaded their horses with supplies brought from town, and walked back down the trail home.

Louis H. Thomas lived for years where the present Oak Creek Lodge is. Shortly after 1900 Lou started work on a road from Flagstaff to his ranch on Oak Creek. He got some money from people of Flagstaff who liked to fish in Oak Creek, but did not like to use a pack outfit to get to the creek. Lou used most of the money he collected to buy blasting powder and other supplies. He did not get much pay for himself.

From where he turned off from the old Verde Road, to as far as Fry Canyon he followed old logging roads. From there on he had to build every foot of the road. It was a slow heartbreaking job. He did hire some help but the money came in small amounts and he never had enough.

In the fall of 1906 Thomas got the road finished to his place at the junction of West Fork and Oak Creek. It was not a highway

Those Early Days.....

but he could drive from his place to Flagstaff with a wagon.

From the Thomas Ranch to Indian Gardens it was said to be eight miles by the old crooked trail. To anyone driving on today's paved highways at forty miles an hour that would seem an insignificant distance. Had they traveled the same part of Oak Creek in 1906 it would have been quite a journey.

The only way to make the trip then would have been to walk or ride a horse. The old trail crossed the creek every few hundred yards. It was grown over with brush and some places it would have been safer to dismount and lead the horse.

One was always in danger of having their hat knocked off by overhanging limbs, or their clothes torn by brush. Three miles an hour was top speed for anyone except cowboys or expert horsemen.

Soon after Lou Thomas got the road to his place, Albert Purtymun came back to live at the old Purtymun Ranch on Oak Creek. It is the present Junipine Resort Ranch. It was two miles from the Thomas Ranch. Through the years of 1907 and 1908 Purtymun built the two miles of road by himself.

I do not think he collected more than $50 from sportsmen, and he used it all for blasting supplies. About 1908 Jesse J. Howard homesteaded the present Todd's Lodge. Frank L. Pendley came to the Falls ranch and Jesse E. Purtymun took the present Mission Rancho. Jesse Howard soon got a road to Banjo Bill Spring, but nothing else was done on the road until 1912.

In the fall of that year Jess Purtymun built a road from Indian Gardens up to the present Spencer place, a short distance from his place. In the first part of 1913 Frank Pendley and Jess Howard got a little money from Coconino County and started working down the canyon from Banjo Bill Spring. At the same time Jesse Purtymun continued to work on the lower end.

In the fall of 1913 Purtymun got enough county money to buy groceries and dynamite and he, Charley and Jim Thompson, Jr. worked the rest of that year on the road up toward Pendley's place.

Soon after the first of the year Jess Purtymun went to Flagstaff to meet the County Supervisors at their regular Board meeting. There had been an unofficial promise from some of the Supervisors, that if the people of Oak Creek could get a trail through the canyon, that they could drive over with an empty wagon, it would be made a Country Road and be maintained by the County.

The Board kept their promise. Purtymun got enough money to

pay the men one dollar a day for the work they had done the past fall and the promise of enough to complete the road at the regular pay of three dollars a day. (That three dollars a day was for an eight hour day. When the Verde Cut-off Road was built the pay scale was one dollar a day for a ten-hour day.)

Jess put on more men and Pendley enlarged his crew. The two crews continued to work toward each other and by the last of May the two crews met at Oak Creek Falls. In the month of June, a wooden bridge was built across the creek. On July 3, 1914 the last work on the bridge was finished and the road was open for travel from Flagstaff to the Verde Valley.

When the road was first opened it crossed the creek 16 times between Sedona and the head of the canyon where it started up the hill. With every flood in the creek the crossings were damaged or washed out. Soon after the county took over maintenance of the road, work was started to eliminate some of the crossings. The last one was done away with in 1925.

In 1918 there was a big flood that not only washed out the crossings, but took away the wooden bridge at the Falls. It was late in June before the road was open for travel that year.

In the spring of 1919 Jess Purtymun, with a county crew, rebuilt the road from Wilson Canyon to the creek below Indian Gardens. The present highway follows almost exactly the road laid out by Purtymun. In 1922 Coconino County started what might be called a highway. It was wide enough for two cars and extended from the crossing below Indian Gardens up to Indian Gardens and eliminated two crossings.

There had been some talk of a highway through the canyon for several years. In 1918 the Forest Service, or the Bureau of Public Roads, I do not know which, sent a lone engineer to scout through the canyon to make a report on the probable cost of building a highway.

In the early 1920's Yavapai County built a graded, but unsurfaced, two-lane road from Cottonwood to the county line just west of Sedona, and a bridge was built across the Verde River at Bridgeport. The Oak Creek Canyon section was called "The Missing Link".

In 1923 Coconino County appropriated enough money to make a preliminary survey through the canyon. From then until 1929 The Arizona Highway Department and the U.S. Bureau of Public Roads made several surveys. In March 1929 the first contractor started work on a stretch of road from Sedona to Indian Gardens.

However the present Midgley Bridge was not included in that

contract. Coconino County built a detour up the canyon to where it is much narrower and put in a temporary wooden bridge.

The next contract was for building the road from the top of Oak Creek Hill down to the creek. Work started there in 1931. In 1932 two contracts started. One from the head of Oak Creek down to Oak Creek Lodge and the other started at Indian Gardens and extended up to Oak Creek Lodge. The project had been taken into the Bureau of Public Roads System by then and a highway was assured.

While work was in progress in Oak Creek Canyon all traffic was stopped. The traffic was detoured up Schnebly Hill. There had been some changes made in the original Schnebly Hill road previously. In 1931 a big change was made in the road all the way from the bottom to top of the hill.

With U.S. Forest Service money and Coconino County equipment, practically a new road was built. At the present time very little of the original Schnebly Hill or Munds Road is in use.

Through the mid 1930's contracts were let for building the Oak Creek Road from the top of the hill to Flagstaff and from Sedona to the Verde River. Also, the Midgley Bridge was built across Wilson Canyon, and contracts let for paving the whole road. As soon as a contract was finished it was taken over by the Arizona Highway Department. The road was first known as State Route 79, but was later changed to U.S. 89 Alternate.

## ROUNDUP OF 1896
*by M.O. Dumas*

  The round ups of the Verde Valley would usually begin in the spring of the year at a convenient time to suit each locality.

  The Upper Verde Valley usually began with the Marr Brothers wagon. The brands for Dan Marr were JH, read bar JH connected. Joe Marr brand was JM, read JM bar connected. Their first camp was at what is now lower Clarkdale, moving down the Verde River to their ranch at Middle Verde. They would work as far south as Grief Hill, just south of Cherry Creek.

  The Wingfield wagon would work from Grief Hill south on both sides of the Verde River to Brown Springs on the west and to Fossil Creek on the east. Their brands were the hatchet ⛏ ; the hoe ⌒ ; the shield ◊ and the bed bug ⋈. George Hance with brand ⋈ , crooked H and Wales Arnold with brand ℧ , flowerpot and others who rode the Wingfield wagon whom I have forgotten.

  The ⊥ , T bar wagon belonging to Frank Andrews of Prescott and the Marr Brothers of Middle Verde would work the Beaver Creek country. The brand ⊥, T bar connected was later changed by adding a lazy S ⪽ under the bar to keep cattle rustlers from working the brand over.

  The Oak Creek wagon, which was more of a community wagon, was the one I worked with most of the time. However, I have worked with the others at different times.

  The Oak Creek wagon taken as an illustration will give an idea of how the old round ups were managed. A few of the cattlemen would circulate the word around the neighborhood that there would be a meeting of the cowmen at a certain time and place. This time was usually around the first of April. The time set for the round up would depend on the condition of the range as to feed. It would take between three and four weeks for this spring round up to be completed.

  At this meeting the time and place for starting the round up was made, elect a wagon boss and make all arrangements for chuck wagon and team. The boss would complete the other arrangements for hiring a cook, horse wrangler and setting supplies for the wagon, such as provisions, hobble ropes and any other necessities.

  In making hobbles a two-inch grass rope of three strands was used. Taking one strand of proper length, doubled in such manner made a soft hobble that would not injure the horses legs. Being

Those Early Days.....

knotted in such a fashion that would make it secure and not easily unknotted, only by hand.

Our first camp would be located just above the old Fain Crossing of Oak Creek and about one fourth mile below the Cornville Bridge. At that time there was no road crossing where the present bridge now stands. We would work four days at this camp, working the west side of House Mountain, Jackson Flat, White Hills and as far south as the mouth of Oak Creek. From there north, covering all the country between Oak Creek and the Verde River as far as Cottonwood. Then we would move to Spring Creek for three days. Each cowboy had his own bedroll consisting of a tarpaulin, called "Tarp" by cowboys, blankets and quilt, called sugins, pillows called goose hair. These were carried on the chuck wagon and at night rolled out on the ground, under the stars, for many tired cowhands.

*Cowboys throwing a steer*

At Spring Creek, one day would be spent riding House Mountain and vicinity. We always had to work House Mountain from several camps, for at that time there were quite a number of wild cattle there. It was also worked from Beaverhead Camp. Before leaving Spring Creek for the Windmill Ranch we would work over the herd giving the cattlemen time to drive their cattle to their respective ranches.

We would then work the Windmill country, now owned by the Millers. Originally Mose Casner and Dave Kelsey had cattle on this range, but the well was dug by Dave Strahan who had it for his headquarters ranch for many years. His brand was Circle S. ⑨. He gathered the cattle and shipped them to Kansas City before the turn of the century. He sold the ranch to Black and Vail, of Flagstaff. The brand they used was DK , originally started by Dave Kelsey.

They ran it for a good many years before selling it to Pat Hurley of Phoenix, Bill Cox and Walter Miller of Jerome (no relation to the present owners). I think it changed hands once or twice before Cecil Miller bought it. We would work here about three days, including the day for moving. The country worked was Black Mountain, Casner Mountain and the Red Rock country, north and east of the Windmill. We then moved into Dry Creek where the real wild cattle lived. We would have to work one canyon at a time, placing the day herd at the mouth of the canyon. When the cattle came out, some of them would stop in the herd, but many would not, and would have to be roped and tied down. The round ups were run much different to the present rodeos you would see today. Every man had to work alone. He roped and tied down his steer by himself. The day herd would then be moved to where each animal had been tied down, so it could be let loose into the herd. Some of them would be glad to stay in the herd, while others would come charging out again. However they never got very far, for the boys would have their ropes cocked and ready for them. Sometimes this would have to be repeated two or more times before the wild critters would give up. At that time there were many ten and twelve year old steers in those canyons.

Few people knew how Brind's Mesa, up Dry Creek got its name, and fewer know of the fate of old Brind. He was an old maverick, brindle bull, unbranded, who lived to be five or six years of age and had ranged on a grassy ridge most of his time between the head of Mormon Camp Wash and Dry Creek. There had been many attempts made to capture him, but he usually out maneuvered them or they had lost their ropes. One time Ed Dickinson and Jimmie Van Deren got their ropes on him, but before they could pull him down, he dragged them into the yew timber thicket, just below the ridge and it was either their lives or losing their ropes. They decided to shoot him, which they did. That was the last of old brind. The boys kept this a secret for some time. It finally caught up with them and the truth became known. The only time I ever saw old brind was his carcass. The mesa was named after him.

From Dry Creek we moved to what is now Sedona, then called Upper Oak Creek. The only family living there at that time were the Frank Owenbys. Roy Owenby now being the only survivor of a family of seven. The family lived just below Sedona in a little three-room board shack near where the old Schnebly two story white house stood. When Mr. Owenby, Roy's father, moved to this place he cut cedar cord wood and hauled it to Jerome and

## Those Early Days.....

delivered it for seven dollars a cord. It would take him one day to cut the wood and two and a half days or three days to make the round trip. Later the Owenbys accumulated quite a large bunch of cattle in the district.

Our camp here was down next to the creek on the upper end of the flat where the George Jordan ranch is now located. There was an old log cabin there in which the Thompsons lived at the time old man Wilson was killed by a bear up Wilson Canyon in 1885 about one half mile above the site of the present bridge on Oak Creek Highway.

After cleaning up the herd and the cattle having been driven to their respective ranges on the mountain and elsewhere, we would work Upper Oak Creek for three days. When we rode Oak Creek Canyon, sometime the evening before, three of us would ride up the canyon as far as Pump House Canyon and lay out all night with only our saddle blankets for a bed. At daybreak we would start driving down the canyon, one on either side and one in the creek bed. The one in the bottom of the canyon would keep the location of the boys on each side of the canyon, so as not to get ahead of them thereby keeping the cattle from cutting back between them. We would round up some where in the vicinity of Wilson Canyon. The other boys would have worked Wilson Mountain, Casner Canyon, and the surrounding country before we got down there and be stationed so as to turn our cattle out of the creek onto Wilson Ridge. Moving our herd across Wilson Canyon and along the base of Steam Boat Rock down to the flat at Sedona.

There was an old wagon trail around the base at that time which Jim Thompson had worked out. He left his wagon at the end of the road at Wilson Canyon for it was too much of a job for one man to build a road any farther. Mr. Thompson would pack his produce that he raised on his Indian Garden ranch, out on horses to the wagon and haul it to Jerome. It would take four or five days to make the round trip. His principal crop was Irish potatoes. On account of the rough roads, he could only haul ten or twelve sacks at a time. He also had to haul his bed, chuck box, and grain for his horses. He would hobble his horses out at night, feeding them grain night and morning. I do not know just what he received for his spuds, but I think they were selling them for about one dollar per hundred pound sack.

Our hobbling grounds at Sedona Camp was about where the Main Street of Sedona is now located. The night herd would be held at the base and just to the south and west of the hill on top of which the water tank now stands. After finishing up here and again driving the cattle to the mountain we would move to Beaver Head, our last camp. We worked here about four days, usually camping near the spring. If bad weather struck us we would move our beds into the old Star Mail Route stage house, which at that time was in very good condition. This was greatly appreciated by the cowboys.

Our largest round up here was held in Big Park. This country covered would be the east and north side of House Mountain, Horse Mesa, Jack's Canyon, Big and Little Park. By ten o'clock A.M. there would be about one thousand head of cattle rounded up. It would take us the remainder of the day to brand the calves and work the herd.

When finished here at Beaver Head, we would set a date for our work to begin on the mountain, giving us enough time to get up and shoe a fresh mount of horses, consisting of seven or more head for each man, making it a point to wind up the round up in time to go to the Fourth of July celebration in Flagstaff. Some of the boys would be contestants in steer tying, bronco riding, calf roping and horse races. There were usually fifteen to twenty men on the round up.

The first round up I was in was in 1896. I was the horse wrangler and now the only survivor of that round up.

I think it would be appropriate to mention some of the old cowboys of the old school that were on this round up. There were the three Fain Boys, John, Dan, and Albert. John, representing his own brand 7X (seven X). Dan worked for Greening outfit 101 (one hundred one). Albert in partner with Dan represented their brand HA connected (H A connected).

The Dickinson boys, Frank, Bill, Alf, and Ed. Frank and Bill were partners, Frank representing them. They had bought up several remnants of brands they used on their increase, but I think it was AZ. Bill worked for Joe Walker and "Boss" Acker whose brand H▷ connected (H triangle connected). Ed worked for Bill Back, his brother-in-law. The brand was ⊥ (one bar half circle).

Charley Bigham represented the Ⅰ. Sol Johnson in partner with Bigham represented the X , campstool.

Bert Maxwell working for Mr. Schroeder brand ⊖ (half circle bar half circle). Tom Hawkins representing M bars and bar JH (Marr Brothers). Wallace Willard representing OK brand owned by John Lee for which Lee Mountain received its name. Ben Clay who was buying beef for a meat market in Jerome and Clay Park got its name from this family. Ed Walker worked for Jim Willard. JW was his brand and 25 (twenty five connected). Con Fredricks represented his Father with brand 7⌄ (seven anchor).

There may have been others that I have forgotten, which

## Those Early Days.....

would not be surprising for that was all about seventy years ago. In my crude or humble way I would like to dedicate this poem to those old pros I have ridden so many miles with.

### ROUNDUP OF 1896 (Poem)
*by M.O. Dumas*

The old boys of 1896
Have ridden their last Round Up
Out in the sticks
They rode over the hill
One at a time.
Though through the dim mist
They left a plain sign,
They rode on and on,
And never looked back.
But we can easily follow
For they left a plain track.
Now there's old Lute, Haydee and Joe,
Who rode with those pokes
Of a long time ago.
That same trail
We shall sometime follow
Up that same hill
And down yon hollow.
Boys keep the camp-fire burning
To light up the way,
For we shall surely join you
And join you to stay.
When we register
For that last call,
It will be on that grand Round Up
Late in the Fall.

Those Early Days.....

## EARMARKS
*by Albert E. Thompson*

There have been pages and even whole books written about livestock brands, but very little has been published about earmarks. Earmarks were used on cattle, sheep and on hogs that were turned loose on the open range. We will confine our remarks here to earmarks of cattle.

On cattle the earmark was the principal means of telling a branded animal from an unbranded one. An unbranded calf was referred to as a long ear. As long as a calf was under one year old and still following its mother it was just a long eared calf. After it was weaned or not following its mother it was a maverick. Mavericks were fair game to the first fellow who could get his rope onto them.

Earmarks were a great help in identifying the ownership of a cow brute from a distance. Earmarks could be read at a greater distance than a brand could. The earmark was the quick identification of ownership but the brand was the final proof. A brand would stand up in court as proof of ownership regardless of what earmark the cow critter might have.

The illustrations below are not meant to represent the earmarks that went with particular brands. They are just given to show some of the possible combinations that could be used. These little ovals are supposed to represent the ears of a cow or steer. I have tried to give the common names of the various cuts and splits of the animal's ears as they are used by cattlemen.

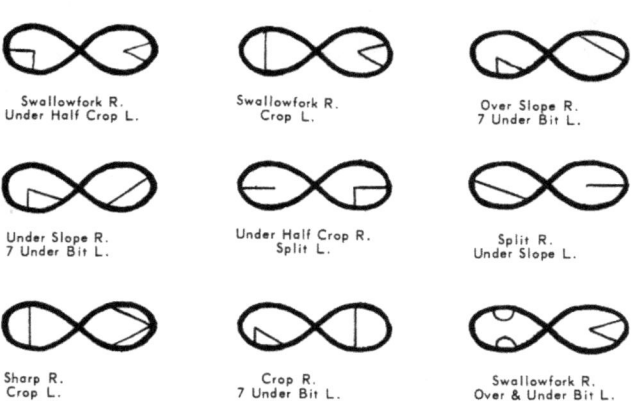

Swallowfork R.
Under Half Crop L.

Swallowfork R.
Crop L.

Over Slope R.
7 Under Bit L.

Under Slope R.
7 Under Bit L.

Under Half Crop R.
Split L.

Split R.
Under Slope L.

Sharp R.
Crop L.

Crop R.
7 Under Bit L.

Swallowfork R.
Over & Under Bit L.

## Sedona Westerners

2 Splits R.
Over Half Crop L.

7 Under Bit R.
Crop L.

3 Bits R.
Crop L.

Sharp R.
Swallowfork L.

Sharp Both Ears

Split Both Ears

Crop R.
Dovetail L.

Under Half Crop
Both Ears

Under Slope
Both Ears

Box Swallowfork R.
Under Half Crop L.

Over Half Crop R.
Under Half Crop L.

Grub Right Ear

Split R.
Over Bit L.

Dovetail R.
Swallowfork L.

2 Splits R.
Crop L.

Over Half Crop
Both Ears

Split R.
Crop & Split L.

Box Swallowfork
Both Ears

Those Early Days.....

## PLACE NAMES IN SEDONA AREA
*by Albert E. Thompson*

There has been much confusion about place names in the Sedona area and some controversy, even among old timers about some of the original names.

Through the Sedona Westerners "Ole-timers'" members, most of the confusion has been cleared up and documentary proof has been found to settle one of the most controversial names - Court House Rock. Practically every one of the "Ole-timers" have agreed that Court House Rock was the original name of the much photographed red buttes at Red Rock near the Red Rock Crossing just south of Sedona.

The General Land Office surveys dating back to 1886 gives the name of Court House Butte to the rocks. In an old diary, kept by John L. Thomas, who was Forest Ranger for the General Land Office Forest Reserve, under the Interior Department, and was forerunner of today's National Forest, he states that Court House Butte is in Township 17 Range 5 East. I will quote the entry taken from his diary. "Jan. 25, 1899 - Rode from Schuerman's Ranch up Oak Creek to post fire warnings and look for tresspassers. A few ranchers have settled along Oak Creek in this Township (T 17 No. R 5 E). Court House Butte is in this township". Today's forest maps show the butte known to the old timers as Court House Rock to be in this township. The place known to old timers as Church Rock or Cathedral Rock is in a township farther east and is north of Big Park. Also, Mrs. Ellsworth Schnebly has a painting of the buttes dated 1902 and giving the name as Court House Rock.

My mother told me that her father, Abraham James named the rock Court House Rock, soon after he came to Oak Creek in 1878. Mother said that he also named Bell Rock, Steamboat Rock, Table Mountain and House Mountain. However, I have heard that Mrs. D.E. "Maggie" Dumas named House Mountain, so I do not know. Since there is no way of proving, which is correct at this late date, we will let it stand at that.

I do not know how the names, Devil's Kitchen and Devil's Dining Room came to get switched around. All of the old timers agree that Devil's Kitchen is west of Sedona up Soldier Wash. My parents were living in Sedona in the early 1880's and heard the crash when the spot caved in. Mother said that the dust from the cave-in filled the air all day and the sun looked like it was shining through heavy smoke. Her brother, Jim James, was the first one to see the new hole in the ground.

I do not know who gave it the name of Devil's Kitchen, but it was much later than the cave-in. Devil's Dining Room is on the east side of Oak Creek not far from the Broken Arrow Subdivision. Joe Lay, an old-timer and SW member, told me that it was named by Frank Owenby, the first person to patent a homestead in Sedona. He lived on the homestead from about 1893 until 1901. Records show that he filed on the place in Jan. 1895. It was likely after Devil's Kitchen had been named that he named it else he would not have given it the name of Devil's Dining Room. This hole in the ground is in Marg's Stable or Morg's Stable. There are differences of opinion about which is correct. Dr. M.O. Dumas and some old-timers call it Morg's Stable and Dr. Dumas says it was named for a Morgan stallion that was owned by William Munds, that ranged at one time in the area.

Now I will give my version of the name Marg's Stable, as told to me by my parents. My dad, Jim Thompson took squatters rights to the Indian Gardens ranch in 1876. Abraham James, mother's father and his family came to Oak Creek in 1878 and to Sedona in 1879. He and his family left St. Joseph, Mo. in the spring of 1868, headed for the gold fields of California. One of the horses in his team was a young mare named Marg, short for Margaret. After a few years in California they started back east again. They encountered poison water at a place in the Nevada desert and lost some stock, both horses and cattle. They were forced to leave the wagons and after much suffering from thirst, arrived on the Muddy River in Southern Nevada near the town of St. Thomas.

After resting themselves and allowing the horses to recuperate, the men folks went back for the wagons to find that they had been robbed of everything of much value. Grandpa James rented a farm on the Muddy River and farmed a few years and built up his herd of cattle and horses. The mare, Marg, was one that did not die from poison water and she raised a colt every year.

About 1875 the family moved across the Colorado River to the mining camps of Mineral Park and Chloride, in Arizona where they cut and hauled wood for the camps for a year. They had met my dad, Jim Thompson, while in the St. Thomas area. He was running a ferry between Arizona and Nevada. Dad sold his ferry to Daniel Bonelli in the spring of 1876 and came to Prescott, Arizona. The James family moved back to Nevada that year and farmed until getting a letter from Jim Thompson telling them of the wonders of Oak Creek.

Those Early Days.....

In May 1878 the family arrived at the present Page Springs ranch on Lower Oak Creek. It is a State fish rearing place now but was owned by B.F. "Frank" Copple at that time. James rented the place from Copple and farmed there that year and moved to Sedona the next winter, to find more range for his horses and cattle. He settled on what was known more recently as the Fred Hart ranch. It is the place on Oak Creek just West of the present King's Ransom Motel. Old Marg, still hale and hearty and raising a colt every year, was still with them. Abraham James allowed all of his stock to run loose on the range, as there was fine grass. When he intended to make a trip to Camp Verde or Prescott, he would hunt up his team of horses and shoe them. Old Marg was smart enough to lift up her foot to have a new shoe nailed on, but she had also learned that new shoes meant a long trip ahead. After getting new shoes she would disappear next night.

James learned that her favorite hiding place was the "Rincon" (Spanish name for a sheltered place almost surrounded by hills or mountains), that lay to the south east of his ranch. As he was a great hand for naming places he named the place Marg's Stable. The names Marg and Morg are so similar it is easy to see how they could be confused. I am not denying that the Munds family called the place Morg's Stable for a Morgan stallion, but I do maintain that it was so named for Marg, the mare, long before it was named for Morg, the stallion.

I will quote again from the John Thomas diary, Jan. 26, 1899, "Started from camp at 8:00 A.M., rode by C. Lincoln's ranch. Adjoining this ranch, J.L. Munds, sheriff of Yavapai County, has a pasture fenced from a point of rocks to another, about a half mile enclosing a large tract of land, several thousand acres of very rough land. Arrived at camp at 6 PM."

Charley Lincoln was the next person to squat on the James claim after it was abandoned by the James family in 1895. The next diary mention of the Munds fence is dated May 25, 1899, "Went to unlawful enclosure of J.L. Munds to see if he had removed the fence, (on reserve section) found that he had not". Some time soon after that there is an entry saying that the fence had been removed. As the Munds fence was built after the James family moved away in 1895, it was only in use about four years. I have no way of knowing whether or not the Munds family had the Morgan stallion there then, but if they did, it was long after the place was named Marg's Stable.

There are two washes in the Sedona area that are sometimes

confused. I will give my version of the naming of each. The first is Soldier Wash: It runs through Sedona and is crossed by what is now called Brewer Road, just before reaching the Sedona School and ranger station. It enters Oak Creek just below the bridge on Highway 179. In the early 1880's, the soldiers of Camp Verde had a summer camp at what is now known as Nelson Shopping Center at the Y in Sedona. They called the place Camp Garden. I think that was the very first place name for the present village of Sedona. The few settlers of the area at that time called the wash near the soldier camp - Soldier Wash.

The other canyon that is sometimes called Soldier Wash is at the north end of Sedona. It enters Oak Creek at the Walter Jordan pump and the little eating place called Fisherman's Wharf. In early days there was a little flat at the mouth of the wash of about an acre in area. Since it was as far up Oak Creek as one could drive with a wagon, it was a favorite camping spot for trout fishermen. One summer in the 1890's a party of men from Jerome camped there. They started jokingly calling each other Mormons, and called the campground Mormon Camp. It became known as Mormon Camp to all of the old timers of the area. John Thomas frequently mentions it in his diary from 1898 through 1903. The wash entering the creek at Mormon Camp became known as Mormon Camp wash or Mormon Canyon. A big flood in Oak Creek in 1903 washed away about half of the campground. Another flood in 1909 washed away the rest of it and Mormon Camp was no more.

The wash is still there and should not be confused with Soldier Wash or Minor Wilson, which is a very short wash at Wilson Canyon. It was named by some of the State Highway surveying crew in 1929, while surveying the present highway 89A. Mormon Canyon heads at the south end of Wilson Mountain, near a pass between Wilson Mountain and the cliffs to the southwest that terminate in Gray Mountain.

There was an Indian trail through the divide when white men first saw the area. C.S. "Bear" Howard, a colorful pioneer of these parts (and the first one to settle at present Oak Creek Lodge) named the pass - Mule Pass. He used the trail often in the 1880's. Doc Dumas has given a very good account of how it got the name of Brin's Mesa (Brind's Mesa ?) I never sound the D in speaking the name and I spell it like I say it. Also, I still maintain that it is more of a pass than a mesa. Anyway, it has been Brin's Mesa so long, let us keep that name and spell it as we wish.

Gray Mountain, north of Grasshopper Flat was, I believe named

## Those Early Days.....

for its color alone, and has nothing to do with Zane Grey. In fact, I think the name is older than Zane Grey's books. The canyon that drains Grasshopper Flat and enters Oak Creek at Red Rock is sometimes called Zane Grey Wash. That canyon has been called Carrol Canyon since the early 1880's. It was named for the Carrol family who were about the first family to live in Red Rock. Henry Schuerman, Sr. bought Carrol's rights and improvements to the present Schuerman ranch in Red Rock in 1885. The road to the present Ambrosio Chavez Ranch goes through a little pass to get down to Oak Creek. That pass was called Jule's Pass for one of the Carrol daughters, Julia Carrol.

Bear Wallow Canyon enters Oak Creek at Steel's trailer park in Sedona. Schnebly Hill road follows it part way up the mountain. The original Bear Wallow was in a side branch of the canyon, where the present road turns right to leave the main canyon. At one time there was a little seep spring there and the bears loved to wallow in the water and mud that collected in the potholes in the bed rock. Mrs. William Loy told me that her father, Dr. M.S. Carrier named the place. He killed a big bear there at one time. Dr. Carrier was living in the east end of Munds Park at that time. He, being the one to homestead in the east end of the park and James Munds homesteaded the west end of the park. Dr. Carrier was married to a sister of Jim Munds.

Almost everyone in Sedona knows that Wilson Canyon and Wilson Mountain were named for the old bear hunter, Richard Wilson who was killed by a bear in Wilson Canyon in 1885.

## HOW SEDONA WAS NAMED
*by Ellsworth M. Schnebly*

Seeking the ideal climate and atmosphere for his health, Ellsworth Schnebly, brother of my father, was inspired by his discovery of the towering red rocks interfused with the forested greenery and the vast valley acreage, all surrounded by meandering clear Oak Creek. These descriptive letters soon became a dominant factor in the journey my father was to make.

On October 12, 1901, my father, Theodore C. Schnebly, arrived in Jerome, Arizona from his home in Gorin, Missouri. He came over the Santa Fe Railroad to Ash Fork where he had to unload his emigrant car to another, which ran over a narrow gauge railroad through Jerome Junction. He had brought furniture, some machinery, and a team of horses with a wagon, which he used to carry his property down the gulch. Parts of this old trail are still visible, which at that time was only a rocky, sandy, rough wagon track, that washed out every time it rained. The last thirty miles from Jerome to Sedona took ten days to complete.

My mother, Sedona, a younger sister, Pearl, and I arrived in Jerome on October 23, 1901. Dad had become partly settled in the old bunkhouse on the land just south and opposite the present Sedona School, which he bought from Frank Owenby. He was soon settled and began to cultivate the land. He had vegetables, which he hauled to market in Jerome in the summer of 1902. He had planted an orchard, which would produce in two or three years so that residents in Jerome, and later in Flagstaff, would have fruit as well as vegetables. Dad marketed his produce and made use of the empty wagon on his return trip by delivering mail and other necessities to the settlers. These items were distributed from our home, followed by the traditional chatter, uniting the warmth of friendliness among the neighbors and a brotherly affection. A further accommodation to be realized was stocking items of necessity and Dad soon was a storekeeper in his own home. He became known as " Father Schnebly " and mother as " Aunt Dona".

There were not many families living here at that time; only the Owenby, Dumas, Schuerman, Armijo, and Chavez plus a very few others. They were concerned about the slow and infrequent mail service and consulted with Dad regarding a solution. Because he was as eager as they to have contact with the "outside world", he wrote to the Post Office Department. A post office was approved and a name requested, to which the reply was "Schnebly Station". Dad was notified by the post office officials that the name was too

Those Early Days.....

long to put on the cancellation stamp; therefore, a second name was requested. My uncle, Ellsworth was living with us and thought of using my mother's first name. He said in the person there was a character that would stand well as a symbol for the community and turned to mother and said, "Sedona, you're going to have a town named after you". The name was approved by the officials, and on June 26th, 1902, Sedona was in business with T.C. Schnebly as its first postmaster.

*Sedona Schnebly and the author at the old age of two months (May 11, 1898).*

After having to ride a mule up Thompson's Ladder or go far to the south over rough country to get out of the canyon, Dad saw the need for a road to Flagstaff. He had an uncanny sense of judging grade and without any instrument, laid out a road, which was later called Schnebly Hill Road. With the help of the county and some local residents, a road was built for wagons up over Schnebly Hill into Flagstaff. The original road, which Dad used to haul his produce can still be seen in many places or is still followed by the newer road. The original road turned to the right above Merry-Go-Round. That slice on the hill is visible although it has not been used since the present road was built around the hill to the right. The view from the old viewpoint is much more impressive and picturesque than the present viewpoint, but has not been maintained and is certainly no place for a car to travel.

Although the Thompsons were irrigating at Indian Gardens, Dad took the first irrigation ditch out of Oak Creek in this immediate area, which is still in use. My sister and I spent many happy hours wading in that ditch or roaming over the hills in search of arrowheads, axes, or other artifacts, which our parents willingly gave to easterners who came to visit us because there were "plenty more all over the country". We did not have to dig for them in those days, and wish I now had some of what we found.

A third child, Genevieve, was born in 1903. Dad set to work and completed a large two story house with a full basement of rock walls, after which my sister Pearl and I took over the old bunkhouse. The old stove and the cupboards were there for us to "play house". One favorite pastime was picking huge, luscious strawberries and making mud pies, which we pretended to bake in the oven (with no fire).

Dad had ample room in that large house for guests to stay overnight. Some of them stayed a week, others a month or longer. This eventually was known as a hotel although it had not been built for that purpose. Two or three times each year Dad would take us with him on his two day trip to and from Flagstaff or Jerome where we always stopped at Uncle Will's place and visited my cousin Lucille Schnebly (now Harlan). Except for those infrequent trips, we saw no towns and only a traveler or an Indian occasionally.

When friends or relatives came, our parents would take them to Montezuma Castle, Montezuma Well, Devil's Kitchen, or to some Indian Ruins or elsewhere. When I was four years old, my uncle carried me up the flimsy ladders into Montezuma Castle on his back and mother told of my letting go of his neck while he held my feet. As Art Linkletter says, "What crazy things kids will do". But those treks were highlights in our lives.

About 1904, my parents loaded a wagon with supplies and bedding and started for the Grand Canyon, with absolutely no roads over which to travel. They walked down into the canyon and back out, except for some who travelled by mule. We made the round trip and returned to Sedona in two weeks' time. My aunt from Missouri was visiting us at the time, as were some other people. She could not realize how scarce water was until she had

Those Early Days.....

carelessly wasted the last drop. The rest of us really suffered one day or more because of her disregard.

Having discovered that my eyes were very poor, Dad took me to St. Louis, Missouri to the World's Fair in 1904 where he had me fitted with glasses, while he and I visited with friends and relatives in Northeastern Missouri. That was really a milestone in my life. Because I knew what such a trip had meant to me, Lucille and Hook our five year old son to the World's Fair in Chicago in 1934, where he saw much that he still remembers.

Dad and Mother had a good old Chinese cook who did not like cats. Pearl and I would thoughtlessly take our cat into the house sometimes. Once the cook, who was very good to us but hated cats, told us in his Chinese lingo, "Takee that cat out of here or me putee him in the lice soup". Thereafter, we guarded the cat and kept it away from that Chinese cook.

We had seen advertisements of automobiles in Munsey's and other magazines, but we had never seen an automobile until 1904 when one of the Miller's drove a car down to our house. Through some miracle the car had made it to Sedona, but it balked on returning. My dad had to haul it back to Jerome with a team of horses.

Pearl and I each had a gentle pony, which we rode all around the area, happily and fearlessly, until June 12th, 1905 when Pearl was dragged to death by her pony. Mother, Baby Sister (Genevieve), Pearl and I were driving the cattle home from the unfenced range that evening when one cow darted from the herd. Pearl's trained pony instinctively started after the cow, throwing Pearl and scaring itself. The pony raced across Oak Creek, dragging the lifeless, mangled body to the corral gate where we found it when we caught up. Mother had been in excellent health but this tragedy upset her tremendously and she began to weaken from grief and worry. Not long after, the doctor advised Dad to sell and move away or risk losing his wife. Seemingly there was no alternative, so they sold the place to my Uncle Ellsworth and returned to Gorin, Missouri.

I, too, missed Pearl very much and the good times we spent together. I remembered the time we had wandered aimlessly to the top of Table Mountain, where we panicked after we thought we were lost. The junipers hid our view and we had lost our directions while looking down for arrowheads and pottery. That taught us to get our bearings thereafter, before meandering off into the thickets.

It took all day to go by wagon from Sedona to Indian Gardens where the school was located. The current road was not built until many years later. Uncle Ellsworth, who was teaching at Indian Gardens enjoyed walking and could hike that distance in an hour or so although he seldom walked,

*This is the Schnebly home in Sedona, about 1902. The first post office was located in the far rear of the building.*

but usually trotted. My parents had sent me to Missouri to live with my grandparents, the Millers, so that I could attend school.

Dad, Mother and Genevieve returned to Missouri after selling the Sedona farm to Uncle Ellsworth. Here in Gorin, Dad "walked" the Standard Oil Company pipeline, which ran from Gorin, Missouri to Fort Madison, Iowa, which is about forty miles. His job was to repair any leaks, which he could mend, and for the major leak repairs he called others. He made the trip once each week until about 1909 when he moved to Memphis, Missouri and went into the clothing business, where he lived until 1912.

The West called again, this time to Eastern Colorado, where we lived until anthrax (an infectious, and usually fatal, bacterial disease) killed the herd of cattle during a December blizzard. This part of Colorado is noted for its severe blizzards. The state law required that all anthrax diseased animals be burned completely. This required staying up day and night for two weeks to keep fires of oil and coal burning under those carcasses. The result was fatigue, which brought on bronchial asthma for Dad.

Dad then realized that Sedona was the place for him. So in 1929, they returned to the beautiful red rock area where they had

Those Early Days…..

become deep-rooted long ago to join their pioneering neighbors and the community that bore the name of my mother.

Dad had lost what took a lifetime to earn, but his health was given back to him, except for occasional bronchial attacks. Mother's health was much improved and with the years our family had increased to include Henry, Clara, and Margaret.

Numerous uninformed, and perhaps well-intentioned people have speculated on how Sedona got its name or what the name means. Sedona is not an Indian, nor a Mexican name. One omnipotent individual explained it this way: When T.C. was courting Sedona, he said. "This weekend I am going over to see Dona".

Dad and Mother were married in Missouri and lived near each other before they were married. Dad and his brothers owned a hardware store in Gorin, Missouri at the time he and Sedona were married. Many people called Mother "Dona". Among them was our grand lady, Mrs. Delia Hart, one of Mother's best friends.

My mother's parents were Pennsylvania Dutch and did not even know any Mexicans or Indians back there. My grandfather, Philip Miller, married my grandmother after the Civil War and bought several acres of land in Gorin, Missouri. Here they reared twelve children including my mother. Grandmother said that she did not know why, but that she liked Sedona as a name and gave it to my mother. She had never heard of the name and after all, there is a first time that any word or name is used. My mother passed away in Sedona on November 13, 1950, just two years after she and Dad had happily celebrated their Golden Wedding Anniversary. Mother loved everyone and I don't believe she had an enemy.

Dad had pioneered and worked hard all his life until he got bronchial asthma, which forced him to slow down. After Mother's passing, he was so lonely that he made his life pleasant by visiting with tourists. Whether they enjoyed it or not, he always did. Many have since told me or written that they did enjoy having talked with him. He was perhaps Sedona's biggest booster. Dad passed away in his little house in Sedona, alone on March 13, 1954 at the age of eighty-six years. My mother, dad and sister are buried in a little plot at the east end of Grasshopper Flat, on land, which was donated for burial of old timers by philanthropic Mr. Jay Cook.

Dad knew the names of many of the rock formations since 1901. He applied names to those not having a name. I believe he named "Queen Victoria", "The Squaw and the Papooses", "King

Herod and the Three Wise Men".

Once while walking on the old road, which Dad used in travelling from Sedona to Jerome, my wife found a half of a broken glass sauce dish which matches a whole one that my mother left. She really thinks that the broken dish is one which Dad threw away near Sugar Loaf on his way to Jerome, and yet she insists that Mother would not put one of her prize sauce dishes in Dad's chuck box, nor would he throw it away. This mystery remains unsolved.

During the early years of the Twentieth century when there was no Sunday School or Church in Sedona, Mother, Dad, Mr. and Mrs. W.F. Wallace (who was the first forest ranger to live in Sedona) and others who might be visiting would gather and sing gospel hymns. Mother enjoyed playing her piano and these gatherings, reminiscent of the colonial days when, as Longfellow wrote in "The Courtship of Miles Standish", "Heard . . . .the musical voice of Priscilla singing the Hundredth Psalm, the grand old Puritan anthem, music that Luther sang to the sacred words of the Psalmist". These gatherings took the place of church services, picture shows, rodeos, and the numerous clubs in Sedona today. Those were the days of non-joiners, since there was nothing to join and very few to join.

The fulfillment of my career as a teacher has been most rewarding. Following my discharge from the army in 1919, I began my teaching career at Chambers, Arizona. I have taught school for forty-eight years with the exception of fifty-two months during World War II which I spent in the Marine Corps. I am looking forward to my retirement from the profession next year.

Those Early Days.....

## RAMBLINGS OF CLARA PURTYMUN
*by Clara Purtymun*

I was born in Sedona, Arizona, April 7, 1887, just under the hill from present King's Ransom Motel, that is where Frank Hart lives now but when I was born, Abraham James and family, (my grandparents) lived there and Sedona had not been named yet. When I was three months old, Dad moved his family to Indian Gardens where he had built a cabin several years before.

When my father first came into Oak Creek Canyon the Indian's garden were still growing there. They had a garden of squash, beans and corn, just across the creek from the present Indian Gardens store, and in front of the old Jim Thompson, (my dad) house. The soldiers from Camp Verde had just been there ahead of him and moved the Indians to the San Carlos Indian Reservation.

My dad and mother were married in Prescott, Arizona in 1880 but Dad did not move his family to Indian Gardens until 1887. The reason was that it was such a wild place where there were no near neighbors and he had to be gone from home a lot of the time.

Dad had taken a temporary partner to help him clear land and raise potatoes. He was the old bear hunter, Richard Wilson. Dad would spend all day working with Mr. Wilson and go back to Sedona at evening to be with his family at night.

When Dad had to go to Prescott on business in 1885, he asked Mr. Wilson to come down and spend the nights near mother and the two small children that had been born since their marriage. Mr. Wilson failed to come down as he had agreed to do and Mother and the little children were alone for eight days.

Some men that mother knew came by from Jerome and stopped to get the key to the Thompson cabin at Indian Gardens to stay there and fish. Mother told them that Mr. Wilson had the key, wherever he might be, and that he must be either sick or dead. The men told her that he had just gotten busy working and forgot to come down. She told them that if he were all right he would have come down because he was a man of his word.

They went onto see. As they were going up the side of present Wilson Canyon, they heard Wilson's dog bark. They turned back then and found the body of Mr. Wilson, lying with his hands on each side of a little pool of water and his face in the water. His dog was standing beside him barking. They did not know whether a bear had killed him outright or only crippled him and he had crawled to the water and passed out and drowned. Mr. Wilson had apparently come upon the bear and wounded it but because his rifle was too small to kill a bear he had tried to climb a tree. Wilson had just bought a new pair of hob nailed shoes. The bear caught him by the heel of his shoe and almost pulled the heel off the shoe before it pulled him from the tree.

Mr. Wilson was wrapped in a blanket and buried at the spot because he had been dead so long. Wilson had some burros packed with little potatoes. They were found far from there and the packsaddles turned under their bellies and the potatoes scattered all along the way.

The first few years I can remember, when we lived at the Indian Gardens ranch, Dad was away from home a lot of the time. He freighted around Camp Verde and Jerome and hauled wood to Jerome. Sometimes he took the family with him. I lived at Mescal Station, Mingus Mountain and at Cottonwood.

Before we had a school in Oak Creek Canyon, we had to move to Red Rock to school. I went to the first school ever held there in 1891. I was five years old and Miss Minnie Maxwell was the first teacher there and also my first teacher. It did not make any difference about my age because I was needed to make up the attendance so they could have a school. This school was a little cabin on the Henry Schuerman place. The teacher used to make me a bed on a bench and I would take a little nap in the afternoon because it was too far for me to walk home by myself. We always had to take our lunch. We studied arithmetic, reading, language, spelling, geography, and copybooks. They were books in which you wrote underneath the words in the book. That is how we were taught writing. Sometimes when the snow was deep, Dad made overshoes for us by wrapping gunny sacks around our shoes. Our feet sure kept warm in those homemade overshoes.

The school in Oak Creek Canyon was built in 1899. It was a log cabin built on the little bench that is now known as Lower Manzanita campground. The desks were home made from lumber and were brought down from the old Pump House School. The cabin was heated by a big wood burning heater when we needed heat. As this was a Summer school we only needed heat for a while in the Spring. It was the children's job to keep the fire burning.

The first teacher was Ellsworth Schnebly. He has a nephew who lives in Sedona now, and is also a schoolteacher.

A daily attendance of eight pupils was required to keep a school, There were ten that first term, all Thompson and Purtymun children. The five Thompson children were Frank, Lizzie, Clara, Fred and Charley. The five Purtymun children were, Albert, George, Dan, Charley and Pearl. We started school in the

Those Early Days.....

first part of March and went until the last of August, as it was a Summer school. We had to walk three miles to school and cross the creek several times. We would walk to school in the morning and when we came home in the evening we would very often find bear tracks made over our tracks of the morning.

One time my sister and I went up onto the bench between our house and Munds Creek to look for a cow with a new calf. As we started across a little canyon, we saw a bear. We thought he went up the canyon in the high brush so we went down the canyon and ran into him again. The hill was covered with oak brush and cat claws and we ran all of the way home. When we got there our clothes were almost torn off and our arms and legs were all bloody from running through the brush. When we got to the house, Mother said, "What in the World Happened?" We said, "We saw a bear". She just laughed and said, "A bear won't hurt you."

*Jim Thompson seated in the doorway of his first cabin at Indian Gardens, in the early 1880's.*

My oldest brother, Frank had to take over the farming as soon as he was old enough, because Dad was gone from home so much. Frank was a harder taskmaster than Dad or Mother either were, and we were more afraid of him. Lizzie, my older sister, helped mother in the house and I had to help in the garden and field work. We had to weed the garden, drop the corn and potatoes when it was planting time and pick up potatoes in the Fall at harvest time.

Once when we were dropping corn and Frank was covering it with a little plow, Fred, my younger brother, spilled a lot of corn. He could not get it picked up before Frank was back with the plow, so he buried it all in one spot so Frank would not see it and scold. A lot of corn came up in that spot!!

Fred and I herded cows, pigs, ducks and chickens. We had to stay out all day and not even come in when we had company or to eat. Someone would bring us a lunch at noontime. We herded the chickens to keep them from scratching up the little corn and garden. Mother and Lizzie tried to make our job easier by sewing old overall rags on the chickens' feet to keep them from scratching. It did not work. Before they got moccasins made for the last ones, the first ones had them worn out. One time Dad bought forty-five hogs and we had to herd them. Sometimes we would get busy playing and forget the hogs and they would get in the potatoes and root them up.

Dad would buy a thousand pounds of flour and a couple of hundred pounds of sugar when he went to market. Mother made lots of sugar syrup before we had any fruit to put up for the winter. We dried tomatoes, corn, pumpkins and even string beans. We strung them like beads on a string and hung them up to dry.

I married Albert Purtymun on July 1, 1903, at my home at Indian Gardens. I was the only one of the family who was married at home. We were married by Juan Armijo, who was a Justice of the Peace at Red Rock precinct at that time. Dad had hauled a load of lumber out from Flagstaff to the top of the Thompson Ladder Trail. The Purtymun boys and Thompson boys went up to bring it down the trail. They nailed about six planks together and put a chain around one end of them and hitched a horse to them and drug them down the mountain. If they were roughed up some on the outside boards they could be turned with the rough side down when the dance platform was built. They got the platform finished before the wedding and had a dance that lasted for three nights and days. Dad would not let anyone sleep but he finally tired out and lay down to take a nap. Pearl Purtymun got a dipper of water and poured it in his face and he jumped up as lively as ever. Mrs. Margaret Dumas, known to all as Mother Dumas or Grandma Dumas, danced at my wedding.

My husband had been cutting wood north of Flagstaff and hauling it to Flagstaff. He was living in a tent. We lived there about a week and then moved into Flagstaff and he went to work in a sawmill. After about a month we moved again, eight miles south of Flagstaff. There he cut wood for the pump house that pumped water

# Those Early Days.....

to Flagstaff. The next fall we moved back to Oak Creek and spent most of the winter on what is known now as Mission Rancho. We intended to homestead the place. Albert cleared some land and did a little work on an irrigating ditch. Our first child, a girl, was born at Indian Gardens that Spring, 1904, and we named her Delia. When Delia was a month old, we moved onto the top of Mingus Mountain and my husband cut mining timbers for his stepfather, Jim Cook. The next fall we moved to Lonesome Valley to a little mine and lived in a little tent that had no floor and was not walled up. The mine was called the Hopkins Mine for the man who owned it. That was a very cold winter and we had a lot of snow.

On New Years Eve they blew the whistle at 12:00 midnight. I had heard that they always blew the whistle when there was an accident. My husband was working on night shift. I was sure there had been an accident and my husband was not due to get off work until 3:30 A.M. I was there all that time by myself wondering what had happened.

Later in the year we bought a bigger tent and moved to Hackberry Wash on the road south of Cherry Creek. My husband worked in two different mines there.

Our next move was to Humboldt, where he got work on a smelter that was being built. While we were living in Humboldt our second girl, whom we named Erma, was born, May 28, 1906. From Humboldt we moved to Oak Creek again in July. We settled on the old Purtymun place, known now as Junipine, and intended to make it our home. My husband, Albert, and his brother, Charley, built a road from the Lou Thomas place to Junipine while we lived there. The Thomas place is the present Oak Creek Lodge. On April 1, 1908, our third girl, Virgie was born at Mother's house at Indian Gardens. When the baby was a month old I moved back to the Junipine Ranch. That summer we kept boarders and roomers and I cooked for them and cared for their rooms.

The following March my husband had a job cutting wood again at the Pump House. He came down to move me and the girls from Junipine Ranch up to the Pump House. He had one workhorse and a saddle mare that was not used to working in harness and she balked and refused to go any farther. We had to leave the wagon there and we threw some quilts on the horses for saddles and I took Delia and my baby daughter, Virgie on my horse. Albert took Erma on his horse with him. There was snow on the ground and it was cold. Albert left the harness on my horse and I hung onto the hames. The horse he was riding gave out and he had to walk and carry Erma. The horse came on the next day. After dark we finally reached an old house without any floor or windows or door. Albert built a fire in it on the dirt floor. The next morning my eyes were swollen shut from lack of sleep and having smoke blown into them from our fire on the floor.

We were back at Junipine in February 1910, when I got sick. My husband and my brother started to take me to a doctor in Flagstaff. It started snowing about the time we left home. We got as far as Fulton Spring on the old Oak Creek road where there was a big log barn. We stayed there all night. They built a fire on the dirt floor of the barn and fixed a bed for me and the children. We made it on to Flagstaff through the deep snow next morning.

My husband got work driving a team for Frank Spear, who had a transfer and livery stable business. The business was later known as Lightening Delivery Co. We never did get back to our Junipine place to live. The next winter we sold our improvements and rights to Andrew Shumway. While my husband worked for Frank Spear, I cooked for the crew.

The next Fall I moved to Red Rock so I could send my oldest girl, Delia, to school. We lived in two walled up tents connected together on what was then the Dumas Ranch. The tent house belonged to my father. I also kept my three younger brothers so they could attend school there. The place is the present Crescent Moon Ranch. My fourth child, Laura was born there on November 9, 1910. During this time I had a tooth ache for three months before the baby was born and for four months after she was born. Finally my husband's stepfather, Jim Cook took me to Prescott in his new car, one of the first cars in this part of the country. I stayed in Prescott for a week with a friend and the Doctor treated my face to get the swelling down and my mouth open. I had had locked jaws. When the dentist finally pulled the tooth he broke the one next to it. I had to go back later and have it pulled.

We moved from Red Rock to Ash Creek in February where my husband was working for his brother. He said he had a nice place fixed up for me to live in. When we got there we found that all he had done was to dig a square hole in the ground and put a fireplace in one end and stretch a tent over it. It was so dark in that hole I had to keep a kerosene lamp burning in the daytime.

The following fall of 1911, we took a homestead on Yarbrough Wash, East of Dewey. Albert worked in the mines during the day and cut brush and cleared land in evenings till after dark. The children and I piled and burned the brush.

Those Early Days.....

On this ranch my fifth and sixth girls were born. We named the first one of them Elsie. When she was two years old she got some watermelon seeds in her windpipe. She coughed up one seed but was still so hoarse we took her to a doctor in Prescott. Traveling with horses and wagon we got to Prescott at midnight. The doctor operated on her about eight o'clock the next morning. She died the next night. The undertaker said she turned black and it was from blood poisoning from unsterilized instruments.

I was never happy at Yarbrough Wash after her death, though we lived there four years more. My sixth girl Violet was born there on September 25, 1916.

When my brother, Charley, was called into the armed service in World War 1, we moved over to his place in Oak Creek Canyon in May 1918. We cared for his place until he got home after the war.

We had sold our place on Yarbrough Wash and we moved to the George Black place in Sedona to send the children to school. It was here that my seventh child and first boy was born. We named him Albert. That winter we bought some land from my brother Frank, who homesteaded the present Walter Jordan ranch. We built a house on the land near where the Robert Jackson house is now. The next fall we moved to a little house that Jess Purtymun had built, on the side of Soldier Wash where present Brewer Road crosses the wash. We kept a small store there and the children went to school.

In July of the next year, I went to Flagstaff where my eighth child, a boy, was born. We rented George Black's place in Sedona and farmed there that year. In the fall of 1922 we moved to Clemenceau, and my husband worked in the smelter and the three oldest girls attended high school in Clarkdale.

In June 1924 my husband wanted to go to California to see his father, who he had not seen for many years. By then my two older girls were married and we all decided to go together and make a long trip of it. We had three old Model T Ford cars.

We first moved up to Stoneman Lake and camped. While the others camped my husband and I went back to Clarkdale to attend some business. On our way back we stopped at Dry Creek to tighten the brake bands. We were there so long that after we started on I reached for Albert's watch to see what time it was. He looked down to see what I was doing and ran off the road and turned the car over twice. We had our youngest boy with us but fortunately none of us were hurt. I caught a ride to Sedona and got a man with a team of horses to pull the car back onto the road. The car would still run, so we went on. We went up Oak Creek Canyon on the old wagon road. I walked up the switchbacks at the head of the canyon, behind the car, carrying my three year old child and a big rock to chock a wheel of the car in case the motor died and the brakes failed. We all got together again on the mountain and started on our trip.

We went first to New Mexico, then to Colorado, Utah, Idaho, Oregon and finally to California. We did not have much money when we started but expected to work as we went along and make expenses. The men worked in hay fields and we all picked fruit when we could get work. Sometimes it was a long time between jobs. Although we did not really go hungry the fare was monotonous at times. In Idaho we lived almost all together on black-eyed peas and prunes.

We picked up tires along the roadside where more prosperous drivers had thrown them away. If we did not have tubes to put in them we stuffed them with rags and tied them with baling wire. In Oregon City, Oregon, the wires wore out and the rags went flying in all directions. The people all pointed and laughed and had fun at our expense, but we did not mind.

We finally reached California about six months after we started. We bought a tent in Cottonwood, California and the men cut wood for a contractor. My youngest boy got sick here and I went down to Fresno on the train to stay with my mother-in-law. I took him to a doctor there but he did not know what was wrong with him, but told me to give him cod liver oil.

The rest of the family got to Fresno about New Year's Day and my husband and unmarried children and I went to North Fork to see his father. My oldest girl, Delia, and her husband and my single girl, Virgie, left for Clemenceau, Arizona. A few weeks later, Albert borrowed fifty dollars from his mother and we started back to Arizona.

As we came through Needles, California, we visited an old friend, Charley Allen. He was the owner of the present Junipine ranch on Oak Creek at that time and we rented it from him. We got back and found ourselves living on Junipine ranch again where we had lived so long ago. Albert worked on the county roads. This job kept him away from home so much the children and I started a garden and had chickens, pigs and a milk cow. In May of that year the fruit was all killed at Junipine and we moved down to present Manzanita Camp and leased some land from the Forest

Those Early Days.....

Service. In November of that year my ninth and last child, a girl, was born. We named her Zola.

We lived at Manzanita for thirteen years. After the big flood of 1938 washed away part of our buildings and farmland, we sold the place and moved down to Cornville, and bought another place. In a few years we sold that place too.

In February, 19.41, my youngest boy, Charley, who was almost twenty years old had a car wreck in Oak Creek Canyon. He died in Mercy Hospital in Flagstaff a few days later from skull fracture and exposure.

In the summer of 1944 we bought some land above Indian Gardens from my brothers. This farm was part of original land homesteaded by my mother many years ago. Here we raised fruit and garden in summer. Since our children were all grown and gone from home by then we spent our winters down on the desert prospecting for gold and having a good time.

On July 1, 1953, we celebrated our Golden Wedding Anniversary at our Oak Creek home. My husband passed away May 6, 1961. I sold the farm a year later and bought a trailer house. I have it parked in my daughter's trailer park, Mac's Trailer Park, near Indian Gardens.

## AN INDIAN SCARE
*by Albert E. Thompson*

On the old Oak Creek Canyon road that follows around the foot of Steamboat Rock, there is a place that might have some historical interest to some people. About half way around Steamboat Rock is a slab of red sandstone that resembles a huge grindstone. At the present time it is lying flat on the ground. Some 50 years ago it stood upright on its edge. It stood about breast high to a man.

The very first trail from present Sedona, started out almost the same as Highway 89A does today. It crossed Mormon Camp Wash and went through the old Mormon Camp, campground. It went through present Brook Haven resort and went at an angle up the hill by the present Red Rock Motel, and up near the foot of Steamboat Rock, where it connected with the old wagon road that was built later. Near the junction of the old trail and wagon road is where the big grindstone rock stood.

Within a short while after my dad, Jim Thompson, first saw Indian Gardens, he was on his way up there one evening. I would place the date in either 1876 or 1877. As he neared the above described rock, by lucky chance, he happened to see two Indians coming down the trail toward him before they saw him. He dropped down behind the rock and rested his rifle over the top of it. As the Indians came closer he could see that the lead one was carrying two rifles and the other one had a deer on his back. Dad yelled "hands up" at them. They stopped and raised their hands. The Indian that was carrying the deer stopped so sudden and threw up his hands that he fell over on his back. They made friendly signs, and showed him a paper. Dad allowed them to come close enough to him to hand him the paper. He was pleasantly surprised to read that they were army scouts from the military post at Camp Verde, and the paper was a permit for them to go on a hunting trip and was signed by the commanding officer at Camp Verde.

Dad said he did not know whether he or the Indians were the most relieved to find that neither side was on the warpath. That was Dad's only experience with Indians after he came to the Verde Valley, and luckily it was just a bad scare and nothing more.

Those Early Days.....

## GAIL GARDNER TALKS TO SEDONA WESTERNERS
*(Taped)*

I think you are making a mistake in asking us because when you ask an "Old Timer" to reminisce, you have to shoot him down before you can get rid of him.

I first came to Sedona in the year 1908. We came over in a party from Prescott four of us - young men - to spend the summer here in Sedona.

Now, Sedona at that time consisted of a little store right down on the creek where the Schnebly Hill road turns up, and that was all. There was no more Sedona.

We stayed at the Schnebly Ranch, which is right opposite where the road crosses the bridge. We boarded at the Schneblys and they had the finest strawberries that was ever known to man. They were about so big (measured with his hand) and they were pink. There were tons of them so we had strawberries all the time. This was in 1908 - There was nothing at all here - not a thing.

This hill right across here (pointing) we called it the Tiger's Head and I won a fine dinner for being able to climb the Tiger's Head before dinner. Another boy and I said we could climb that before noon. So we climbed it before noon and waved our hands there and the other boys had to pay for our dinners at the Schnebly Ranch that night. So we called that the Tiger's Head.

I couldn't tell you too much about the names of other landmarks around here, but I certainly discovered a great many of them in the year 1908.

The second time I came back was in the year 1910 and I remember—with a buckboard and a team we left Sedona at 6:30 in the morning and it was past noon when we got that willow tail team up to the top of Schnebly Hill. So the traveling wasn't quite so fast as it is today. The Schnebly Hill was a little bit different than it is now, but it was a steep climb and a little bit on the tough side.

I forgot to tell you a little bit about myself perhaps. My father came to Arizona in 1879 - when the railroad stopped at Trinidad, Colorado, and he came the rest of the way with a pack outfit. He headed straight West from Trinidad, Colorado or rather he came through Santa Fe and Taos. When he got to- - oh possibly- - to where Holbrook is now, he stopped on the road and somebody said, "Where are you boys going?" He said, "Oh, we're going to Silver City, New Mexico." He and his partner. This man that stopped said, "Oh, you don't want to go there. Why don't you go to Prescott, Arizona? That's the gambler's paradise. Why, there's more money there than there is any place in the West. Now, you fellows head for Prescott, Arizona and you'll be alright."

So my father headed for Prescott, Arizona in 1879. So, anyway, I have a great interest in Sedona having been here in 1908 and again in 1910.

I have another sort of an offbeat interest. My brother-in-law owned Lolomai Lodge up the creek. Some of you might know where it is. The old tumbled-down house was quite a beautiful place, built of logs, a fine stopping place for the Sisson family. My brother-in-law Bill Sisson, died a year ago this last October. And this Lolomai- - the four acres that's left now belongs to my son and my daughter.

There's no access to it. What they're going to do with it - I don't know. Some day they will do something with it. So I have that precarious interest in Sedona.

But I've always had this great interest - we used to come through here when we were going turkey hunting. We came through Sedona and went up Schnebly Hill to the top of the mountain and when we got there, we would go through Munds Park. My God! Have any of you seen Mund's Park recently? What's there? A man behind every bush! That's fine, I suppose, it may be progress but that kind of progress does not appeal to me! I like fewer people and, let's say nicer people - scattered over a wide area, which is something I would prefer.

Now I don't know - Tex, are you going to call this organization Westerners or something? I just want to mention that there is a national organization of Westerners if you happen to be interested in it. And the Westerners headquarters are in Stockton, California. There's a chapter of Westerners in Phoenix, Tucson and in Prescott. There's one in Los Angeles, San Francisco, and one in Chicago. The headquarters in Stockton, California - the dues are very nominal. It doesn't amount to much.

We have a great deal of fun out of our organization in Prescott. The idea is that you have talks either recorded or published of the things that do not occur in history books. Now you take Don Bell's talk here - you won't find that in any history. You "dog-gone" right you won't! That's first-hand!) Which the historians like to call primary research.) When you talk to Don and me you'll get some primary research in history!

Well now, in the Westerners' meeting, you get that kind of

## Those Early Days.....

performance talk or whatever it is. (This thing is being recorded and that embarrasses me no end! (Anyway that's historical facts. Of course you might stretch your facts a little because historians are apt to if the occasion is good and the audience is attentive. You may stretch it a little bit, but not too much. You can be checked on that.

This Tiger Head now, you see you come in to the difference of thought, which has got to be resolved someway. Don said, maybe it's Camel Head. I say it's Tiger Head. I say I won a dinner climbing the damn thing and I wore out a good pair of levis - the seat of them - coming down! So that was something too.

So, you see us visitors have an interest. Lots of you fellows are in Yavapai County - all of you! You don't know that, but you were. You're in Yavapai County so we have a great interest and I think we have a community of interest with all of us.

And that's about all the lies I can think of, so I thank you very much for your kind attention.

AFTER APPLAUSE HE RELATED THE FOLLOWING STORY: and was asked to sing a song of his called, "Tying a knot in the Devil's Tail," by Gail Gardner.

You see, I was a cowboy for many, many year and then, you know you stomp a cowboy's brains out and you got a postmaster. I was a postmaster at Prescott for 21 years.

So when I was a cowboy - why - to amuse the friends I worked with, why there'd be some things happen that would be amusing. So the cowboys would want me to write about it. So I had a "gigs" or propensity for writing doggerel verses. So I wrote a few of these songs, and of course the cowboys would come around and give me the words. Well, I hated to type worse than anything, so finally I published a little book. These cowboy songs that I wrote - farfetched - as they might be, they are all founded on facts.

This one is about - TYING THE KNOT IN THE DEVIL'S TAIL -Another old boy and I (Bob Heckle, maybe you might know him). Bob Heckle and I were riding out West of Prescott in the Sierra Prieta Mountains. The old boy out there called them the "Sierry Petes." So this is what the name of the song is. Bob Heckle and I were riding out there - branding calves and catching wild steers, tying 'em up to trees and leading them in. (We won't go into that 'cause nobody knows how to do it any more - anyhow.)

So anyway, we went to town and "partook" of all the amusements that a cowboy had in those days. (And the amusements was plenty and varied!) So we're going back to about along where that Thumb Butte picnic ground is now. One of the boys said, "Why, the Devil gets cowboys that do what we're doing." "Oh, let the Devil come along and get us! We'll neck him up to a Black Jack sapling, the way we're tying up these outlaw steers. So we don't care if the Devil jumps us."

So I forgot all about that little conversation. I was going back on the train on the Santa Fe Limited — in 1917 — went back in World War I to make the world safe for Democrats! And we went back there.

On the train I passed through this old Canders, Nebraska and my God! Cattle that broad across the beam (measuring) - not an ear mark on a one of 'em and men walking around among them on foot. Well, I'd like to see some guy walking around among them cattle on foot, the kind we'd been tying up. And they weren't broad. They ran out this way (made a "V" with his hands) to the rear and had horns on the other end. And we tied 'em up to trees and then led 'em in. So, I got to thinking about the difference in those cattle and the ones we'd been catching.

So I sat down and wrote this little bunch of "doggerel" verses and sent 'em back to my sister who was back home in Prescott.

When the wars were over I came home and happened to think about this thing and a friend of mine said, "There's a little girl that's ill in the Mercy Hospital and she's never seen a cowboy. Now, you go on and put on your boots, your spurs and your hat and what not and go over and see this gal," I said, "What am I gonna talk to this kid about?" Well, I happened to think of this verse. So, I went over to my sister's desk and dug it out and took it over to the hospital and read it to this girl. While I was there, there was an old cowboy, Billy Simmons', some of you know him. You probably know him Howard. (Howard said, "I went to war with him.") "You went to the war with him? That was making the world safe for Democrats!"

Well anyway, Billy said, "Gail, that'd make a good song. Why don't you make a song out of it?" So Billy, he put some old wore-out tune to it and he started singing it. So the song got out and the first thing you knowed these drug store "punks" got to singin' it over the radio and it kinda got away from me. I did have the sense to get a copyright on it. So, I think. (God help you all, I'll sing it for you - (Tune - Polly Wally Doodle All Day).

## GAIL GARDNER SINGS A SONG TO SEDONA WESTERNERS
*(Taped)*

Away up high in the Sierry Petes,
Where the yeller pines grows tall,
Ole Sandy Bob an' Buster Jig,
Had a rodeer last fall.

Oh, they taken their hosses and runnin' irons
And mabbe a dawg or two,
An' they 'lowed they'd brand all the long-yered calves,
That come within their view.

And any old dogie that flapped long yeres,
An' didn't bush up by day,
Got his long yeres whittled an' his old hide scortched,
In a most artistic way.

Now one fine day ole Sandy Bob,
He throwed his seago down,
"I'm sick of the smell of burin' hair,
"And I 'lows I'm a-goin' to town."

So they saddles up an' hits 'em a lope,
Fer it warnt no sight of a ride,
And them was the days when a Buckeroo
Could ile up his inside.

Oh, they starts her in at the Kaintucky Bar.
At the head of Whisky Row,
And they winds up down by the Depot House,
Some forty drinks below.

They then sets up and turns around
And goes her the other way,
An' to tell you the Gawd-forsaken truth,
Them boys got stewed that day.

As they was a-ridin' back to camp,
A-packin' a pretty good load,
Who should they meet but the Devil himself,
A-prancin' down the road.

Sez he, "You ornery cowboy skunks,
"You'd better hunt yer holes,
"Fer I've come up from Hell's Rim Rock,
"To gather in yer souls."

Sez Sandy Bob, "Old Devil be dammed,
"We boys is kinda tight,"
But you aint a-goin' to gather no cowboy souls,
"'Thout you has some kind of fight."

So Sandy Bob punched a hole in his rope,
And he swang her straight and true,
He lapped it on to the Devil's horns,
An' he taken his dallies too.

Now Buster Jig was a riata man,
With his gut-line coiled up neat.
So he shaken her out an' he built him a loop,
An' he lassed the Devil's hind feet.

Oh, they stretched him out an' they tailed him down,
While the irons was a-gettin' hot,
They cropped and swaller-forked his yeres,
Then they branded him up a lot.

They pruned him up with a de-hornin' saw,
An' they knotted his tail fer a joke,
They then rid off and left him there,
Necked to a Black-Jack oak.

If you're ever up high in the Sierry Petes,
An' you hear one Hell of a wail,
You'll know it's that Devil a-bellerin' around,
About them knots in his tail.

Those Early Days.....

## DON BELL TELLS HIS STORY TO SEDONA WESTERNERS
*(Taped)*

I was between 9 and 10 years old when I first came to Sedona. It seems as though it was appropriate to write this article for the Independent in view of the fact that there was so much controversy in the names of the peaks and mountains around Sedona. And to touch briefly about what I wrote in the Independent - if you take the Independent – I'll go back a little on my family history. My mother was born in Cape Elizabeth, Maine. She came West with Don Willard's aunt, Mrs. Munds - later. She was a girl of about 21 years of age and they came to Kansas City on a first class train. And when they got there the train broke down, and I didn't learn until about two years before Mack Willard, Don's father died, that they transferred to an immigrant train and came on to Ash Fork on an immigrant train which wasn't very becoming to two fine young ladies. (They never told that, but Don's father told it later on.)

Anyhow, they came to the Verde Valley where her brother, Frank Jordan, was in the bee business and milling business. (He had a gristmill there). She taught school at Clear Creek several years then at Middle Verde and then at Upper Verde. Some of the pupils she had were the Willards, the Scotts and down on Clear Creek she had the Wingfields. She taught Howard's and the Tompkin's Mothers/Later years, she taught even the kids of those people. So she was an "old-timer" schoolteacher.

I came into the picture in 1894 in Bracksville, Ohio. And Horace Greely said "Go West young man." So at the age of 3 months my folks decided to come west. And we landed in Jerome where my uncle, Frank Jordan, then was interested in what is known as "The little Daisy". And it seems he was the first finder of the discrepancy in the survey that gave the Verde Extension a separate mining claim than the United Verde. So we came on to Camp Verde and there I stayed and was raised until 1939. Then I went to Prescott and was superintendent of the County Hospital for nearly 25 years.

However, going back to my childhood in the Valley. In 1903, a young man by the name of D.Ellsworth Schnebly was a teacher at School District #2. He was one of the most industrious men I ever saw in my life. Very likeable fellow. He boarded at my father and mother's house. He paid the sum of $20.00 a month board and room. He walked *2 1/2* miles to school everyday. He got the magnificent sum of $70.00 a month for teaching which was a big salary in those days. Every Friday evening, he would walk from Clear Creek to Sedona, where he and his brother, Carl, had a ranch. He'd work all day Saturday and Sunday and he went back to Clear Creek Monday Morning. He never missed a shift. Well, when it came Thanksgiving in 1903, (I checked the date at the County Superintendent's Office) the Bell family was invited to Sedona for Thanksgiving dinner.

We started before daylight and ended up down here at Beaver Head at noon, where we had lunch. And we pulled into Sedona with our plow horses and wagon along in the evening. And there we were greeted by Carl Schnebly. By the way, Ellsworth Schnebly came with us in the wagon with my father and mother, myself and two brothers.

Then the next day being Thanksgiving, we had the regular traditional Thanksgiving dinner and I ate too much as I usually do. (You can verify that because we just had a big supper down here tonight). For one that's been looking after his weight - well, I neglected to do that tonight.

And, that's the same thing that happened in 1903. I overate and of course, was sick. Well, fortunately, as you can see I recovered.

Then the next day Ellsworth Schnebly took us to a big cave in Capitol Butte, over here north of Grasshopper Flats. A big Indian Cave and there were several metates. It hadn't been visited by very many people, but anyway Ellsworth packed a metate down about ½ mile. The metate must have weighed about 100 pounds. He brought it in.

He also took us over by Coffee Pot. He pointed out Coffee Pot Rock. As I remember I was about 9 or 10 years old at that time (If I get twisted up on telling these things - you can look back and time will make you not remember like you used to.)

Anyhow we went by Coffee Pot Rock (he pointed them out to us) and went back to what is known as the Devil's Kitchen, And that is very vague in my mind, but as I remember it was about half as big as a football field and it was 30 or 40 feet deep. Now, it might not have been that deep but from a kid's standpoint, that's the way I remember it. And he pointed out this Capitol Butte where this cave was. Then he pointed out to us Steam Boat Rock. Also he pointed out Camel's Head, which my brother and I prepared to climb up the hill and visit. And we figured that we were the first white men - (mind you he was 12 and I was 9 or 10) to ever visit this place, but we found that there was plenty of other visitors before us. And Mr. Schnebly also pointed out Court

Those Early Days.....

House Rock, which is down here North and East of Bell Rock. Now that's the controversy of today. And coming up with Gail Gardner, who is a great friend of Andrew Baldwin's, why he said that Baldwin always called this rock down here by the crossing Court House Rock.

Dr. Dumas ought to know something about that. I have a picture of his father and mother sitting on a homemade bench with these rocks back of them. He probably knows whether that's Court House Rock or not. "What did your folks call it Doc?" "Courthouse Rock."

Anyway that was the sum and substance of my visit to Sedona and as I mentioned in the article, there was a man named Thompson here. He brought a mess of trout to Schneblys, which gave us boys the idea that we were going to do a little trout fishing. I had never seen anything but a "Verde sucker" or a "bony tail" in my life but we went trout fishing with poles and improvised fishing gear. And we couldn't get a bite. We could see 'em down there and finally we rigged up a snare out of fine wire and we snared one. We sure thought we had a trout but he turned out to be a "humped-back sucker". The humped back suckers today, I think are extinct in this area. I've never seen one in the last 30 years. Now that's my remembrance of Sedona.

Later I went with Mr. Schnebly. He had a goat ranch down at what is called Cold Water. He had goats down there and he had a herder by the name of Ray Palmer, and on below the M.T. Ranch was Tinsley's place. They also had goats and a nice fruit orchard. We got down there and hit there the day that Wes Durfey got bit by a rattlesnake. He reached down to pick up a rock to throw at the goats and got bit right near the vein in the pulse.

We went down 7 miles - horseback and brought him back. His arm was swelled up as big as the thigh of your leg and underneath his arm was as big as a water bucket. And this bite, I can remember there was green liquid oozing out of it. Well, they sent to Camp Verde for a doctor. Ray Palmer went for the doctor and they brought a doctor back and I've forgotten what they called the doctor but I think it was either Wiley or McGeimis. And also the father of Wes Durfey came back with them. And they brought five quarts of whiskey — started with it but when they got to Tinsley's Ranch, they had one quart left! Mr. Durfey, the father, brought some flax seed and some Japanese oil and put flax seed poultices on it. Naturally Wes Durfey recovered from the snakebite.

Coming home from the Schnebly place, I rode behind the saddle of Mr. Tinsley on a mule - rode like that for 30 miles. I couldn't sit down for about a week afterwards!

That's my early recollection of Schnebly's and Sedona. I'm probably wrong on some of the names of these things but that is how I remember it.

Those Early Days.....

## A FOLLOW-UP TALK BY DON BELL
*(Taped)*

This is a saying a kind of aftermath of tying the steer up, Andrew Baldwin, you've probably heard of Andrew Baldwin that lived down here at the Crossing. He was a friend of mine and a great friend of Gail's. We went on several hunting trips together. And I was in high school in Prescott at the time and Andrew and I decided to go over into what is known as Copper Basin.

Coming back on this side of the rim, we saw a steer tied up to a Black Jack Oak. And he was poor and his horns were bloody and the poor devil was about starved to death.

I said to Andrew, "I bet some cow puncher has forgotten where that steer is. I'm gonna go over and cut him loose."

"Now it happens that when they find a steer that won't lead, they'll tie him up to an oak for two or three days and then go back and lead him.

Forty years later, after I cut that steer loose, I was telling Gail about it.

He says, "I've often wondered what son-of-a-#@$%$#@ cut that steer loose!"

## HOWARD WINGFIELD TALKS TO SEDONA WESTERNERS
*(Taped)*

Good evening, it's a little bit embarrassing to have to get up and talk after those two (Gail and Don). I didn't get to Sedona until, oh, a couple of years after Gail, here. And Don beat me here about ten years. But the first trip I made to Sedona was with my father and four mules to a wagon. He brought the whole family, by the way, and there was three girls and myself, and Mother and Dad. And all the way from Camp Verde it took us two days to Bacon Rind Park (Indian Gardens). I think we called it Bacon Rind Park in those days. Is that right? (Someone said, "correct.")

The first night out we camped at the Schuerman Ranch after traveling all day over the road out to Big Park at Beaver Head Flats and we camped there at the Schuermans. The next day we spent going up the canyon, and the end of the road was at Bacon Rind Park.

Well, I had about the same experience that Don did only I'd catch the fish without snarin' 'em. I dug some worms and thought I was going to get a trout. I could see these big fish and had a wonderful time catching these big suckers.

My Dad went on up the creek and came back that night with a good string of trout. But we had a wonderful trip - spent about ten days on it -two days traveling each way and saw a lot of country. We passed Bell Rock and Court House Rock. My Dad, being very familiar with the country, was able to name 'em to us. And, in all, we had a fine trip.

I think it's very commendable here the work you people are trying to do, or, are doing, I should say. And I think you might be interested in knowing what Camp Verde has done in the way of preserving these stories that your Old Timers tell. They published a book - VERDE VALLEY PIONEERS. We just now have completed the third edition of it. And we are taking the proceeds - the profit - and giving it to the Camp Verde Museum, which the most of you, I think, is familiar with.

Now, Camp Verde could use something more of this nature though. I understand that you are locating points of interest and getting the correct name for them and "signing" them. We have a number of places down here that people are interested in. They come and ask about them. It's awful hard to direct a man - you go up the road, take the first left turn, then you come to the end of that, you park your car and go up this canyon and off to the left and you come to the spot. Now one particular place is the Grief Hill

Those Early Days.....

Massacre Grounds.

A few years ago, after the Black Canyon Highway was completed through the valley, somebody mentioned it and the State became interested, that was the time Howard Pyle was Governor. Hardly anybody in town knew where it was. I, of course, had been historically minded all my life and those things made an impression on me and I was able to take the engineers from the State Highway Department up to the Massacre Grounds, where the graves were and at that time there were a number of marks of the old wagon train. But since then they have been all carried away. Nothing left there but the graves. That, now, is creating a lot of interest. People are in the store every few days asking. I tell 'em how to go to Grief Hill Massacre Grounds. As I said before, it's hard to tell 'em how to go.

And then we do have Old Fort Lincoln there that pre-dates Camp Verde - the fort there - by about two years. The old cemetery is there -one or two graves left. The soldiers were exhumed and moved to military cemeteries back when I was a small boy. I don't remember how old I was. But, there is two of these scout's graves (Indian Scout's Graves) still in the old cemetery. The old foundation of the old fort is still in existence there if a person knows where to go.

You have that and I don't know whether you folks have discussed it yet. But you have, out here on Beaver Head Flats, you have the old stage station site. The last time I was there, there was the chimney standing. That is on the continuation of the Santa Fe Trail to the old immigrant trail into the Verde Valley which continued on down across the Beaver Head Flats over to the Verde and out over the mountain over by Grief Hill and on into Fort Whipple. And that should be marked so that our younger people will know where that was located. You can barely discern on this hill where it is now. It's quite plain going out of the valley on the West. And we do have a number of spots in our locality that should have a marker placed on 'em.

I didn't come up here to make a speech. I hadn't prepared one. I came to listen. But I'm glad to express my self in those words.

## FLETCHER FAIRCHILD MAKES A TALK to SEDONA WESTERNERS
*(Taped)*

Well, I am a new one, I feel like one because there's so many more "Old Timers" or "Older Timers" here than I am. The first time I saw this valley was in 1908 from the top of the hill up here - Schnebly Hill -and I thought it was the most beautiful place I ever saw.

I was with Charlie Woolfolk - a lot of you remember him. He was an old sheep man and every place he went that he could take me, he took me. We were on this buckboard and we were headed for Thompson's Ranch. We got down to Sedona, stayed over at Schnebly's Hotel; Charlie Wool-folk's mother was spending the summer there. And then we started on up the creek in this buckboard. And we got up here somewhere and slid off the road. I think it was up around where Wilson Canyon is now. However, the road didn't chance to go right along there. There's some controversy about where the old road went. I think I can mark it out with the help, probably, of Albert here.

We slid off the road and the right front wheel - the hub of the wagon-hung on this big tree and we were going down hill a little bit. So the only way to get the wagon out of there was to cut the tree down. So, Charlie Woolfolk usually tried to refrain from cussing too much around me 'cause I was just a kid. He thought an awful lot of me. But, I learned an awful lot of words there while he was cutting the tree down, and getting the wagon out, that I have remembered ever since. And I'd like to say he used them profusely. We finally got on up to Indian Gardens. We had two more people with us but they fished up the creek - they walked from Schnebly's up to Indian Gardens - fishing up the creek. One of them was Frank Brooks who a good many of you remember, he had the office bar and later a bottling works in Flagstaff.

And while we are on the subject of business buildings, I might say that Gail Gardner scuffed the seat out of his Levis coming off Camel Head, which he calls Tigers Head. He could have easily gotten another pair from his Dad, J. I. Gardner Mercantile Co. over in Prescott, whom I knew very well. I went to grammar school in Prescott a few winters owing to the fact that I had an uncle who lived down there. So I knew old J.I. We used to call him Old Jay. We'd go up to his store. It was down below the old Head Hotel. What was the name of that

Those Early Days.....

street? Cortez. (Someone said, "Jake was my nickname when I was a kid"). Well, anyway we finally got to Indian Gardens and it seems like every place I went, kids tried to whip me because I was too small. Of course I've gained a great stature since then. We got up there and I thought I would be immune to play down in this remote country. Ah, some of the kids started showin' up. You probably know who I mean - the Thompson brothers. I thought they never would quit chewing me out.

We got very friendly, however, and they didn't beat me up too much. I was real surprised. I want to say in a statement that they were very, very friendly. And I thought it was funny for kids to be so friendly. But we had a great time while we were down there. And Mrs. Thompson had a little milk house down along the little creek that ran from the Thompson Spring. And I think it was either Charlie or Ab told me the other day that this spring is just as productive as it was in those days. And Mrs. Thompson had this milk house down there. In those days they had coolers that were built of a little wooden frame with burlap over them so the air could get through. Of course there was a cool stream running underneath.

Mrs. Thompson had big old pans of milk in this place and we used to slip in there and skim the cream off, you know, and eat the cream. I remember that one day I ate so much cream and then I think we went and picked wild blackberries, which I don't think grows up there any more. Anyway the mixture of all this I couldn't eat too much dinner. But, that was my first trip down here.

I came back each summer, however, that was the only trip with Charlie Woolfolk. But my Uncle, Billy Rodin, which many of you know of the old Pitch Fork cattle outfit, came with me. From the summer of 1908 on - I think - until about 1915 - he and I were on the banks of Oak Creek at Indian Gardens (Bacon Rind Park) the night before fishing season every year - just Billy and I. Of course you haven't had any fish stories so I guess I'll tell you a fish story. This "hump back" sucker, you know, we didn't use to call that a fish, with due apologies where they belong. Billy, my uncle Billy Rodin, wasn't a very big talker. He didn't talk too much. If he had something to say, he said it and if he didn't, he didn't say too much. That is, until after he retired, and stood around on the streets of Flagstaff after he got a little older - say like a few of us - and then he could really tell you some good ones if you could stand it. We used to come into camp one day to fish up the creek and he would fish down the creek and then the next day we would change. He would fish up the creek and I would fish down the creek. So we got in quite late in the evening. By the way, we would have plenty of trout.

I don't think there was any limit, but there was a season. In those days you didn't need a license. So this particular evening we got in late and fried some of our fresh trout. The others we would pack in fern (these mountain ferns) and we would salt them down and pack 'em in the ferns and keep them in a cool place. They will keep for a long time. We would usually take them back to town. Or, if anybody else would fish up there which was seldom, (Old Jack Smith would fish up there a lot and several others), we would send 'em to town by whoever was going while we were there.

They would usually take them where they belonged. This particular evening (getting back to it) we leaned our fishing rods up against a tree in our camp and hung our creels up. (We did have those; we happened to to have something fancy in order to carry the fish in). And we had dinner, or supper as we called it then, and so after supper it was dark and Billy walked back over to the tree and got his creel and hung it on his shoulder and started to pick up his fishing rod. "Well," I said, "Just what do you think you're going to do?" (Or words to that effect). "Well", he said, "I spotted a big fish down there in a hole today and I'm goin down and get him." I said, "You mean at night?" He said, "Sure at night is the best time to fish." (I'd never heard of fishing at night before.) Well, this story is true - believe me or not, I don't care how many of you do or how many of you don't. I'm goin to tell it anyway. You'll have to bear with me.

So, I said, "Now I'm going with you." "No", he said, "Now kid, you can't make it." He said, "There's some awful steep places and some rocks you have to scale over - all this stuff - so you'd better just stay in camp." He said, "I'm gonna get that fish." I said, "If you're gonna get that fish, I'm goin' with you." So, I finally talked him into it, and we started out. I never had such a rough trip in the dark in my life! (Except one other time that I won't mention). So, we finally got down to the place and I think I can still spot the hole up here in Oak Creek. I gaze longingly in this direction. (I'm pretty sure it's the same place every time I go up that way.) So we got down to this kind of a big sandy hole - a lot of you guys probably know where it is, but this fish isn't there anymore. So, we got down there and it was real dark and Billy built a big fire right on the bank of this hole. So we started fishing and we fished and we fished and we fished and I thought this is crazy. This man, they say, is "blowing

# Those Early Days.....

his top" or something like that. About the time I was beginning to believe that he was a little off his rocker, boy! Something hit his line and he had the darndest wrestling match there I ever saw and I watched it for 5 or 10 minutes or something. He didn't want to lose him. He was takin' his time with the thing and then in the meantime, something hit mine! Well, the outcome of the story is (and this is the part you don't have to believe if you don't want to) the biggest fish I've ever seen out of Oak Creek. (Maybe the Thompson boys can "top" it or some of you other folks). That fish was 26" long. It was a regular old native trout and this thing looked like a whale to me! Well, mine, I think, was 14" or 16" or something like that. (I liked my fish better than I did his.) It was really a wonderful native trout. So, when Billy caught his fish and I landed mine, he just picked up the stuff and started back up the creek - didn't cast in the hole another time. So we got on back to Indian Gardens and about two days later (I don't know whether to mention his name or not, a good many of you know him I know, but oh, maybe I can.) Old Man Heckethorn was camped up there. He was going to town the next day or two. So we sent the two fish along, with some smaller ones, to Flagstaff with Heckethorn, to give to Billy's wife, my aunt, who would distribute them around. When we got back to Flagstaff, we asked my aunt, "What do you think of that fish?" And she said "what fish?" The fish was never delivered! Well, Old Man Heckethorn was one of the finest people I've ever met, but, by gosh, he just couldn't resist the temptation, I guess. That wasn't bad enough, but we heard later that he showed it around up there and told other people he caught it. (Well, now you see there was larceny in those days too.)

As I say, there's many here like Doc Dumas and Joe Lay and Don Willard and so many. And my good wife over there whom I met here in Sedona about 1911 or 1912 - somewhere along there. (We still argue when it was). We've almost been together ever since. Ah, by the way, the ones of you that don't know her, I'd like her to stand at this time while I have the floor and take a bow. And now I'll tell you who she is. She's Lee Van Deren's daughter, Iva Van Deren. Of course she's the one who forced me finally to move back to Sedona. And we've been back here now for two years. We were away from Arizona for 40 years however, we made from one to two and sometimes more trips back on vacations each year and watched Sedona and Verde Valley and all this county progress. And of course we have been back - it'll be two years in March. We've lived here on Van Deren Road and we'd be pleased to have any of you come to see us. We don't say that we'll return the visit because Lanora Mack was up to visit us and several others - Charlie, Albert and a lot of the old

Sedona Westerners

timers - Myrtle Smith and a good many. And dog gone it! Fred Metz lives right down the street and we don't ever go to see him, and Fred and I were raised together. But, we just work all the time. In other words, I retired and went to work.

When I get back off to the coast nowadays, I tell my "higher ups" this - - I can tell them anything now I want to. I've worked for them for so long.

And so that's what's happened. We don't get around a lot. However, we are getting around more lately. We went down to Camp Verde to Howard's store about a year ago. And - getting back to Camp Verde - I think it was 'round the summer of 1906, Howard tried to tell us, but there was the Wingfield Saloon and the Bill Lane Saloon in Camp Verde those days, and we went down with old Tom Drum, and we stopped the first night at Blacks' Ranch down on Beaver Creek by Montezuma Well. And then over to Camp Verde and we spent a couple of weeks down there. And the 4th of July celebration, which we went for, was quite an affair. (Howard could probably put the date on this.) They were trying to get "local option" in Camp Verde. I'll never forget this "Verde Valley Local Option Social Club" - V.V.L.O.S.C. I was then a kid, of course, and what they did down there was pin this little ribbon on me, which I kept for years. It was a little red ribbon with black letters on it. - V.V.L.O.S.C. I don't know whether they ever got local option or not. I think they did, I'm not sure. They shouldn't have. I was down to the celebration - the 4th of July. The local option people had a big picnic and everything was free - this was a sight you know - everything was free - so the kids had all the soda pop they wanted and pink lemonade, sandwiches, and pie. You know how these people are - they go all out. (We went to a school picnic down here last year, I never ate so much in my life.) Everybody brings this stuff, you know. (We just go to eat).

So that's the way it was at Camp Verde. So then the following day on July 4th the "Wets" - or whatever you call it - the ones who wanted to retain the saloons etc. - they had their picnic. And, of course, they were the "aftermath" so they could out do the others - or tried to - and I'm not sure but I think they did from what I recall seeing around there. (What year was that, Howard? "That was the year 1909," Howard said.) I thought it was before that; I remember it pretty well though so it must have been later.

Then we moved down to Oak Creek and my stepfather was one of the Harts and our first ranch was down below House Mountain there. I think they bought it from old Juan Armijo there. I think we moved down here in the fall of 1911. From then on for several

## Those Early Days…..

years, I was back and forth in the Valley, but, as I say, we used to punch cows a lot here and tied some wild steers once in a while. I didn't do much of it - I watched the other guys. I was a little "chicken", I guess. I tied up a few I guess, but I didn't stuff any cotton in long ears or the old cows either. (Course maybe you guys know what I'm talking about.)

Well, anyway I've taken up enough time, I think. We old timers owe these old Westerners a vote of thanks for getting us all together. I've seen people here and tonight by the way, and prior evenings we've been here that I never expected to see again in my life. And I'm not a person that is very nostalgic. I've always been interested in history of old times. I can remember 50 or 60 years ago better than I can remember things that happened today or yesterday. Of course that's probably caused by something being missing above my chin.

Anyway, it's very interesting and I do think that the Westerners have done a wonderful thing to get us all together and to give us these Life Memberships in the Westerners. And to let us get up here and express ourselves the way we do. (I know I get a kick out of it.) And I'm sure the other "boys" and the "old timers" that I've talked to do. And I'm sure there are many more that should have been at the table tonight. But Tex called me and said that Albert had asked for me to give my moral support and would I sit at the table with Albert? So I'm not apologizing in that sense. And somebody says 1879 and stuff like this - I think my father came to Flagstaff about that time; but my first sight here, as I said before, was 1908. It's awfully nice to get to talk to people and to see all of you. It gives you a great feeling to see all these old timers that you've thought many times that you'd never see again.

Thanks to the Westerners.

## A TAPED INTERVIEW WITH DAN PURTYMUN
*by Laura McBride*

"Good morning, Uncle Dan. I would like to have you tell me a few things about Grandpa and Grandma Purtymun and Grandpa Howard if you would."

"Could you tell me how they came to this part of the country and where they came from?"

"They came from California about 1880, and I think they came from Ventura, because Jess, my brother, was born there in 1879 and he was a baby when they came to Arizona."

"How many children did Grandpa Howard your grandpa, have?"

"They had three. There was Uncle Jess Howard and Mother and Johnny. He died when he was a baby. Mother was the youngest of the three. She was just a baby when her mother died and she was raised on goat's milk."

"Did Grandpa Howard, "Bear Howard", come to Arizona with your father and mother?"

"Yes he came with them but he did not travel with them. He had just broke out of jail in California so he stayed off the main trail and just came to their camp at night when he ran short of grub. Father and mother had two children when they started, Jess and Emory. They did not travel in a wagon train. They were by themselves. They ran into some Indian trouble along the Colorado River. They came to a little settlement, I don't know just where it was, but the Indians had been there the day before and killed everyone there. They said it was an awful mess. The Indians were gone when they came along and they ran into some soldiers near there and the soldiers brought them safely into Arizona and out of the danger of Indians."

"Where did they come to first in Arizona?"

"They came to Phoenix first, or towns around there, Tempe and Mesa, and then they went to old Pinal. That is where your father, Albert, was born, he and George too."

"Well when did they leave the Southern part of Arizona and come north? About what year?"

"It was in '87 I know, because I was born there in '86 and I was just a year old when they moved."

"Where did they move to and what did Grandpa Purtymun do for a living at first?"

"They first came to Flagstaff to find out where Grandpa Howard was. He had come on ahead of them and had squatted on

Those Early Days.....

a place on Oak Creek. It is the present Mayhew's Oak Creek Lodge. They went down and stayed with him for about a month and then came back to the mountain and Father took a timber claim homestead near the old Pump House, 8 miles South of Flagstaff. He got a job in the tie camp making and hauling ties. He also cut and hauled wood for the pump house. After he got some land cleared he started farming and had a few cows for our own use."

"What did you raise on the farm and what did you have to eat back in those days? You could not go to the store every day."

"We raised potatoes, peas, carrots, lettuce and cabbage. We raised lots of cabbage and put up lots of kraut. We dried some vegetables and also fruit when we could get it. Father would buy flour by the ton and salt pork by the sack full and several hundred pound sacks of sugar. He bought coffee by the barrel. That was green coffee and we roasted it. I can see Mother yet sitting in her chair in front of the oven door roasting her coffee. It was hard to roast. You had to be careful or you would bum it. Then we had lots of wild game and often the sheepherders would lose sheep and we would find them and butcher them. We really lived better in those days than we do now."

"Grandpa Howard was a bear hunter and killed lots of bears, did you ever eat bear meat?"

"Yes, we used to have bear meat at times but I never could eat it. I would take a bite of it and the more I chewed on it the bigger it got. I just could not swallow it."

"Well what did Grandpa do with the bears he killed? He was always called "Bear Howard"?"

"He would butcher them and take them to Flag and market them. They were sold over the block in the butcher shops. We always raised some hogs to kill every year and Father would buy or trade for a beef every Fall. We had lots to eat."

"Where did you go to school up there?"

"Well we had a school house right on the lower end of our place. They built a big log schoolhouse. It was there for years and finally burned down. I have a picture of it."

"Was it a winter or summer school and about how many kids were in the school?"

"There were from eight to thirteen kids. You see there were a lot of ranches there and they all had children and there was quite a bunch of us. It was a winter school. I can remember that well because I was not very old and they had to pack me part of

*This is the first schoolhouse on upper Oak Creek. The teacher was Miss Frances Miller who later married Will Bristow.*

the way at times or pull me on a sled over the snow."

"Was that the sled that is still up at the old Purtymun place?"

"No it was one that Jess built. It was smaller than that one. You could hitch a team to it and haul us kids. I remember the old sled that is up there now. Charley was telling me that it was still there. Emory and Jess and Albert built it. Charley was telling me about the time he fell off of it and one of the runners went over his leg. It just skinned the hide off of his leg but did not hurt him any."

"How many of the children were born while you were living at the Pump house?"

"There were three born there, Charley, Pearl and Ida."

"Where did you go when you moved from there, and about what year was that?"

"It was in 1897 and we moved to Oak Creek. We moved to the Banjo Bill place. It is called Junipine now. Banjo Bill had already gone before we came down and I never did see him"

"When you first moved to Oak Creek didn't you farm on Bootlegger Flat or Slide Rock Camp as it is known now?"

"Yes, before we got a ditch on our place we farmed there a while. That spring used to run quite a lot of water. We raised squash and pumpkins and corn and other things there."

"How did you move to Oak Creek? There was no road was there?"

## Those Early Days.....

"Well we moved to the rim and had to make a trail down the mountain. That was a job. Father would bring a whole wagon load of flour and other groceries to the rim and we kids would have to pack it down the hill. We usually brought it down on Indian drags. We made them by getting a couple of poles and nailing slats across them. Then we would pile some stuff on them and tie it down with a rope, like packing a horse and take off down the mountain - - right straight off. The trail came in right in front of the present Junipine Store. It was later called the Purtymun Trail. We did not have much of a trail at first. It came right straight down the mountain over the tops of the brush."

"Why did you give up the place on the mountain and move to Oak Creek?"

"We thought we could raise more and have fruit and such things. We could not raise fruit on the mountain. Uncle Jess Howard was with us part of the time but at other times he was out working."

"He took up the place below where you were didn't he?"

"Yes, he took that place where Todd's Lodge is now, but that was years later. He took it up and proved up on it. He was the first one to live there."

"What did you kids do for entertainment back in those days when you were just kids?"

"We went fishing and swimming and running around over the hills barefooted through the Manzanita brush and knocking our toe nails off. We used to have dances - - especially on Christmas and the 4th of July. We would get together with the Thompsons and either all go to their place or they would come to ours. We would dance and the mothers always cooked up lots to eat. We had pie and cake and lots of other things, especially meats."

"Where did you go to school when you moved to Oak Creek?"

"They built a school house half way between our place and Thompson's. We each had three miles to walk to school. Just the two families had enough for a school. There were seven or eight of us going to school all of the time."

"Was that a summer school or winter school?"

"It was a summer school. We never had school in winter because of high water and snow,"

"Did you help build the road into the canyon? There was no road there then. Was there?"

"Yes, I helped to build the road. I worked for Lew Thomas. He lived at present Oak Creek Lodge. I worked on the road until it was finished to his place. The road was started about 1902 or

1903 and finished to his place in 1906. I stayed on at the old Purtymun ranch for a while after the rest of the family moved away. Charley was with me part of the time".

"Before the road was built, how did you get your produce out and get supplies in?"

"We packed it on burros to the rim and hauled it from there in a wagon."

"Did you have many bad storms then and much snow?"

"Yes we had some pretty big storms and some big snows, but not nearly as deep as we had when we lived on the mountain. When we were snowed in up there and wanted to go to Flagstaff we would go on skis and pull a small sled to haul light groceries home on."

"Where did you get your first job away from home and how old were you?"

"I was 14 years old and I never lived at home very much after that. I went to work for a fellow that ran a dairy near Flagstaff and I delivered milk around logging camps and other places. I worked around logging camps a lot till I was eighteen years old."

"Can you tell me some of the experiences you had when you were in the logging camps?"

"No I never had any experiences that were worth telling. I started working in the kitchen. I was a flunky and washed dishes and waited on tables."

"Did you ever go and live with Grandpa Howard when you were little?"

"Yes, I used to live with him some. I used to go and stay with him for two or three weeks at a time when he lived in Fry Park. I was with him when he was lion trapping there once. He caught two lions when I was there but I was never along. I went with him every day for a while to the traps and he did not catch any thing. Then I would get lazy and sleep in and he would go and he would bring in a lion. I always wanted to see a lion in a trap. I would go with him again for a while and he would not catch a lion and I would sleep in again and he would catch another lion. I never did get to see one in a trap."

"Did Grandpa Howard have horses on the range? Where did he range them?"

"Yes, he had range horses. He ran them in Fry Park and Barney Pasture country in summer and in the Red Rocks Country under the rim in winter. He moved them down and back over the Mooney Trail."

"Where did you meet Aunt Viola, your wife?"

"I met her in Oak Creek. Oh, I first met her in Flagstaff but we got better acquainted when she was cooking at the old Lolomai Lodge. I was doing some plumbing work there, putting in some pipe and she would come down and keep me from working."

"Who was running the Lolomai Lodge then?"

"Mrs. Ike Wheeler was running it then, in 1912. Mrs. Sisson built it and ran it first but it was leased out all the last years it was run. Art Vandevier and his wife were the last ones to run it in the 1920s."

Note - Dan Purtymun started work for the Arizona Game and Fish Commission in the early 1930s. He was in charge of the trout rearing ponds at Sterling Spring at the head of Oak Creek for a few years. Later he was superintendent of the Page Springs rearing ponds and hatchery until his retirement about 1960. He and his wife, Viola bought a home in Cottonwood, Arizona. Viola passed away in a few years.

Dan sold their home and he now lives alone in a small house in downtown Cottonwood.

## A TRAGEDY
*by Albert E. Thompson*

Sometime in the early 1900s, I would guess about 1905, a small group of sportsmen, or "sports", started from Jerome for a fishing trip on Upper Oak Creek, with a wagon and team. They were to be gone for a week or more, so they had with them a generous supply of "snakebite medicine", as well as several cases of beer in quart bottles.

They crossed the Verde River at Cottonwood and went up the old Lime Kiln Hill. That old road crossed Spring Creek far above the present 89A Highway, so there was no water between the Verde River and Oak Creek at Sedona. When they got well into the sand hills near Spring Creek a tire came off of a wagon wheel.

It was well known at that time, that in the dry, hot weather of summer, the wood parts of the wagon wheels shrank and let the tires get loose if they were not watched carefully. When a tire came off it was necessary to stop at once before the wooden parts of the wheel collapsed.

The only real remedy for such bad luck was to "set" the tire. But you cannot set a tire without water to cool the iron tire quickly after it has been heated and put back on the wheel. They had only a very small amount of water in a canteen for making coffee, but they had lots of beer. It nearly broke their hearts but they had to use beer to cool the wagon tire when they set it.

The only one of the party that I know the name of at this late date is Jack Duff. Jack was known to all of the pioneers of Jerome and almost all of the Verde Valley. Duff Flat near the mouth of Sycamore Canyon was named for him.

Those Early Days.....

## ONE OLD TIMER'S REVIEW
*by Don Willard*

While there may be some question as to whether Arizona settlers and natives since, 1890, the date used by the annual Pioneers Reunion in Phoenix, should be known as pioneers, there is probably little doubt that those whose experience began earlier than statehood are at least entitled to be called "old-timers". In any case their numbers and their proportion of today's population are less and less each year. Sometimes it is only by turning back and viewing again, in recollection, the people, places and activities of the early days that one can avoid the feeling of being a stranger in his own land.

In the case of the Verde Valley, the most complete list of pioneers and families of old timers with many of their stories is to be found in Pioneer Stories of Arizona's Verde Valley, published by the Verde Valley Pioneers Association. The Ghosts of Cleopatra Hill by H.V. Young is the best story of Jerome's important figures of the old days. The Camp Verde historical museum has made available a pamphlet, which relates the story of the old army post and its men.

Each individual in recounting his personal experiences can represent little more than a single thread in the pattern of a historical period. It has always seemed to me that a background of events and places of origin, together with circumstances leading to arrival, is necessary to portray accurately the wide variety found in the telling by different people about what they consider to be of interest in the Valley's history and their part in it.

The following is simply such a background and one family's bit in the scene, together with a one-man collection of observations and impressions.

The year was 1804. President Jefferson had decided that a great exploration was to be undertaken into what was then a vast unknown space. A group of selected young men was organized under the leadership of two of the most capable officers he could find. Theirs was to be an adventure scarcely less dangerous in their day than that faced by the first space explorers of our times. They were to be not only cut off from all communication with home and their friends, but left entirely to their own resources for any hope whatsoever of safe return.

Young Alexander Hamilton Willard at twenty-six years of age had become skilled with guns and with ironwork at the forge and anvil. His father, Lt. Jonathan Willard had been in Washington's army; and he, himself, had already ventured into that wilderness which Washington had helped to win from the Indians before the Revolution. When the Lewis and Clark expedition was being planned, he was one of the "young men from Kentucky", and was chosen for his special ability, to maintain their equipment in usable condition.

The story of that famous trip up the Missouri River, over the Rocky Mountains, to the Pacific, meeting with Indians who had never seen white men, all the hardships they had to overcome, and then the return to civilization, has been recorded in detail. In western Montana alongside a modern highway there stands a bronze memorial on which appears a list of some thirty names - - all members of that band of men. The first name in the second column of that list is that of Alexander Willard. It was not far from this location, according to records, that a hundred miles of forbidding mountain front was searched before finding a pass through which they could cross to the West.

Encountering situations, which tested the endurance, both of the leaders, and of each man, it was November 1805 when they reached the Pacific, and many months more before the successful completion of their assignment. They had unlocked a door no less significant, to their day, than the first space journey of our times.

After Willard's return, he settled near St. Louis, Missouri, where he married and raised a family. Later he moved to Wisconsin and lived there for many years. But it seems he must not have been satisfied with what had come to be a dull and uninteresting way of life. As years passed and his sons grew to manhood the time came when they decided to join their father in seeking a new home in California, the "promised land", where gold and excitement were said to be so easy to find. The long journey was made in 1852 when he was nearly seventy-five years old. Its details are not on record, but since no easy ways were available in those days, it was probably neither more nor less difficult than those experienced by others. Finally the families arrived in the Sacramento Valley, where it seemed others had already dug most of the gold. They turned to farming and raising livestock. Grandchildren were born, some at Sacramento, some at Georgetown, later to be called Franklin, and others including my own father, at Clear Lake.

In the run-down cemetery of the once active town of Franklin, among a number of graves with the name Willard on their stones, I found, several years ago, a bronze marker placed by a California historical group, honoring Alexander Hamilton Willard as the last

Those Early Days.....

survivor of the Lewis and Clark expedition to the Northwest. He died, full of years, in 1865. It seems hard to realize that nearly two centuries have passed since his birth in 1778, and that the last century has seen more changes in our way of living than in all the previous centuries of recorded history.

In 1870 the time came when my grandfather, Joel Willard, and his brother Lewis A. Willard, with their families, moved from California to northern Nevada, hoping to build up a cattle business. They lived there several years in Pine Valley, west of Elko. Winters were very severe, and at last it seemed desirable to look for a milder climate, especially since my grandfather's health seemed in danger. My uncle, the late Charles D. Willard took the responsibility of seeking a new location. In 1878, having heard of a wonderful green valley far to the south in Arizona, he traveled to the Verde Valley on horseback.

There was an army post at Camp Verde and a few ranches had been cleared there and also in the upper part of the valley. He wrote to the family back home stating he intended to go on to the Pleasant Valley, later to be famous for the feud between the Grahams and Tewksburys, before deciding what to recommend to them. Toward the end of the year plans were made that the entire Willard clan in Nevada would move to Arizona. First there was a cattle drive on which my grandfather was accompanied by five of his sons. This drive of several hundred head of stock took place during winter when water was more available than in hot weather. One of their stopping places was the Pahranagat Valley in the southeastern part of the state of Nevada. This was, and still is a verdant and well-watered oasis surrounded by as barren desert as one can imagine. Even today there are many hundred cattle grazing the pastureland there.

From that place they continued to the Virgin River near the present farming community of Overton, and then on to what has become known as the Bonneli Ferry, which had at one time been operated by Jim Thompson who was later a pioneer of Oak Creek Canyon and the father of Charles and Albert Thompson of the Sedona Westerners. Their wagons were ferried while the cattle and horses swam the Colorado River. After crossing the river their next stop was at Dolan Springs in Mohave County, Arizona. This was a station on a trail, which came to be used by Mormon immigrants from southeast Utah to northern Arizona. It was located five or six miles from where the highway from Kingman to Lake Mead now runs. It was while there that my grandfather's condition became worse and his illness ended with his death from pneumonia. He was buried there and Uncle Charlie had to write back to Nevada informing his mother of their loss.

Their drive continued to the upper Verde near what was later to be Perkinsville, and from there through Baker Pass above where the Clarkdale cement plant now stands. They ended their trip just across the river from the present location of Clarkdale, their herd having been considerably reduced along the way. It was near here in June 1879, while a rock and brush dam was being built in the river, that a boat or raft was being used to transport rocks from up the river in the deep water above the dam to increase its height. Two of my fathers brothers, were in the boat when it capsized, probably from being overloaded, and the two boys who had not learned to swim, were drowned.

In order to feed cattle the year round the brothers followed the custom of the other ranchers and drove their cattle to the mountains in springtime. Summer camp was at what is now called Willard Spring north of Munds Park on the Black Canyon Highway.

An 80-acre farm was acquired between what is now the North end of Main Street in Cottonwood and the river, which then flowed considerably to the northeast of its present channel. All but a small part of that farm has been washed away by floods. As soon as they were able to do so they built a home for their mother. Brick was burned on the farm and lime from the white hills across the river was burned for mortar. The house, still standing, had five fireplaces, with one in each bedroom. My father's uncle "Lew" and his family arrived a little later and located a farm below what we now call Bridgeport.

At first supplies and mail were to be had only at Camp Verde, which was an army post, or occasionally from Prescott over the road through Cherry Creek. By 1883 the new mine at Jerome was getting started with a small smelter, and a mining camp was under way. In 1885 the upper Verde ranchers were able to secure their own post office. It was in a small frame house just to the west of the Willard home, the two-story brick house seen on the north side of the highway as it turns west from Cottonwood's main street toward Clarkdale. The name Cottonwood came from a group of large trees under which a wagon camp ground was in use for many years, a little north of where the Justice Court is now located. My father, G.M. (Mac) Willard, received his appointment as the first postmaster on July 6, 1885.

As indicated earlier, two of Alexander Willard's sons reached Arizona, and a daughter, Aunt Ellen, joined her brother Lewis's

Those Early Days.....

family. My grandfather's remains were in later years removed from Dolan Springs to the Cottonwood cemetery, where Lewis A. Willard who died in 1911 is also buried. My grandmother, "Aunt Mary" Willard, died in 1921 and is buried in the family plot at the same cemetery.

Back in California another family had heard glowing reports of the Verde Valley. My maternal grandfather David Scott's former neighbors in Glenville had come to the valley and had sent word back. Deciding that if the Van Derens had pronounced it good, that was enough for him; he proceeded to sell out. With three sons, three daughters, a son-in-law and several grandchildren, they undertook the trip by wagon across the Mohave Desert in 1883. A farm was acquired at what was to be known as Scott's Crossing, a mile or so above what is now Bridgeport. On that farm he later built a gristmill and ground corn and wheat for several years, using waterpower from the "big ditch". One of the Scott daughters, best known as Birdie or "Aunt Bee", was to marry "Mac" Willard. They became my parents.

So in 1896 in that old brick house of my grandmother, "Aunt Mary" Willard, I came into the world a fourth generation westerner. That was the year William Jennings Bryan made his "Cross of Gold" speech, which won him nomination for president on the issue of free coinage of silver at "sixteen to one"; so my middle initial is the letter B.

From this space age in which I find myself, it seems such a very short time, but such a long, long way back to the horse and buggy age.

Some random scenes from my mental scrapbook begin with my recollection of our arriving one time in Prescott when I was about five crossing led to the mouth of Oak Creek at the Indian ruins and from there by Middle Verde to the mouth of Beaver Creek and Camp Verde. The first automobiles in the valley had only one road to Prescott or Phoenix, by way of Cherry Creek. On some of the sharp curves were warning signs reading "Sound your Klaxon".

It was not until 1912 when we moved to Phoenix, that I was able to start high school. That was the year Arizona became a state. The high school had just outgrown its original location in a single building converted from an old brick residence that had been the "Churchill Mansion". The enrollment had become 425 pupils. That year I had the opportunity of seeing and hearing "Teddy" Roosevelt, W.J. Bryan and Eugene V. Debs. Also, I was one of two high school students invited by the first governor of the new state, Geo. W.P. Hunt, during the first of his seven terms, to visit the new state prison at Florence. During this visit we saw the notorious Wm. Faltin who would have been executed that morning except for Hunt's reprieve, pending abolition of capital punishment. Also we were conducted around the top of the prison walls at sunset, dined in the prison mess hall, and inspected the gallows with its gruesome rope noose-framed pictures of those who had been executed, arranged on the walls of the death chamber.

A classmate, who was a football quarterback, often needed help with his algebra and geometry and sometimes called on me for sudden help, and this was as close as I came to sports participation. His name was Frank Luke, who, during World War I was to become second only to Eddie Rickenbacker as a flying hero and whose monument now stands in front of the state capitol. Luke Air Force Base is named for him. A great thrill for kids those days was seeing the automobile races on the fairgrounds track with such great racers as Barney Old Field, Teddy Tetzlaff, and Earl Cooper.

In 1913 a state game department was organized with a naturalist from Cottonwood, Frank Rogers, as the first state game warden. He served only a short time and at his death my father was appointed to the position. Except for Tom Campbell's term as governor and a short time afterward, he served until his death in 1926. Shortly before that, he had accompanied Zane Grey, representing the state, on Grey's ambitious but unsuccessful experiment attempting to drive Kaibab deer across the Colorado River to the south side where there was a scarcity. Grey was to finance the drive, using Indian riders, hoping to realize profit from film and story rights. He learned what my father had contended, that deer are not as easily driven as cattle.

While in Phoenix High School I made the acquaintance of Amos Yates the son of a minister, who had brought his family to Arizona from Guthrie, Oklahoma by covered wagon. He had a sister, Ruth, also in the class. After finishing high school the three of us attended the old Tempe Normal School, which has now become Arizona State University, graduating with the class of 1918. Soon afterward the Yates family moved to Missouri, and it was there that Ruth and I were married in Sedalia, June 17, 1919.

We made our first home in Cottonwood, where I went to work driving a truck. Our first daughter Donna was born in 1921, our second daughter Meredyth in 1924, and Robert in 1932. We lived successively in Phoenix, Flagstaff, Jerome, and at last in Sedona. In 1946 we started the first motel and with our son-in-law, Joe

Those Early Days.....

Moser, we opened the first full service station in 1947.

No recounting of Cottonwood's early days should fail to mention some of the facts of Charles D. Willard's part in them, a continuous resident from 1879 until his passing in 1957 at the age of 99. He had been liked and respected by all who had known him. In the early days of Jerome he operated a dairy supplying milk to that town by running a "milk wagon" twice a day from Cottonwood.

Years later, when the United Verde Copper Company started the smelter and town at Clarkdale, some employees wanted their own homes instead of renting "company houses", so he laid out lots on the west side of what is now the main street, clearing a mesquite thicket in which I had often hunted quail. The first business started on Main Street was a garage and repair shop on the site now occupied by the Ford agency. I helped Uncle Charlie haul the first load of lumber for it one summer about 1914 or 1915, and when completed it was operated by P.D. Neff for a few years, until taken over by Ersel Garrison in 1919.

My uncle who spoke fluent Spanish had many Mexican friends. At one time when they desired a panteon or cemetery of their own, he donated the land for it adjoining the original Cottonwood cemetery, and they showed their appreciation in an unusual way by erecting a monument to the living.

It bears the names of Charles D. Willard and George Kingdon then general manager of the Douglas-owned United Verde Extension Mining Co., who they also considered their benefactor.

As the town grew, a water system was needed, so Willard began piping water from his artesian well, and this became the start of the Cottonwood water system. After the death of his wife in the year 1923 he became interested in an experiment in dry farming. He planted fruit trees on land, which he cleared for the purpose in what is called Red Canyon. They produced fine crops as a result of his special methods of cultivation to conserve moisture. The Red Canyon ranch is today a cattle ranch.

It has been said by some that he might be called the "father" of Cottonwood. Two of his daughters, now living there are Mrs. Alice Hancock and Mrs. Jennie Garrison, my cousins.

Years ago I spent a very special day with Uncle Charlie. He had asked me to drive him to certain places that marked the former locations of cabins and corrals of early day cattle ranchers he had known. We talked of the great changes to be seen since the times of the pioneer settlers. It almost seemed that some spots were haunted by memories vividly imagined as part of those men and women. A certain old fence-post corral in particular drew our attention and we speculated as to the possible stories it could tell. The idea stuck with me. Later I tried to put into words the nostalgic emotions of an old cowboy returning after many years to the scenes where he had ridden the range and taken part in round-ups and branding. At the risk of whatever may be the penalty for failure to obtain a poetic license, or for misrepresentation of the article as poetry, the following product of my imagination is submitted as a sort of verbal picture frame.

## THE OLD CORRAL

The old corral is haunted and another round-up's due;
The ghosts of the range are here in their lonely rendezvous.
The branding iron and horseshoe are but crumbling bits of rust.
My pony's thudding hoof beats stir memories from the dust.

I hear saddle leather creaking and the tinkle of the spur,
And farewell words once spoken the day I rode away with Her.
A voice, a face, a handclasp reach out from the long-dead past;
Just the old corral is left and it has not long to last.

I pause where stood the 'dobe ranch house underneath the trees;
The bawling of the yearlings seems to echo in the breeze.
The howl of a prowling coyote gives me a sudden start; - -
I sit in star-lit silence, while an ache creeps round my heart.

(Lonesome Valley, the cowboy's trail, - -A passing scene, now - - For Sale.)

It was not until after 1930 that a highway first made Oak Creek Canyon easily accessible and its scenic grandeur began to be known to a few motorists. During the depression and even until after World War II there was little to indicate the growth and development that have since taken place, and tourism had not commenced to approach today's levels. A day on Oak Creek still offered a quiet, restful afternoon in the solitude of a rustic spot with shade by the running stream. What more could be required to set a contemplative mood? Such an occasion was my excuse for trying to depict some of the feelings inspired; and since no professional poet happened to be around, the following was the result. So, I am prepared to close the pages of my scrapbook with the words that came to me at that time.

## OUR CANYON

Our canyon is deep and ruggedly sublime;
It didn't cost money, it cost only time.
No man can take credit for its design,
Nor artist can copy nor poet define
Its lights and shadows, its tints and its lines,
From its rocky creek bottom to skyline of pines.
Upward the mountain, like a symbol of strength;
As shadows foreshortened, the hours in their length.

No words can describe, only feeling can tell
of the rest to our spirit when under its spell,
or the voiceless melody sung by its stream
As it lulls and enraptures our midsummer
dream. The call of the canyon with its
echoes shall bring our hopes for renewal
like flowers in the spring. And when the
rocks and mountains shall fall, in no other
place would my soul wait its call.

## MORE ABOUT COWBOYS
*by M.O. Dumas*

A horse wrangler is usually an old broken down cowboy or a teenager whose one aspiration is to some day become a real cowboy. His duties are to take care of the saddle horses when they are brought to camp after they have had the hobbles taken off. He herds them throughout the day and returns with them in time to be hobbled again for the night grazing.

**Horse herd or remuda at Pool Wagon — Oak Creek roundup. About 1910**

Each cowboy has a "night-mare" which is a horse he keeps tied up at night for use in night guarding of the day herd. Each man has to take his shift for singing to the herd, as it is called. They call it this because you have to sing, whistle, howl and yell or make some sort of noise to keep the cattle from going to sleep. If they should sleep and some sudden noise might be made, as a horse stepping over brittle sticks, or stumbling on a rock, maybe causing a spark of fire, all the herd seem to jump to their feet at the same time and be on the run. Then the night herders try to get in the lead of the running cattle in order to circle them. Once getting them to circling or milling (as it is called, they won't go anyplace but in this circle) no matter how fast they are running. When the cattle start running they make quite a roaring noise and the boys in camp are awakened and are on their "night-mares" and gone to the assistance of the night guards. This does not take them long for all they remove on going to bed are their chaps, hat, boots and spurs. The chaps are leather covering that buckle around the waist and snap over their pants to protect their levies when riding in brush. It takes them about two minutes to do all this and get on their "night-mare", which is always saddled, and they are off. The guard is usually divided up into four shifts and the number of men on a shift depends on the condition of the weather. If it happens to be a dark stormy night there will be five or more men according to the size of the herd. If the weather is nice and all clear, three men can take care of a shift. I might explain how the hobbles are used. A horse is hobbled by fastening the horse's two front legs together just above the fetlocks with the hobble rope. This will allow the horse to take one step of one foot at a time which is sufficient to let him move around enough to go in search of food grass, but will keep him from going any great distance during the night. After being hobbled at night, many times after dark, they are all headed in one direction, which serves to make them more easily wrangled next morning.

The boys are up and out a mile or so by daybreak or when it is light enough so they can see a few hundred yards in the distance. They begin unhobbling and heading the horses toward camp picking them up and un-hobbling other horses as they work toward camp. When they reach camp each man looks over the horses and if any are missing, after breakfast one man is detailed to look for the missing horses, as might be the case. They take into consideration as where the horse might have been missed or whether he might have headed for his old range. The man detailed for this job is usually the person whose horse is gone. He will go out and cut for signs and if he picks up his tracks he can easily be over-taken, and soon returned to the horse herd.

There are two or three left to hold the day herd, fortunately most of the time they were the only ones who got anything to eat around the middle of the day, however, they all dreaded the day when it came their time for this duty. The horse herd is called the remuda.

## A COWBOY'S PRAYER
### In Commemoration of "Rimmy" Jim Giddings
*by M.O. Dumas*

O'Lord I never called on you before,
But I need you now or I'm a goner shore,
Old Paint just fell and pinned me down.
If you don't come quick, I'm eternity bound,
He busted my lag and broke my wing,
And I really can't do a doggone thing.

Flies are crawling in my ears, eyes and nose,
I'm in misery down to the end of my toes.
You gotta do something about these damn flies,
O' just send me some screw worm medicine,
Down from the skies.

Now you better come down for shore
For old Satan's kicking in my door.
O' you just help me to my feet and I'll
Go kick that old devil right in the teeth.
I'll tie knots in his tail and saw off his horns.
I'll trim him up in proper form,
I'll tie him down, I'll cut his throat,
That's what I'll do to that damn'd old goat.

When you come, just ask for Bob.
Don't send your little boy, Jesus
For this is no boy's job.
Now I'm one of the best at tying a steer,
At ridin' a bronc, I have no fear.

You better get down here quick
Before old Gabriel turns the trick.
If you wait till he toots that old horn,
You're gonna lose the best durn cowpoke ever born

## THE LAST LONG TRAIL DRIVE
*by M.O. Dumas*

In the spring of 1905 the King Brothers, John, Sam and Blan had contracted to buy some range horses from Tom Carrol. Any amount that he could gather and pay $9.00 a head for them.

At that time there were a great number of wild horses on the range and as you can see they were not worth very much, but the owners figured anything they could realize out of them was just velvet to them.

There were quite a number of other stockmen who had horses on the same range and were also willing to get rid of some of them.

Dan Fain took the contract to gather them for $2.00 per head, plus what mavericks that could be rounded up. At that time I believe at least one-fourth of the horses on the range were unbranded or mavericks. Dan hired a bunch of cowboys who were quite familiar with the range. The men working for Dan were George Casner, Charlie Hawkins, Fred Back, Frank Heath, Con Fredricks and myself. Others who rode with us, having horses on the range were Charley Hollingshead, John Scott, Lew Willard and Dave Brollier. We started the work to ride some time the first part of April. This time was chosen as a most advantageous time as there was some snow on the ground, which was thawing during the day and that made the terrain quite soft and in some places even boggy. Under these conditions the broncs would be at their weakest time of the year and their feet would be worn down and become very sore. This would prevent them from running as fast as they normally could.

We were all riding stout grain fed saddle horses, which gave us quite the advantage over the range animals. We had only ridden three or four days when a storm blew up and we had to move to the valley for a few days. It was very disagreeable weather, half rain and half snow. I remember the day we were driving off the mountain, down through the cedars. I could see that Sam King was disgusted because we had to suspend the work. He was cold and very wet and all out of sorts. We all had slickers on but if it rains on you all day, as it had that day, your slicker will usually begin to let in a little dampness and moisture creeps through in spots. Just to break the monotony, I thought I would ride around to where Sam was riding and kid him a little bit. Sam always used a lot of profanity. He had just been looking straight up and letting it rain in his face, saying, "Rain!

You old so and so. Rain!" As I rode up I said, "Sam, this is sure the making of this country". He blurted out, "The hell with the country, it's horses I want".

We stayed in the valley for three days at Beaver Creek. The weather clearing, some we moved back to the mountain and started work again. We worked until the 26th of April and on April 27th, 1905 we left the Apache Maid Ranch, which is located not more than 20 miles from the geographical center of Arizona, going to Holbrook where John King was receiving another bunch of horses. We started with something over 380 head of horses and reached Hay Lake the first day. We night guarded them that night.

Our crew was made up of eight cowboys, Sam and Blan King and Jim Tate, the cook, who drove the chuck wagon, drawn by four horses. The wagon carried our bedrolls and provisions, as well as three boys (night herders), who slept in the wagon during the day and night guarded the horses at nighttime. However, when we reached the plains the horses were turned loose at night and rounded up and counted next morning. Charley Glispee, Marion Hall and Dave Sanders were the night herders. The balance of our crew were Frank Heath, Charley Hawkins, Port Adair, John Sharp, the two King men, Sam and Blan, and myself.

The next day we came to a place called "Old Bed", on the Little Colorado River, which was the headquarters ranch for the Hash Knife Cattle Company. Here we picked up some more saddle horses for our use. The next day we went on to Holbrook and stayed there for five days, receiving the other horses making over eight hundred and fifty head of horses in the herd, plus about fifty head of saddle horses.

After leaving Holbrook, the first night we camped in the Petrified Forest. At that time it was not a National Monument but was all wide-open range. The second night we camped at Seven Springs and the fourth night we came to a place called "Stinking Springs". This spring was in a white sand formation in a funnel shaped hole. The water was very clear with a variety of fern growing in it, with thousands of tiny red things living on the ferns and smelling like rotten eggs or sulphur. However, there was another good spring near by and a very nice residence and bunkhouses for the cowboys who worked for the "Long H Outfit". (X brand). This was the headquarter ranch for the cattle company. A man by the name of Knight was the foreman. This place was not far from the Zuni River. We followed up the river for two or three days to Ramah. From there we climbed out on the mountains. The first night on top was dark and cloudy and it rained a little together with some thunder and lightning. Upon counting the horses next morning we found that the night herders had lost one of our markers, which was a black mule. We had several markers, probably between thirty or forty head. These were certain colored horses, mules, pintos, buckskins and appaloosas, etc.

I was detailed to hunt them and return them to the herd. I made a wide circle and found their tracks. I tracked them for a couple of hours or more and finally located them. As I had said before it was cloudy and threatening to storm. Concentrating on the trailing tracks for that length of time I had sort of lost my sense of direction and having no sun to direct me, I started driving in such direction as I thought was right. I drove them for what seemed many hours and was about to give up and go find my way out, but thought I might go a little ways farther in this direction. I had not gone more than two hundred yards when I came upon the trail of the herd. After getting my bunch of horses on this trail I had no more trouble for the horses seemed to sense that they were on the right trail of the herd. I overtook the drive about two o'clock that afternoon and we made camp in a clearing in the cedars that night. For the next few days the drive was more or less of the same nature.

We had at times some very rough roads and sometimes no road at all. I remember in one such place our chuck wagon turned over on its side. The night herders, sleeping in the wagon at the time came out yelling their heads off, some yelling "help", others "what has happened?" One of them said he thought they might be rolling down a mountain side and we all had a good laugh after it was all over and we soon got the wagon straightened out and upon its wheels and were on our way again.

I always felt sorry for the night herders, for it took some time to become accustomed to sleeping in the rough rolling wagon and they saw very little of the country. That was one of the main reasons I had decided to go on the trip. Everything went along very smoothly again for a few days. We had crossed the railroad but were still in the cedar country and camped in a clearing for the night.

Along about twelve or one o'clock in the morning the horses stampeded and came running toward our camp. They split, some going on one side and others on the opposite side of the camp. We, who had night horses tied up, started after them. The cedars were very thick and it was a dark night.

Those Early Days.....

*Mack O. "Doc" Dumas at the age of 87 (left) and Mack O. "Doc" Dumas at the age of 26 (right).*

I could hear their noise as they ran so I just followed the sound, riding as fast as I could among the thick cedars. I had to ride low in the saddle and do a lot of dodging. Finally all noise stopped because they had come to a canyon with steep perpendicular sides and they could go no farther. I rode around them and discovered what had stopped them. I thought by chance the night herder had kept in front of them and so stopped them but I could find nobody with them so I hollered and no one answered me. I called several times, again louder each time but no answer. The other boys had followed the other bunch that had passed on the opposite side of the camp. I was at a loss as to how I could drive them back to camp alone, without taking a chance of losing some of them. I had about decided to try to hold them against the bluff until daybreak and just thought I might call aloud again any way. As it was, about this time the other boys had gotten their bunch back into the clearing and heard my call so came to my rescue. Every once in a while they would holler and I would answer them. We continued this until they found me and came to me. None of them seemed sure that they could lead us to camp. I told them that I might be able to do it, so I took the lead and ever so often would call back to them so they could follow the direction I was going. In about thirty minutes or longer we made it back to camp.

We never knew just what caused the herd to stampede, but a short time later a Mexican or Indian with a dog passed camp. I always thought that whoever it was with that dog was responsible for the act. I also thought it had been done thinking some of our horses might get lost and after we had left camp they could pick them up and claim them as their own; however, it was doubtful if we had lost any for that morning we checked them very thoroughly and found none missing. But it was a miracle that some had not been lost.

Sometimes a colt would be foaled and as it would be impossible for it to keep up with the drive, it would have to be destroyed. The only way it could be put away was by shooting it or cutting its throat. It just seems to be unable to knock one in the head and kill it. You can knock one down and it seemingly will be dead but in a few minutes it will be on its feet again. At one time, I thought John Sharp was going to kill Sam King. Sam had taken out his pocketknife and cut a small hole in the colt's throat and it was trying to follow its mother slowly bleeding to death. John Sharp pulled out his pistol and shot the colt. He was so mad he was threatening to shoot King but we talked him out of doing such a dangerous thing that could have caused very much trouble.

Over near Grants, New Mexico we camped on an old Indian road, being much more like a trail, than a road and upon it we came to a deep dry wash with an old pole bridge across it. One of the boys riding on the point, (this meaning that two men riding along each side near the front to steer the drive in the direction we wanted them to go would be called riding on the point). This point man came back and reported it would be unsafe to try to cross the horses or the chuck wagon on it. King looked at it and said he thought we might make it by letting a few horses cross at a time. We got about twenty-five head across and down went the bridge with about fifteen horses aboard. This looked like a mass of scrambled horses, some with their feet up in the air, others lying on their sides covered with logs and poles, some were really screaming, I think more from fright than anything else. We had to destroy only one animal due to a broken leg.

We had to drive them down the wash about a mile before we could find a place to get them out. We also had to drive the rest of the herd down the same distance to get them across. Now to get the chuck wagon across . . . . We cut some heavy cedars and pulled them down near the wash using a team of workhorses that were used to pull our chuck wagon. Some of them were pulled with our saddle horses.

We filled the wash about half full of cedars and dirt that we cut down from the banks of either side. The wash was about

## Those Early Days.....

twelve feet deep and fifteen feet across. We cut the opposite bank down as much as we could so as to make it easier to pull out of. Our fill was rather wobbly so we pulled the wagon down into the wash and up the opposite side with our saddle horses using our lasso ropes. Then we hitched the workhorses back on the wagon and pulled it out.

We had unloaded the bed rolls to lighten the load as much as we could, so after getting the wagon across we had to pack the bed rolls over and reload them into the wagon, then we were on our way again.

We were now getting quite well into open country, so did not have to night guard the herd. This gave us more help in the daytime.

In this wide-open country where one could see for a very long way and still not see much of anything we would try to break the monotony. One of us would pitch our rope on a bronco, drag him out of the herd, ear him down, get a saddle on him and have a bronco busting show. If you were thrown off, you were dis-qualified, so another fellow would take his turn. However, there were very few of the boys ever thrown.

We got along very nicely until a few miles from the Rio Grande River. The horses were getting rather dry and the ones in the lead began to sniff water and started off in a trot. I had an idea what would happen if they were not checked. I was riding on one point and Charley Hawkins was on the other side. I hollered for Charley to cross over to me and when he came I told him I would circle the leaders and for him to make the other horses follow or hold them up until some help came to him. By the time I reached the leaders they were on the run but I managed to circle them and bring them to the back of the herd. The boys all got up to the front of the herd and held them up so as to take a few head into the water at a time, in order to prevent them all going at once. If there was quick-sand, which there most always is in a large stream, even by doing this we had quite a number mired down and had to be pulled out.

After getting them all watered and pulled out of the quicksand our next problem was to get these eight hundred head of horses across the river. There was an old wooden bridge, which was very shaky and the river was almost up to the bottom of the bridge. It was either to try to cross them on the bridge or swim them, and the distance was more than two hundred yards across. We were just opposite the small village of Bernalillo. Sam King went across to find out the safety of the bridge. He came back with a Mexican leading an old bell mare, so with the aid of this animal it was decided to try to cross a few horses at a time. This was working very nicely and the horses were stringing out and getting across in good shape until the last bunch. They seemed to get frightened and started to run. In this way, too many horses started over the bridge when one panel of the bridge gave way and some of them landed in the river but it was near the end and they could all swim out. We had all of them across except thirty or forty head and we drove them back to the side we had started from and then drove them upstream far enough to make a safe landing on the opposite side. We had some trouble getting them started across the water but once we did, we swam them across landing about a quarter of a mile below on the opposite side. The current had carried us that far below the starting point.

From there on for two or three weeks it was something of the sameness. Grazing them along during the daytime and camping at night, rounding them up and counting them each morning.

Somewhere along the drive evidently some one thought that they had lost some horses and maybe that we had picked them up. When we reached Clayton, New Mexico we were held up and had to have the herd inspected. There were four head that the inspector thought were not on our Arizona inspection papers. He released the balance of the herd and they started on their way. It seemed that there had to be some court proceedings regarding the four head. Sam King, Dave Sanders and myself remained for the court proceedings. There were two of the horses that I could swear to as belonging to the King Brothers and the same was the case of Dave Sanders. There was no one there who would claim the horses so King sold them for what he could get for them and we started out to overtake the drive, which had about three days ahead of us. The first day we went as far as daylight would permit. It looked very stormy and the wind was blowing, looking as if it might rain at any moment. We unsaddled our horses and hobbled them. We placed our saddles so as to break the wind as much as we could, at our heads, then gathered some broom weed and placed them as to make a sort of a mattress that would keep us a little above the ground in case of rain. Placing our saddle blankets on top of the broom weed, using one army blanket as a cover with our slickers over that to shed rain. King was a big fat fellow so he said he would sleep in the middle, so in case of rain he would act as a ridgepole to shed rain to each side. The blanket was hardly big enough to cover all three of us too well, so Dave and I stuck out a little on either side. However, it did not rain much and it was not cold so the cover we did have helped quite a bit.

Toward morning Dave asked me if I had enough cover. I said, "Oh yes, I was doing fine", which I was not as one side was hardly half covered. I thought I should be as courteous as he, so asked if he had plenty. He answered in a drawling way saying, "I haven't got a damned bit". So I had to pretend that I was releasing some of my cover. I think old Sam was the only one who got any sleep to amount to anything, as he was well covered and kept warm on each side by Dave and I.

By the first crack of day, we were out after our horses and glad to be on our way. We caught up with the drive about two o'clock that afternoon. This was the last mishap to amount to anything and in about ten days more we reached the end of our drive and very glad that it was over, reaching Garden City, Kansas, 14th day of July 1905.

The King Brothers would pasture the horses until they were in good shape then they would take a car load at a time and ship them down to the Southern States and auction them off. The negro farmers bought the most of them. King would advertise a week or so ahead stating the date the auction would be held.

In explanation of the Loco Animal:

Some years if range feed is not so good and it happens to be a year when the Loco Weed is plentiful, animals eating it will sometimes become "locoed". It is like hop to some people, when horses or cattle find it and acquire a taste for it, they will continue to hunt for it. They become crazy and act queer. A loco horse never will lead, you can't get them to lead and if they are going to water they will start trying to drink several yards before they reach water, and walling or rolling their eyes around, some stagger and fall to their knees. An old cow or steer will roll their eyes around and shake and shiver and if they get too close to a person they will lower their heads and charge, usually falling before they get very far, however. If they are not too far gone and are taken away from the weed, or if you can get them fat, they will not show the loco. If they are not fattened or if they become poor again the loco condition returns to them.

John King told me that he had shipped a carload of "locoed" horses to a small town in Alabama and sold them as locoed horses. Of course, down in that country, they know nothing about locoweed.

Several years later he shipped another carload down to the

same part of the country and had forgotten about the locoed horses that he had sold before.

An old negro man walked up to him and said "Mr. King, do you have any more of them loco stock of horses?" He continued, "That is shore a good stock of horses, but they shore have some funny ways. You know you never can learn one of them to lead and they start to drink before they get to the water trough, but if you get them hooked up, they shore will pull. They will never balk. They just stand and pull all day and they usually make something move."

From the time we left the Apache Maid Ranch, April 27th and reached Garden City, Kansas, July 17th and returned home it was well over three months. Some days, while riding, when finding good feed we would sometimes only travel about five miles a day.

We were only a couple days by train, coming home to Arizona. At this date, I am the sole survivor of that drive.

Those Early Days…..

## HOWARD WINGFIELD MAKES ANOTHER TALK
*(Taped)*

As you know, back in the early days doing business as a merchant you didn't have much cash. It was simple barter. If you came in and you bought something you charged it. You probably paid it off with corn, hay, hogs or beef. So it wasn't a cash business but it leaves a good record of the old customers of the Wingfield Commercial Company. At that time, the store was operated by C.P. Head. An Indian at Camp Verde called Captain Smily was credited with personally capturing Geronimo on the campaign into Mexico; bringing him out of Mexico to General Howard when he surrendered. He had a medal that verified that it was procured for him by Senator Ashurst. Well we called him Major after he got the medal! Well it went on about a year or so and he was granted a military pension. Of course that was more money than the Major ever had in his life. He got one hundred dollars a month and he opened a little account with us just like a white man. And he felt pretty important. But he wasn't very careful with his money and usually run out before the month was over and we had to be careful for him to see that he had money enough to stretch his account every month. Well this day he was standing there by the counter and looking pretty glum. So one of the clerks walked by and said, "What can I do for you Major?" He grunted. He kept standing there and Mr. Wingfield walked over and said, "What's a matter Major?" He said "Yesterday no charge 'em and today no eat 'em". He'd gone broke.

Entries in old 1873 account book - not the oldest he had: 1872 the oldest. Captain Carpenter bought 2 sheets of emery paper 50¢. He was a surveyor for the government. He surveyed old trails and roads in the county and he surveyed the land of a lot of old deeds in Camp Verde.

Bowers Richards bought 15lbs of sugar $5.00 and 10lbs of coffee $4.50, probably green coffee that had to be roasted.

3 boxes of powder $1.00

Tobacco $2.00

Box of Matches 50¢

Tobacco and cigars $1.00 was purchased by Lynn Piet.

Al Seiber was a government scout for the army there. Well when they were not on scouting trips they had to keep those Indians busy or they would get into some kind of "devilment." So they would contract with us to cut wild hay or wood. And this note book I have is an account of so many cords of wood delivered to the hospital, or so many to Troup K or Troup C or which troop it happened to be and to the store and the commissary or so many tons of hay to the different stables around. He was the most famous of all Apache Indian Scouts on their work in Arizona. Seiber was killed at Roosevelt Lake. There is a monument where he died.

    2 gals, of whiskey $16.00
One can of pineapple $1.00
Jug of whiskey, doesn't say how big the jug was, was $3.00
2 bottles of ale $4.00
Jug of whiskey $3.00
Plug of tobacco $1.00
Plugs of tobacco $1.50, doesn't say how many.
Box of cartridges $2.50
7 drinks 50¢

In the store they had an officers' clubroom; that's where they met to have their drinks and play cards. This room was partitioned off from the store and the room rented for $1.00 per game.

Those Early Days.....

## BEAR TREE JIMMY
*by Albert E. Thompson*

Sometime in the 1890s there was a young Englishman by the name of Jimmy Prosser working at his trade of carpentering in Jerome, Arizona. He had left England only five years before and had been in the far west a very short time.

A group of Jerome men decided to come to Oak Creek for some trout fishing and asked the English carpenter to join them. It may have been that they knew already how credulous he was and asked him mainly for the fun they could have with him.

They camped at the present Indian Gardens camp ground, known then as Bacon Rind Park. One evening soon after arriving at camp, some members of the group had been fishing up the creek. On their way back to camp, they decided to try to scare Jimmy Prosser. They came in and told him that a bear had got after them, but they had managed to escape. They made the story so convincing, Jimmy decided to climb a tree. They told him that a bear could climb a large tree by hugging it with his fore legs, but could not climb a small tree. Jimmy picked out a slender box elder tree, hardly six inches in diameter but quite tall. He not only climbed it, but took a good stout club with him for protection. The tree was so slender it bent with his weight and caught in the limbs of a larger tree.

It was so funny to the men, they decided to go across the creek to the Thompson house and tell about it. They told Jimmy that they were going over to get my dad to kill the bear. The men came to the house after my folks had gone to bed. They called Dad out of bed and told him the joke. Dad would not believe that anyone would be that scared. He said that when they got back to camp they would find Prosser in bed. They went back to camp and told Prosser that they had found another bear before they got to the house and had had to come back without seeing Dad.

Jimmy was really scared then. Although the other men slept on the ground all night he roosted in the tree till morning. When Dad found out in the morning that a man had actually spent the night in a tree for fear of bears, he decided to help carry the joke along. He went out and made some bear tracks in the loose dust with his hands.

When they showed the tracks to Jimmy he was sure he could not spend another night in camp. He came over to ask permission to sleep in the cabin for the rest of his stay. I remember hearing Mother tell that he came up to the house and said, "Oh Mrs. Thompson I spent a miserable night last night."

It was midsummer and as hot as it ever gets here. All of our family had moved their beds out of the cabins and were sleeping out in the open under the trees. Just the same Jimmy Prosser slept in the cabin with the door and windows closed tightly until time to go back to Jerome.

He did not learn for several years that he had had a trick played on him. When he did finally find out he took it like a good sport and did not hold a grudge against the ones who had tricked him. He remained a life long friend of my dad. After he learned more about the ways of the West he loved to tell the story on himself. Several years after Jimmy spent the night in the tree, some vandal camper cut the tree down. When Jimmy found out about it he was quite put out to know that someone had cut his tree down. He was known all of the rest of his life by old-timers as "Bear Tree Jimmy".

This story is taken from a series of bear stories written by Albert E. Thompson as yet unpublished. Used by permission of Albert E. Thompson.

Those Early Days.....

## HOW TO DISMOUNT FROM A HORSE
*by Albert E. Thompson*

Joe Lay can sit and tell one interesting story after another, if he has the right kind of listeners. Not long ago he was telling me some yarns about experiences that he and Doc (Dr. M.O.) Dumas had had together during their long acquaintance.

The best that he told that day, in my opinion at least, was about when Joe was a mere boy, not many years after he came here from Tennessee. It was sometime in the late 1890s, about 1897 or 1898.

Joe and Dumas happened to be riding together when they saw a little bunch of cattle with a calf among them that roused Dumas's curiosity. Joe was riding a well-trained, gentle horse and Dumas was riding a young half-broken horse. Dumas wanted to catch the calf for a closer examination. He asked Joe to trade horses with him long enough for him to catch and examine the calf. Joe agreed. Dumas chased the calf down near the creek and caught it and tied it down. Joe came along more slowly on the "bronc". Joe started to dismount near the tied calf but every time he made motions to do so the horse would start acting up and trying to buck. Joe said, "How do you get off of this crazy so and so?" Dumas said, "Just thumb him and he will buck you off."

I might explain here for the benefit of the uninitiated, that if a horse was inclined to pitch at all, thumbing him would get results. To thumb a horse all that you need do is hold both thumbs straight out and rigid and reach down and rake the horse up his shoulders with your thumbs.

## THE MUNDS FAMILY
**The Family That Has Had So Many Landmarks Named for Them.**
By Sedona Westerners Book Committee, from information supplied by Inez Loy Lay, Jennie Munds Wingfield and Sally Munds Williams.

As there are several landmarks not far from Sedona that are named for the Munds family, we should know a little more about who the Munds' were.

William Munds, the father of the family, was born in Kentucky, September 25, 1835, and went to Oregon when he was still a young man. He married at Roseburg, Oregon, and their four children were born there.

In 1875 he and his family started traveling down the coast of California. They had two covered wagons and drove 110 head of cattle and fifteen head of loose horses. There were three boys, Jim, John and Neal, and one girl, Melvina. They went inland into Nevada and stopped at intervals along the way.

In October 1875 they reached the old Stone's Ferry on the Colorado River. The family and wagons were ferried across the river but the cattle and horses had to swim across. They only lost one steer.

They continued on across Arizona, not knowing exactly where they were going, but finally arrived in Williamson Valley, northwest of Prescott on November 22, 1875. William Munds leased the "Bean House" ranch there and fenced it with the first wire fence ever used in that part of the country. They raised hay there and sold it to the army post of Fort Whipple and at Groom Creek.

After a year there they moved to Verde Valley. They stopped first on the east side of the river just below the present Bridgeport but soon moved to Spring Creek. Mr. Munds homesteaded there, but as they had range cattle and horses they moved them to the mountain in the summer time.

James or "Jim" as he was called married Harriet or "Hattie" Loy in 1882 and in 1883 he took a homestead in what became known as Munds Park, south of Flagstaff. Jim and his father were principally interested in farming and cattle-raising. John, a younger brother, was more interested in raising horses. He built the first trail onto what is now known as Munds Mountain. It is the high mountain just southeast of the present Schnebly Hill. John pastured his horses on the mountain in the winter when there was snow for water as there was no source of water there at other times. He lived in a cave there at times while looking

Those Early Days.....

after his horses.

As all of the stock had to be driven from the valley to the high country each spring and back down each fall, Jim Munds did most of the work on a trail that was known as Munds Trail. Years later the Schnebly Hill road was built in about the same place. The road was known locally as the Munds Road for a few years after it was built. The big canyon that drains the Munds Park vicinity and empties into Oak Creek at Indian Gardens became known as Munds Canyon.

Neal Munds did not live long enough after coming to Arizona to have anything named after him. He was a rather bold and reckless cowboy and bronco rider. In 1886, when he was only 18 years old he was dared to ride a mean outlaw horse. The horse bucked so hard, Neal's head was almost snapped off but he was still riding when the horse ran into a tree and fell with him.

The accident happened at what was known as Willard Spring Park, a few miles northwest of the Munds ranch at Munds Park. Neal's brother, Jim, made a fast ride to the ranch for a wagon to bring Neal home but when he got back Neal was dead. Neal's father picked a burial spot on a hillside on the Carrier homestead just north of the park. (Dr. Myron A. Carrier had married Melvina Munds, daughter of William Munds, and had taken a homestead in the east end of the park near the Munds ranch).

On March 30, 1890, John Munds married Frances Willard, daughter of a pioneer family that also ranged cattle on the same range the Munds family did. The Willard Summer quarters were at what became known as Willard Spring, a few miles from Munds Park.

John Munds and his bride lived at Willard Spring for three years in the summer months. Their first child William Harold was born in Flagstaff while they made their home at Willard Spring.

In September 1892, Jim Munds was accidently shot and died from the wound at the Munds Park ranch. He had come in from a ride on the range and set his gun down by the gate and rode around to drive some horses into the corral. When he came back he reached down for his gun, a .44 Winchester rifle, and the hammer struck something and it discharged. The bullet struck him in the head.

Mack Willard, a brother-in-law of John Munds, was with him and saw him fall from his horse. Mat Black, a cattleman from just south of Flagstaff and his nephew, George Black Jr., came to the ranch soon after the accident. Mat Black went at once to Spring

Creek where Dr. Carrier was, to have him come up, and to notify the womenfolk who were at the time at the Mid Campbell ranch at the foot of Mingus Mountain. Dr. Carrier left at once on horseback by way of Jack's Canyon Trail but Jim Munds was dead when he got there.

William Loy, a brother of Mrs. Jim Munds, was on Oak Creek a few miles above the Cornville post office. Mat Black notified him and he started with a buckboard to get the womenfolk and take them to Munds Park. The only way to get to Munds Park at that time with a wagon was by the old Beaver Head Road. Young George Black was sent from Munds Park with a team of fresh horses to meet William Loy and the families. George said in later years that he was only twelve years old at the time. It was well after dark and George was beginning to get scared when he heard the sound of the buckboard coming up the rocky road.

James Munds was buried by his brother, Neal, on the hillside at Munds Park. The same year a girl child, daughter of Dr. and Mrs. Carrier, was buried there. The graves were fenced and markers put up. Many years later, after Charles Burrus became the owner of the Carrier homestead, he deeded the burial plot to Hattie Munds (Wingfield) who was the widow of Jim Munds. Jim and Hattie Munds had two girls who were quite young at the time of their father's death. Hattie's brother, John Loy, came to live with her and farm the place.

She sold her cattle and continued to live on the ranch through the summer months. The girls attended school at Camp Verde in the wintertime. When they reached high school age they had to move to Tempe to attend the Tempe Normal School, now Arizona State University. Both of the girls, (Getha, who later married Oliver Benedict, a Camp Verde rancher, and Jennie, who later married Dave Wingfield, a cattleman), earned teacher's certificates and taught school for several years. To make a trip from Munds Park to Tempe at that time took six days with a wagon and team.

John Loy later homesteaded land joining the Munds homestead. After the Munds children were grown, their mother married again. John Loy also married just before he took his homestead.

In 1894 John Munds moved his family from Willard Spring to Prescott, though he still had livestock in this area. He served as under sheriff for three years under sheriff George Ruffner. John, himself was elected sheriff of Yavapai County in 1898 and served two terms. He was on some pretty dangerous manhunts while he was deputy sheriff and sheriff. He spent several days on the trail of "Blackjack" Ketchum, the bandit who held up the Camp Verde store and killed Clint Wingfield and Mack Rogers.

John Munds also had some experience in law enforcement while he was still quite a young man. There was an outlaw - or as some of the folks thought - a crazy man, who was stealing horses, raiding ranch houses and molesting women between Munds Park and Flagstaff. There had been two or three organized parties that had tried to find and capture or kill him but all had failed.

Young John Munds was out riding the range one morning when he saw the bad man run a bunch of horses into the corral at Willard Spring Park. John saw that most of the horses belonged to the Munds family. When he rode up the man said, "Watch the gate kid while I catch me a fresh horse". He had his rope down ready to catch a Munds horse. John pulled his rifle and drew a bead on the horse thief and said, "Throw up your hands", but the bad man who was known as Jimmy Wilson, reached for his gun instead and John shot him. The outlaw was buried right near the corral. The present Black Canyon Highway is built over the grave.

John's wife, Frances, also entered politics after her children were grown. She was active in woman suffrage, and was instrumental in getting voting privileges for women in 1912. She was the first woman elected State Senator in Arizona and the second in the U.S.A.

In the 1890s, William Munds, father of the family, moved to Jerome and opened the first butcher shop there. At the time Jerome was a wild, disordered town. The garbage was thrown down the hillside and the burros roamed the town. There had been five bad fires, so it was decided to incorporate the town. William Munds was the first Mayor.

Although Jerome was his home he liked to get out to Oak Creek to spend his summers. In 1903 he was on his way to Indian Gardens for a camping trip. He got sick on the way and stopped at the Schuerman ranch, at Red Rock. He died there June 11, 1903.

John Munds returned to Verde Valley in 1919 and served as deputy sheriff until he retired. They lived in Clemenceau. His wife, Frances, died in 1948, and John died February 2, 1952. Sally Munds Williams, Iva Carrier Shaw and Jennie Munds Wingfield, are the only living grandchildren of Wm. Munds.

## A BEAR HUNTER WHO LOST
*by Albert E. Thompson*

In the spring of 1885, John James Thompson and his young wife and two small children were living in a log cabin on the present George Jordan ranch in what is now Sedona, Arizona.

He had taken squatters rights to a claim at Indian Gardens, four miles farther up the creek some ten years previous. The Indian Gardens ranch was in such wild country and so inaccessible, he had built the cabin at the Jordan ranch when he married, so his wife could be near her parents. They lived on the present Fred Hart ranch, about two miles down the creek.

The previous year, Mr. Thompson had taken a temporary partner to help him farm the Indian Gardens ranch. He was an old Arkansas bear hunter, by the name of Richard Wilson. He first came to Tucson, Arizona in 1864. Mr. Wilson and a man named Jim Woolsy had built a neat hewed log cabin at Indian Gardens, but Wilson himself, camped in a hut about a half-mile from the cabin.

In June 1885, Mr. Thompson was called as a witness in a court case of some kind to Prescott, the County Seat. (Remember, at that time, Coconino County had not been made from part of Yavapai. Yavapai County extended to the Utah border).

Mrs. Thompson's family had moved from Sedona with their cattle to the mountains for the summer. Mr. Thompson did not like to leave his wife and small children alone while he was gone to Prescott, so he asked Mr. Wilson to come down every evening while he was gone and spend the night near the family.

Mr. Wilson had been telling Thompson about seeing the tracks of a monstrous grizzly bear between Sedona and Indian Gardens. He said he intended to kill the big bear. He had broken the sight on his large caliber bear gun and had only a small rifle to use. He asked Thompson to take his big rifle to Prescott and have the sights repaired. Thompson told him to leave the big bear absolutely alone until he got back from Prescott with the big rifle and the old man agreed to do so.

The evening of the very day that Mr. Thompson left home, Mr. Wilson failed to show up at the Thompson cabin in Sedona. Not only did he fail to appear the first evening, but for eight days Mrs. Thompson had the two little children, a boy of three and a girl of one year were alone. The nearest neighbor was about five miles away by trail down the creek.

Mrs. Thompson said later that she was both worried and

frightened, but she was almost helpless to do anything about her plight. She did not even have a horse. The only livestock she had were milk cows and pigs. She had to tend the stock and rustle wood for cooking and carry water from the creek for house use and for the pigs.

On the ninth day she was happy to see two men riding in on horseback. They were Judge John Goodwin and his son Tom from Jerome. They asked Mrs. Thompson for the key to the Cabin at Indian Gardens, as they wanted to spend a few days trout fishing there. They were old friends of the Thompsons, and Mrs. Thompson said she would be glad to let them have the key, but Mr. Wilson had it. She told them that she was dreadfully worried for fear that something serious had happened to Mr. Wilson or he would not have stayed away so long.

Judge Goodwin tried to reassure her by telling her that Wilson had just got busy with his farm work and forgotten about his promise to come down of evenings.

Mrs. Thompson stoutly denied that and insisted that Mr. Wilson was an honest and trustworthy man and would not have broken his promise if it had been humanly possible for him to keep it.

The Judge told her that he and his son would ride on up the canyon and investigate and come back and let her know what they had found out.

As Mrs. Thompson used to tell it, "They had been gone only a short while when she saw them coming back, riding pretty fast." She knew they had bad news.

They had got only as far as Wilson Canyon. It is the big canyon that Highway 89A now crosses over Midgley Bridge near where it enters Oak Creek. It is about halfway between Sedona and Indian Gardens.

The old trail used to cross the canyon much farther up in the hills. The Goodwins had crossed the canyon and started up the steep north side when they heard a dog bark. They went back to the bottom of the canyon, past the forks and up the left hand branch into a box canyon with a high cliff fall ahead. There they found the battered body of Wilson, the bear hunter. His faithful dog was still with him.

The Goodwins came immediately back to the Thompson cabin and reported what they had found. Judge Goodwin then sent his son Tom, back to Jerome for help. He told Mrs. Thompson that he would stay with her because he knew she had already had it plenty rough, being marooned there alone. She was very grateful for the

*Jim Thompson standing by the grave of Richard (Bear) Wilson in Wilson Canyon, about 1885.*

offer. Tom went to Jerome and brought back enough men to hold a Coroner's inquest at the scene of the killing. The Judge, being the Justice of the Peace at Jerome, presided at the inquest.

The story, pieced out at the inquest, and from what Mrs. Thompson could tell them is as follows: Mr. Wilson had quit work early enough in the evening to get to the Thompson cabin before dark. He had two pack burros that he had loaded with little potatoes for feed for the pigs at Thompsons.

Apparently he and Mr. Thompson had dug potatoes previously and packed the marketable ones out and Thompson had taken them to market in Prescott.

It appeared that Wilson had got as far on his way as Wilson Canyon. (Of course it did not have that name then). He caught sight of the big bear there. In spite of the fact that he had only a light rifle and a young untrained dog, he could not resist the temptation to kill it. He, an old experienced bear hunter, had lost all fear of the big brutes. He shot the bear and wounded it. Very foolishly he followed it up a brushy canyon with an untrained dog.

It appeared from sign that the bear had gone up the box canyon and stopped in a brush thicket. The hunter followed it by tracks and dripping blood, expecting to get another shot and kill it. He stepped past some Arizona Cypress trees and the bear jumped at him so close he had no chance. He ran for a tree and dropped his gun. He tried to climb the tree but the bear caught him by the heel of his shoe and pulled him down. He was wearing heavy hob-nailed mountaineer shoes. One shoe had the heel almost pulled off

Those Early Days…..

and showed the marks of the bear's teeth. The Cypress tree that he had tried to climb had a limb almost as thick as a man's wrist almost twisted off. It showed how desperately the old hunter had clung to the tree to try to save his life.

The body was found some ten or fifteen feet from the tree. It was lying face down in a little pool of water. It appeared that the bear had pulled the hunter from the tree and either bitten part of his face off or knocked it off with his paw. The belief was that the bear had then gone away. The hunter had then regained consciousness and crawled to the pool of water to try to get a drink. He had passed out again and fallen in the water and drowned. At least that is what the jury decided from the evidence at hand.

The old man's body was too badly decomposed to move any great distance. Bedrock was too near the surface to dig a very deep grave. They just wrapped him in his blankets and buried him in a shallow grave and piled a big mound of boulders on top of his grave. At the base of the cliff they cut his initials, R.W. into the rock.

The old man's burros were found grazing on the slope of the mountain north of there. They had torn holes in the potato sacks and scattered little potatoes far and wide, but still had part of the pack rigs on them.

When Mr. Thompson returned from Prescott, his old friend and partner was dead and buried.

Some years later, some of the old man's friends from Jerome dug up the bones and reburied them at the Thompson ranch at Indian Gardens, where they have lain all these years.

Some fifteen years after the killing, Frank Thompson, who was the little three-year old boy when Wilson was killed, found the skeleton of a very large bear in high brush near the top of Wilson Mountain, some two miles from the scene of the killing. He brought the bear's skull home to his father's house. His father asked him if he had looked for Wilson's hunting knife there. He went back several weeks later but could never find the skeleton again. Mr. Thompson knew that Wilson always carried a large hunting knife. As it was never found, Thompson always believed that the old man had stuck it in the bear and the bear had carried it away with him and died from his wounds, but we will never know.

This story is taken from a series of bear stories, written by Albert E. Thompson, and as yet unpublished. Used by permission of Albert E. Thompson.

## THE FIRST SHERIFF OF COCONINO COUNTY
## and SOME POEMS
*by Lenore Francis Dumas*

John W. Francis was born in Springfield, Missouri on March 27th, 1856. He graduated from the Kirksville Normal School and then decided to seek a career in the open west. He and a brother, Dan M. Francis started for the West.

In 1881, the year that the Atlantic and Pacific Railroad (now known as the Santa Fe) tracks were being laid in Arizona, the boys arrived in Flagstaff. At that time, Flagstaff was a small camp, more or less, with one boarding house, saloon, general store and a flagpole. The boys split ties and worked on the railroad. Later John taught school in Flagstaff, being the second teacher. Mrs. Eva Marshall was the first teacher.

During the "Tewkesbury-Graham Feud", John became a deputy sheriff under Sheriff Mulvenon of Yavapai County, where he saw much action. On August 23rd, 1887, Sheriff Mulvenon called Deputy Sheriff Francis to meet him. Such men as Constable E.F. O'Dell, Fletcher Fairchild and John Weatherford went into Payson County to meet Sheriff Mulvenon for the first invasion. Deputy Francis and men returned to Flagstaff and on September 2nd, date of second invasion, they spent many days and returned to Flagstaff September 22nd, 1887. Many arrests had been made according to the story in "Arizona's Dark and Bloody Ground", written by Earle R. Forrest.

Yavapai County was divided in 1891 and John Francis became the first sheriff of Coconino County. During the years he served as sheriff of Coconino County, the only record of him having to kill anyone was on one account, and that was while making an arrest.

He was on the trail of a horse thief and trailed him into a sheep camp. Leaving their horses at a safe distance, he and his deputy walked into camp. Quietly he asked the sheepherder if he had seen a man of a certain description, and without any comment, the herder pointed to a tent. Sheriff Francis could see the shadow of a man in the tent and told his deputy to jerk the tent-flap back and he would have him covered. When the deputy jerked the flap, Sheriff Francis called, "Throw up your hands", but instead the man reached for his gun and the sheriff shot him in the neck. The sheriff said, "Why did you reach for your gun instead of throwing up your hands?" "Didn't you know that I would shoot you?" The man said, "Yes". He was bleeding profusely and the sheriff told

Those Early Days.....

him he could never live to reach town, and asked him if he would like to send any word to his family and he said, "No, my folks are all well respected and honorable people and I never want them to know what happened to me". He died without giving any names or making any recognition of who he might be or where his family lived.

One of Sheriff Francis' duties was to make the arrest of R.W. McNeill, a store and train robber operating in Navajo and Coconino Counties. The Santa Fe train was held up near Canyon Diablo. The Canyon is very deep and the railroad trestle over the canyon is long and very high. Me Neill left his horse and made the robbery while the train was moving, very slowly. He made his haul, and riding a fine horse soon disappeared, going in the direction of East Clear Creek Canyon. Word came in to Flagstaff and Sheriff Francis with two men, started in pursuit. The deputy, possibly E.F. O'Dell and Mr. Jacoby, a saloonkeeper was the other man.

Clear Creek is a very deep and rugged canyon, running east and west coming into the Little Colorado River about six miles east of Winslow. Sheriff Francis and his men were riding along the north side of the canyon when a shot rang out, then the gun battle across the canyon began. Me Neill, riding on the south side, spied the three officers and opened fire. The battle began, each firing at the other across the canyon. All men took refuge behind large boulders, but bullets were coming so fast on every side, that the boulders seemed to be no larger than an orange.

Finally, McNeill called over that they would never take him alive and the shooting was a waste of time, so if Francis would ride ten miles down the canyon, he would find a crossing and a path leading to his camp, a good dinner would be waiting for them with plenty of hot biscuits in the dutch oven. Sheriff Francis called back, "No shooting in the back". McNeill called on his honor: "No shooting", so all was well. McNeill went his way and the men started down the canyon. Some say that Mr. Jacoby really had his excitement, as one shot passed through his derby hat, and he headed back for Flagstaff.

It took many hours of riding to reach the camp from where they were, having intervals of rest for the animals. This was rugged terrain and very steep along the rough hillside. They had to cross the canyon after finding the trail leading into his camp.

On arrival, the sheriff found things just as McNeill had said, good food, hot biscuits and coffee. But McNeill was well on his way for parts unknown.

Sheriff Francis found the following poems and note from

McNeill, on top of the dutch oven.

R.W. McNeill was a well-educated man, good manners and most honorable and from a very fine family, he was never an outlaw at heart. He served time either in New Mexico or Utah, having surrendered of his own accord. Many years later after John Francis' death in 1925, Mr. McNeill came back to Flagstaff, a free man, to shake Sheriff Francis' hand.

## DUTCH OVEN POEM
*By R.W. McNeill*

Here's where Clear Creek deeply flows
From the melted mass of Mogollon snows
Here I lived and fain would roam
O'er the country that I for years, called home,
Hunted continually like some wild beast
Until I reach my ranch, I know no peace.

While strolling on the canyon side
Three men on the opposite side I spied,
They were officers, bold, brave men,
Who dared to brave the lion in his den.

They little dreamed of the danger near
Until a report which startled all
Quickly followed by a whistling ball.
Nothing could excel the leader's grace
As he threw his rifle to his face
And as my carbine rang out crack
He quickly sent an answer back.

In fighting, these officers were well skilled
Yet strange to say, none were killed.
But among the pines, birds whispered that
"A bullet pierced Jacoby's hat
And as the battle held its course
Another struck John Francis' horse".

Although my name is badly smudged
Toward these men I hold no grudge.
And hope someday, a free man to stand
And grasp my combatants by the hand.

**A second poem as follows:**

> I'm the Prince of the Aztecs
> I am perfection at robbing a store.
> I have a stake left me by Well's Fargo,
> And before long I will have more.
> On trains, I have made a good haul
> Stages are things I hate
> My losses are always small
> My profits exceedingly great.
>
> I will say a few words for my friends
> You see I have quite a few
> And although we are at daggers ends
> I would like to say "How do ye do"!
> There are McKinnon and Larson
> Who say that robber's have no honor,
> I think in a test of manhood
> They will have to stand back in a corner.
>
> There are my friends, the Schusters
> For whom I carry so much lead
> In the future to kill this young rooster
> They will have to aim at his head.
>
> Commodore Owens says he wants to kill me
> To me, that sounds like fun
> It's strange he would thus try to fill me
> The red-headed son-of-a-gun.
>
> He handles a six shooter neat
> And hits a rabbit every pop
> But should he and I happen to meet
> We'll have an old "Arkansas hop".
>
> My friends, I will have to leave you,
> My war horse is sniffing the breeze
> I wish I could stay here to see you,
> Make yourself at home, if you please.
>
> I will not say very much more
> My space is growing so small
> You are always welcome to my share
> "That's that", "Much obliged" - "Not at all".
>
> > Yours in luck,
> > R.W. McNeill

Those Early Days…..

Dear Friends:

I hope you will not be insulted at the reception I gave you, for you see that it was my birthday and I thought I would celebrate it with a pyrotechnical exhibition on a small scale. I have so few visitors here that I am glad to see somebody come around, no matter what his business is- I am always ready to welcome him by firing a few shots from my Winchester as a salute. Some people do not admire this style of greeting, but they cannot see a joke. But I hope you, (my running friends) will appreciate it at its full value.

R.W. McNeill

## AN OLD TIME DOCTOR, DR. M.A. CARRIER
*by Inez Lay*

Dr. Myron A. Carrier was born in Onieda County, New York, December 22, 1842. When he was quite a young man he joined the army at the start of the Civil War. He was soon captured and spent four months in Libby Prison before being exchanged.

After the war was over he hired out to a wagon train going West, to help take care of the stock. Young McGuffy, son of the McGuffy who wrote some of our schoolbooks, was also on his way West for the benefit of his health. Carrier saved him from drowning and they became great friends.

*Dr. M.A. Carrier and wife Melvina, daughter of William Munds. Dr. Carrier was the first Doctor to practice medicine in Jerome, the market place for all of the Upper Verde Valley.*

Those Early Days.....

They left the wagon train at Salt Lake City and stayed that winter in a cabin about twenty miles out of the city and trapped. They sent the pelts East to sell.

While Carrier was in Libby Prison, there was so much sickness and death he became interested in medicine, so in the spring he returned to New York to study medicine.

*Dr. L.A. Hawkins, the first dentist of Jerome, and his motorcycle. Dr. Hawkins was a son-in-law of Dr. M.A. Carrier.*

On September 30th, 1867, he married Jane Lindsay and they went to Nebraska and then to Michigan where he practiced medicine for seven years.

After the death of his wife, he left his little girls with relatives in New York and came to Arizona in 1881. Not long after his arrival here he filed on a homestead in the southeast end of Munds Park. He built a log cabin and corrals near the head of Munds Canyon. He got a few head of cattle, and his brand was DC bar. He later sold the cattle to Frank Owen-by.

On September 24, 1884, he married Melvina Munds, daughter of William Munds and a sister of Jim Munds, his near neighbor. They were not able to spend the winters on the mountains so they all spent them together at Spring Creek.

His daughter, Eleanor, called Nellie-who later married William Loy-came from New York in 1888. His other daughter, Ethel, later married Dr. Lee Hawkins. Dr. Hawkins was the first dentist of Jerome. He came to Jerome in 1889.

On one of his trips to Verde Valley by way of Munds Trail, Dr. Carrier saw a bear wallowing in a rock tank. He followed it out and killed it, taking the hide home, and later had saddlebags made to fit behind his saddle. He carried his medical supplies in it. The rock tank and canyon below have been known as Bear Wallow ever since.

As Jerome began to grow his profession kept him busy. He established an office in the Red Cross Drug Store, owned at that time by Elwin F. Tarr. In 1898 he sold his Munds Park ranch to E.S. Gosney, a sheep man.

**Dr. L. A. Hawkins, first dentist of Jerome and his car — the first one in Jerome, about 1905.**

One year he was health officer there. Smallpox was very bad in Jerome that year. The doctor was called in the night and found three men in one bed. He quarantined the place and told the sick man to stay in bed and keep warm. The next morning the man got up early and dressed and got on the bus, going to the depot. The other passengers took one look and piled off the bus and walked. The bus driver phoned from the depot. The doctor hurried up there and brought the sick man back.

Down at the foot of the "Hog Back", a "pest house" was built. The people were frantic and kept the doctor busy. When the epidemic was over, someone was sent to fumigate and bum the bedding, but found it had all been stolen. At the livery stable a horse

Those Early Days…..

was always kept ready for the doctor when he had to ride into the country, day or night.

The big fire of 1897 burned most of the town. The doctor's house was third to burn. The next winter many people lived in tents and it was very cold. Soon after that the town was incorporated.

Dr. Carrier was one of the 13 charter members of Verde Lodge No. 14, F&AM. It was with brothers, William Nichols, E.A. Gilmore, S.J. Perkins, J.C. Duff, G.B. Niblock, David Scott, J.M. Campbell, Chas. F. Fisher, Geo. O. Wagner, D.E. Dumas, J.W. Sharp and William Munds, that organizing a lodge for Jerome was started in June 1897.

A pioneer doctor having to go on horseback or by buggy, and lots of times be nurse too, would spend many hours with his patients. In those days malaria and typhoid fever were very bad, sometimes going through the entire family. Long and tedious doctoring was necessary to save the patients, as there were no "wonder drugs" in those days.

When the doctor was no longer able to work, as he had developed a heart condition, he moved to Camp Verde, to a lower altitude. His death came December 8th, 1907.

## THEY WERE AFRAID OF EACH OTHER
*by Albert E. Thompson*

Joe Lay and Doc Dumas like to tell stories of cow punching in days gone by. Dr. M.O. Dumas told this one not long ago.

He was out riding one day when he saw a big calf that was unbranded. It was big enough to be past a year old but it was still following its mother. The mother cow did not carry Doc's brand.

When I asked Doc's permission to write this story he said that these new comers might not understand that it was legal to steal in those days, providing you did not get caught. That was his joking way of saying, that if the old time cowmen did not brand every long eared calf he could get away with, he would come out on the short end of the deal. Almost every one of them followed that practice, so the ones who would have liked to stay honest had to do the same to stay even.

Now we come back to our story.

Doc knew that if he could get the big calf away from its mother and keep it out of her hearing for a while it would forget its mother. He was riding up a ridge that slopes down from the foot of House Mountain when he jumped the big calf. He took down his rope and started after the calf. Just as he was about to throw his rope and make his catch, he saw another man chasing a calf down a ridge on the opposite side of a wash that divided the two ridges. The other fellow was too far away to be recognized but Doc did not take any chances that it might be the owner of the calf s mother. He gave up the chase and rode into the bushes in the opposite direction.

A short time later he met with Joe Lay and told him of the incident. Surprisingly enough, Joe told him that he was the other fellow chasing a calf, and when he saw Doc on the other side of the wash he gave up the chase and slipped away in the opposite direction also.

Those Early Days.....

## THE LOY FAMILY
### Another Family With Many Landmarks Named For Them
*by Inez Lay*

Samuel Loy was born near Columbus, Ohio in 1820. He joined the gold rush of 1849 and went to California by ox team. He spent four years there but he farmed rather than dig for gold. At the end of four years he came back by ship to New York, bringing a fair amount of gold and a strong desire to make a home in the West.

The next year he married Jane Sennette and they went to Missouri and bought a farm. They stayed there until after their five children were born and the youngest child, a daughter, was 12 years old.

He sold his farm in 1876, and in the summer of that year he joined a wagon train headed for Oregon. In the meantime they heard so many reports of Arizona's fertile Verde Valley they came here instead. He drove horses to his wagons but there were others in the party who used oxen and they all had to travel at the same pace, so they did not make many miles in a day. They were 3 months and 13 days on the road and reached the Verde Valley on August 13, 1876.

Hauling freight was good business in those days so they went on to Prescott and stayed that winter, using their horses and wagons to haul freight to the Verde Valley. The five children of this family were, James, John, William and Mary, (twins) and Harriet Ann, who was known later as Hattie. Soon after coming here, Mary, called Molly, married Conway Bristow. William and Harriet went to school in a log schoolhouse in Prescott during the school year of 1876 & 77.

The next spring they returned to the Verde Valley. As farming was the occupation he chose the valley looked promising to him. He bought some land from Riley Casner, near the mouth of Oak Creek. As this was unimproved land, they rented the Anderson place near Bridgeport and farmed there while building a ditch onto their own land.

So many families were settling along the Verde they had to begin thinking about a school. Alexander Strahan gave a piece of land, near present Cottonwood, to be used for a school and a cemetery. John Hawkins' grave was the first in the cemetery. He was killed when thrown from a horse when he was only 18 years old in the year 1876.

In the school year of 1877-78 Harriet and William Loy,

together with the Munds and Wingfield children and many others attended the school built on that land.

Some histories list the building as adobe, but others say it was made of poles set closely together and fastened in a rough framework. The roof was made the same way and plastered with mud and covered with sod and dirt.

The teacher, a Mrs. Rheubottom, and her children lived in one end of the same building. She used her dining table for her teacher's desk. A fireplace supplied heat for the school and she also did her cooking on it.

When the first pioneers came to the Verde Valley, they found a stockman's and hunter's paradise. There was however one bad fault with it. The high grass that grew everywhere acted as a sponge and held most of the rainwater back from reaching the river and causing floods. The Verde River was more or less a series of pools that were grown over with moss and made good breeding places for mosquitoes that spread malaria.

There were very few kinds of medicines available then, quinine and calomel being the main ones used. Blue mass in cake form was also used. They would cut off a small piece, according to the size of the patient, and rolls it into a pill. Also a salve made from the soft pitch of the pine tree mixed with mutton tallow was quite healing, but once on, it had to wear off.

Very few people came to the Verde Valley without bringing horses, cattle or sheep. In a few years the stock ate the grass down and trampled the spongy land down to solid ground, thus causing the rain water to run into the river channel, which was only about 100 feet wide. Soon the high water was making a wide channel and malaria was not heard of any more.

Jim and Ben Barney had land joining the Anderson place where the Loys lived. In the spring their cattle and horses were taken to Secret Mountain. Many landmarks were named for these people. On our present maps you will find, Anderson Butte, Barney Pasture and Barney Spring. Also there are Loy Butte, Loy Canyon and Loy Trail.

Jane Loy was never very well so Samuel Loy and his son James hewed logs and built a cabin up in Loy Canyon where it was cooler and the water was purer and malaria was not so bad. Loy Canyon is one of the main tributaries of Spring Creek.

The Loys built a cabin on the slope of what is now known as Woodie Mountain arid moved their stock there for the summer months. They milked cows there and made butter for winter. To preserve the butter they would mold it in small rolls and wrap it in clean cloths and pack it in containers surrounding it with coarse salt. That would keep it from getting strong.

In the winter months Samuel Loy would work on furniture. Some of his chairs were in the family for many years.

However this pleasant and easy life came to an end when the big drought of the late 1880s came and they had to move to Oak Creek where the water never fails. It was well they did for the drought was followed by a depression so great you could buy a cow for eight dollars. But by raising a garden and feed for the animals and with a gristmill nearby to grind corn into meal, they were able to sell enough eggs to buy sugar, salt and coffee.

On February 12, 1894, Jane Loy left this world. Samuel lived on with his youngest son, William, and family. He always raised a garden. He worked in the morning and evening, and under a peach tree he had a chair that he had made, where he would rest through the heat of the day. He also had a rainproof box where he kept his garden seed that he would gather. The little homed toads learned that he was their friend and the grandchildren were warned to leave them alone as they caught insects.

On March 29, 1901, he passed away and was laid beside his wife in the Middle Verde cemetery.

## PIONEERS OF THE RED ROCK PRECINCT
*by Frieda Schuerman Loy*

John George Heinrich (Henry) Schuerman was born in Melle, near Osnabruck (West) Germany March 17th, 1852. He was educated in German schools, and was a baker by trade. He was a member of the Lutheran Church in Melle, Germany, which is still standing today, and was visited by a grandson in 1955. The old home and some of the relatives were also visited.

At the age of 17 years, he and another young man the same age, Heinrich Beinke, came to the United States by way of Quebec. This new life was not an easy one for these young men in a strange country so far away from their home. Neither could speak the language or knew the ways of a foreign land. Where to go or what to do next was indeed a problem. Many hardships confronted them in their early years.

These two young men traveled together from place to place, working their way in various bakeries or at anything, which was available to do. Several years were spent together in St. Louis and New Orleans. After eight or ten years they felt the urge to go west. This was in the days of 1876 - 77. They walked together from Pueblo to Lake City, Colo., sleeping under one blanket, which was hardly large enough for one to sleep under. Such things were not soon forgotten. Later they drifted apart. Heinrich Beinke went back to St. Louis and later to Staunton, 111., where he married and made his home. He was a very successful businessman. They kept in touch the remainder of their lives thru correspondence.

Heinrich Schuerman went to New Mexico and then to Prescott, Arizona, where he met a cousin, George Schuerman. They rented the old Pioneer Hotel, then owned by Dan Hatz. They worked and lived there together until 1884.

In 1883 he became a charter member of "Aztlan Lodge, No. 1, F. & A.M." Also a charter member of "Hall of Golden Rule", Chapter No. 1 order of Eastern Star, Prescott. Later transferring to Verde Lodge No. 14, F. & A.M. Jerome in 1899.

Thru the years he had kept in touch with his lifelong sweetheart in Melle, Germany, where they had been neighbors and went to the same schools and church. She was Dorette Johanna Carolina Titgemeyer! After many years of correspondence she finally consented to meet him in New York City in company with several of the wives of our late old timers here. The group sailed from Bremerhafen and bid a farewell to their homeland, never to return. They were Mrs. August Thorbecke and children,

Those Early Days.....

whose husband and father had a bakery in Jerome for many years, Mrs. Bismeyer who met her husband here. They later moved to San Diego, Calif.; and Heinrich Brinkmeyer, a young man of 17 who for many years operated a hotel and bakery in Prescott. It is still operated by members of his family. A daughter still lives in the old home.

The Schuermans were married in New York City June 29, 1884. The party came by train from New York City to Ash Fork. From there they came to Prescott by stagecoach. His wife's baggage came free from Germany to Ash Fork. From there to Prescott it cost $10.00!

After living in Prescott for several months George Schuerman purchased the hotel from Dan Hatz. He changed the name to "The Sherman House."

*Schuerman house at Red Rock before it burned in 1900.*

Heinrich Schuerman (who had Americanized his name to Henry Schuerman) settled an old debt of five hundred dollars for a 160-acre farm on Oak Creek from a man by the name of Tom Carrol. Where was this place in no man's land on Oak Creek? Was it real or just a dream? They purchased a wagon and team, packed up their belongings with a supply of groceries, hired a driver and started out to find this place. They traveled five days over roads, which were merely cow trails. What an experience this was for a bride from a city, and who could not speak English! She could only make signs to be understood.

They came by way of Cherry Creek, Camp Verde, Beaver Head, Big Park, Little Park and across what was called Oak

Creek. Here they found the place, to be true, nestled there in the Red Rock Country.

They asked if any of the rocks and old landmarks had names. Yes, the one directly to the east of the place, just across the creek, was "Court House Rock". Later the peak west of the old home place was named Schuerman Rock and Schuerman Mountain was in the back. There were many other places around which were already named also.

There were no roads, no schools or churches. It was all beautiful, but so wild, quiet and strange to them. They did not want to stay. They could not even give it away. No one else wanted it. Time went on and what could they do with it? They just stayed, as they did not know where else to go. Progress had to be made if they stayed. They were not farmers or of the old frontier stock. Every thing was learned and earned the hard way with hard work and perseverance. There were many good people who helped. At that time people, far and near, were neighbors and friends.

There was only a small log cabin in which to live. A home had to be built. Irrigation ditches had to be made. A crude ditch was already on the place. They were told it had been made by the Indians, who had farmed the land many years before.

Large orchards with many varieties of fruit were planted. They were mostly apples and peaches. They also had a large vineyard. Wine was made from the grapes and sold to the miners in Jerome.

Roads had to be built to market the fruits and vegetables, which grew in abundance. In 1885 Mr. Schuerman made his first trip to Flagstaff by way of Beaver Creek road. The trip was made in 6 days.

Later there was the opening up of the United Verde Mine, which provided a good market for the farmers. They still needed better and shorter roads to Flagstaff and Jerome. He always carried a pick and shovel, along on his trips and worked the road when he stopped to let the horses rest.

Feb. 17, 1902 the people of Red Rock and Sedona donated their time and money and started the work on what was then called the Rim Road or Munds Trail Road. On Aug. 27, 1902, the first wagon went over this road to Flagstaff. In later years the road was renamed Schnebly Hill.

Those Early Days…..

*Erwin Schuerman, hauling fruit to market before the days of motor trucks. About1912.*

A few years later, after they purchased the 160 acres from Tom Carrol, it had to be bought again, from the Atlantic and Pacific Railroad Co. After it was surveyed it was found to be railroad land.

Six children were born to the Schuerman family. They were Erwin, Clara, Helene, Henry, Fritz and Frieda. All were born at the ranch. Mrs. Schuerman had only the help of a midwife, who was Mrs. James, mother of Mrs. James Thompson. There was only one civilian doctor in the whole Verde Valley, Dr. Myron Carrier of the horse and buggy days, and who was impossible to get in time for a birth. The mid-wife came and stayed a couple of weeks before the birth.

When Erwin was six years old, a school was established - Red Rock School District #27 - in the fall of 1891. For many, many years the teachers boarded and roomed at the Schuerman home. Many happy times were spent there. Friends gathered for dances and church services there and in the schoolhouse.

Mother taught the scriptures from her German Bible to the children in the home. It was hard to translate it to the English.

Clara passed away with Cholera Infantam when she was 4½ years old. She was the first one buried in the Red Rock Cemetery. Dr. Myron Carrier picked the location in the pasture on Sept. 3, 1893.

On June 12, 1900, their first home burned down and everything was lost except a few pieces of the old furniture which was shipped from St. Louis, Mo. and a few things which Mother brought here from Germany such as some of her old bustle dresses which were a part of her trousseau. Everything else was lost. Again their good friends and neighbors came to help.

This time a strong rock house was built because they thought this would be safe. It was fireproof and over a quarter of a mile from the creek. But again in Feb. 1920 Oak Creek went on a rampage and washed away all the land up to the edge of the house. Another home had to be built. This time it was built higher up on the land where it was safe from high waters.

Henry Schuerman passed away Oct. 26, 1920 after a long illness and was laid to rest in the Cottonwood Cemetery by many of his old time friends and neighbors. Dorette lived in her new home until she passed away Aug. 4, 1940. She was also laid to rest in the Cottonwood Cemetery. Henry Schuerman, Jr. and family now live at this home. They have two daughters, one grand daughter and one grandson.

Erwin passed away June 21, 1929 in Jerome Hospital. He was also laid to rest in the Cottonwood Cemetery. His son, Fred, and family now reside at his home.

Helene Owenby passed away July 6, 1962 in a Prescott Hospital after a long illness of paralysis. She was also laid to rest in Cottonwood Cemetery, July 11th, on her mother's birthday. She had two daughters, four grandchildren and six great-grandchildren.

Fritz and his children live in Phoenix. He has a daughter, a son and seven grandsons.

Frieda and husband live in a little old homestead house and farm by the side of the road, which was homesteaded by her father in 1908. They have two children; a daughter in Phoenix, a son, who is a major in the Armed Forces, and five grandchildren.

An additional 40 acres was homesteaded across the creek in 1898. This is located southeast of the old place.

Since this was written, Henry Schuerman Jr. passed away in a rest home in Prescott, Arizona, May 8, 1967.

## MYSTERIOUS GRAVES
*by Albert E. Thompson*

Many of the Sedona Westerners are familiar with the graves of unknown persons in the Sedona area. There is some evidence of Americans in this area before the first settlement was made at Camp Verde. I have never heard of any written evidence of these people, but there is other evidence that cannot be overlooked.

When my Dad first came to Indian Gardens, in 1876, he said that he found two gold rockers near the creek in the vicinity of the present Rocky's Cottages. They were no doubt small enough to be carried on packhorses, but large enough to be much faster than a gold pan. Dad asked some of the very first settlers of Camp Verde if they knew anything about the rockers and none of them did.

In Daniel Ellis Conner's book, With The Walker Party in Arizona, he mentions several excursions, some of them many miles from the Prescott area. One mentioned was to the northeast of Prescott as far as the slope of San Francisco Peaks, where they had a battle with Indians. As Conner only relates his own story, it could easily have been that the other small groups could have ventured to this area and had battles with Indians, and Conner made no mention of them.

There is pretty good evidence, that Spanish prospectors and miners were in the Verde Valley, long before any Americans visited it. There are what is thought to be graves in many places scattered throughout the Verde Valley. Some of them could date back to the time of the Spaniards, others could have been American prospectors, and still others could have been after the army post of Camp Verde was established.

I know of only one grave on upper Oak Creek that there is any certainty that it is the grave of an American.

When the Purtymun family were excavating to build a house at the present Junipine Ranch, they dug into a grave. There were metal buttons, an iron lash cinch hook and a small piece of baling wire. Dan Purtymun told me that the skeleton was thought to be that of a civilian rather than that of a soldier.

Not far from there, in Barney Pasture, is a place known now as East Pocket that was once known as Dead Man Point. Several old timers have told me that there were several graves there, and I believe there was evidence that they were soldiers' graves.

Almost all of this is speculation, and the best answer yet is on the marker of the grave near Coffee Pot: Quen Sabe? Who knows.

## A FOREST RANGER'S EXPERIENCE IN SEDONA
*by Fred W. Croxen 1st*

Request has been made that I quote my duties and experiences while District Forest Ranger in charge of the Munds Park-Sedona District, on the Coconino National Forest. This was from May 1912 until October 1915.

Conditions were much different back in those days than they are at the present time. There were no automobiles or trucks. All transportation was by saddle horse, packhorse and wagon. Each Ranger owned his saddle and pack animals. Teams and wagons were hired in construction work or to transport a Ranger and his family—providing he had a family—from one part of a forest to another.

Forest Ranger Claude Thompson had been in charge of this district. Due to ill health, he had resigned and I was transferred from the Flagstaff District, where I had been Assistant Ranger, under Lewis E. Benedict. My personal possessions were few, consisting of camp equipment, bedroll and three saddle and packhorses.

This part of the Coconino was new to me, and I found my assignment much to my liking. I stopped at the new Munds Park Ranger Station. This was an entirely new station. House, of two rooms, and barn were of un-peeled logs and shake roof. Mr. and Mrs. Fred H. Grant were there, he being the Fire Guard that year.

From the Munds Park Ranger Station I rode to the John Loy ranch and met these fine people. They directed me to the road to Sedona. When I came to the Rim, at the top of the Schnebly Grade Road, I was amazed to see such a wonderful view of the Red Rocks below me and the view across the Verde Valley with the Black Range beyond the valley. The six-mile ride down the Grade, as it was called, was one of continuous and unsurpassed scenery.

At the Sedona Ranger Station, a day was spent with Claude Thompson. He acquainted me with work throughout the district. He then left for Flagstaff and I was on my own.

The Oak Creek Pool Roundup was on, and I joined it at their camp in Little Park, east of the Henry Schuerman Ranch. It being my desire to become acquainted with the local stockmen (grazing permitted), and to secure knowledge of that part of the District below the Mogollon Rim. So, I threw in with the roundup.

"Biscuit Bill" Dickinson was roundup boss. I believe Walt Van Deren or Dick Mason was the cook. A regular chuck wagon

## Those Early Days.....

with a drop leaf chuck box, sixteen inch Dutch-ovens, large pots, pans, and coffee pot and pot rack was the cook's domain. Those whom I can recall being on this roundup were: Charlie Dickinson, one of Johnny Lee's sons, Bill Loy, Joe Lay, Ira Hart, Haydee Lane, Edgar Page, Harry Stephens, Fritz Schuerman, "Pretty Bill" Back, from Beaver Creek, Alf Dickinson, Con Fredericks, Dutch Dickison and a "D K" man, who was "rep" for the "Windmill" outfit and the MAT's. I do not recall who was wrangling the remuda that year. All horses except the night horses were hobbled out over in Big Park Pass. Some took their beds over there so they could wrangle earlier. It's a real job, or chore, to hobble 75 or 80 or more horses every night and un-hobble them the next morning. It took two burlap sacks to hold these rope hobbles.

    The next move was to Sedona. Camp was made under the big cottonwoods on the east side of the creek, just below the Joe Farley Fruit Ranch. This was the last roundup camp. Grasshopper Flat and all the country east to Woods Canyon was worked. Cattle were drifted up the Schnebly Grade and up through Jack's Canyon. Quite a few had already headed up for the summer range, always with a mother cow in the lead; the bulls taking their own lazy time. After reaching the top, different outfits cut their brands from the bunches and trailed them to their respective ranges. The same in the fall, cattle drifting down to the winter range - an old mother cow always in the lead. This was true with every bunch, large or small.

    I would like to tell about the Sedona Ranger Station. This was a small two room Arizona Cypress log building, with a small fireplace in the west end. The location was on the south side of Soldier Wash and across from Soldier Point, where the details of soldiers, from Camp Verde, had camped. It was built by Billy Wallace, one of the first ten Forest Rangers on the Coconino National Forest. Billy had learned the carpenter trade from his father, as well as being a good cowboy. He was one of Teddy's Rough Riders and received a wound in the charge of San Juan Hill, in Cuba, in 1898.

    The barn at the Sedona Ranger Station was a very old log building with a pole corral adjoining. This was not far from the Sedona Hotel and horses were watered there or taken to Oak Creek. Domestic water was taken from an irrigation ditch that ran in front of the station.

    During the summer months, the principal duties of the district, was watching for and working on any forest fires that might break out. These were caused by lightning, this being in the pine timber and volcanic malapai formation area. We did surveying, by compass, and pasture and water developments. Several homesteads were on the district and annual reports had to be submitted pertaining to cultivation, improvements and residence on each homestead site. The telephone line from Flagstaff to Camp Verde was maintained by the District Ranger. This was soft 12 gauge copper wire easily broken. The poles in the pine timber area were pine poles, and under the Rim was of Arizona Cypress. Neither, the best for telephone lines.

During the First World War, this copper wire was valued at several thousands of dollars, because of the scarcity of copper. Due to the lack of other wire (iron) to replace it and to the scarcity of labor nothing was ever done about it.

Another duty of the District Ranger was the handling of cord wood sales. Several Mexican woodcutters had sales on Black Mountain. These were of Utah Juniper wood only. After cutting this wood, it was packed to the vicinity of Clarkdale and racked in long tiers. Every three or four weeks a trip was made there, and this wood was measured. The woodcutters left payment for the sales with Lyons Grocery store in Jerome, and contracts left there, because of uncertainty, of contacting these parties. These were good hard working Mexicans. They had good pack outfits and their burros were always in good condition. (Years later, while working along the U.S. Mexican border, it was much different. Mexican woodcutters packed wood into the border towns on the Mexican side of the border (International Line). All too often these burros were abused, under-fed and their backs one solid sore. When they drifted onto the U.S. side of the line, they disappeared, which was a blessing for these poor animals. I saw this while a Border Patrolman.) The wood cut on Black Mountain was sold in Clarkdale, Cottonwood and Jerome. This was unusually hard work and I doubt if many Americans would have done it.

During the winter months, the Ranger's work was similar, although there were no forest fires in the Juniper and Cypress types of timber. The telephone line had to be maintained. This line was originally built by the Overland Telephone Co., and was later turned to the U.S. Forest Service because of financial difficulties. The line was quite often used by other than forest officials, which was a real accommodation to all.

The Sedona settlement was small and all lived on ranches nearby. The owners grew fruit, vegetables and alfalfa hay. The

## Those Early Days.....

Sedona Hotel was owned and operated by Charles Stemmer and his mother; but was sold later to George W. and Stella Black. Across the Soldier Wash, on Soldier Point, lived Mr. and Mrs. Johnny Lay. After this good woman passed away, the ranch was sold to the Lee Van Deren family. Approximately one mile north on the west side of Oak Creek, lived the Frank Owenby family. They had cattle in Dry Creek and branded ONB.

On the east side of the creek, Joe and Mrs. Farley had a homestead and developed a fine fruit ranch. Farther down the creek was the Elijah and Dave Lay ranch. This was later sold to Mr. and Mrs. Ed Hart. Farther down the creek was the Ambrosio and Tommy Chavez's ranch. Their parents lived with them. They were descendants of early Spanish-Americans from New Mexico. On down was the "Dad" and Mrs. Dumas ranch. Below it was the Henry Schuerman vineyard. The last three named ranches were in what is called the Red Rock School District.

In order to take advantage of the Sedona Public School, Joe and Inez Lay had a winter home nearby. Their summer home was at Willard Spring, a few miles north of Munds Park. One winter, Ben Taylor and family made their home at Sedona and sent their children to this school.

Six miles up Oak Creek, at Indian Gardens, the Jim Thompson and Purtymun families had their homes. These folks were real old settlers and were among the first families to settle in Oak Creek Canyon. Several of their children attended the school at Sedona.

The principle means of entertainment was the dances held at the schoolhouses at Sedona and Red Rock. Local music was made by Walt Van Deren, a fiddler, Frank Derrick, also a fiddler (left handed), Jess Purtymun and Albert Thompson who played accordions. Waltzes, two steps and Varsouvians, with some doing the polka and schottish were the sets at that time. Occasionally a square dance set was a change.

Come Christmas and the teacher, Edith Lamport, gave a fine entertainment at the Sedona School. All the pupils did their parts well and the real Christmas entertainment was enjoyed by all. Most dances had a potluck supper with coffee made over an open fire outside the school building.

I can remember cutting a 14 foot spruce tree up on the side of Munds Mountain one year and packing it down for the Christmas tree. The school decorated it nicely and many gifts were dispensed to all the pupils with candy, etc. for all those present.

One night, the teacher, Miss Lamport and I, rode up to Indian

Gardens to talk with Jim Thompson about the Christmas program. Several of their children attended the Sedona School. The night was really dark and we were returning on the road, which at that time followed around the base of Steam-Boat Rock, a big rock, perhaps several, let loose above us. Then it was, leave there in a hurry or maybe get hit. Fortunately, the rocks came down behind us. Until one has heard or experienced a rockslide, one can't realize the terrific noise accompanying it.

One winter, Asst. Supervisor Thomas McCullough and I made a pack trip up into Sycamore Canyon. It is hard to realize just how rough and brushy this canyon really is. The trail took us out on the west side of the canyon and across Cow Flat. We camped there one night. Water was really scarce and cattle came in to water all hours of the day and night. I have never seen anything like it. It certainly was strong for camp use. Then the trail dropped off into Cherry Creek before coming back into the main Sycamore Canyon. At the rim of Cherry Creek were several rock monuments that had been used by the Indians for defensive purposes while their women and children made it down to the rough country as the soldiers were hot after them. This was in 1875, prior to removing the Indians to San Carlos. (Now, in 1966, Sycamore Canyon is a wilderness area, because of its beauty.)

Back in the days of which I am writing, before parcel post, the mail was carried by saddlehorses from Cornville, Arizona on lower Oak Creek. Each patron had a small mail sack in which the mail was placed. This sack was hung on a post or placed in a box at its destination. The mail rider gathered them on his return trip and hung each over the saddle horn as he came to them. The Post Office was at the Jim Thompson ranch at Indian Gardens, six miles above Sedona settlement. The mail riders, during my three and one-half years at Sedona, were Tom Hunt, a nephew of Mrs. Lee Van Deren and Wallace Willard of the early day Willard family in the Verde Valley. He also was one of Teddy's Rough Riders and was in the charge up San Juan Hill in Cuba.

Back in those days few travelers came through the Oak Creek country. As a rule they were looked upon with suspicion, until they were found to be reliable. A Mexican horse thief was apprehended on lower Oak Creek. At another time a Mexican, riding a large black horse, shot and killed old man Mulligan, without cause. His two small sons were in camp waiting for their father to come in with the team of horses he had gone to wrangle. The Mexican was not apprehended.

The fall of 1912, Camp Verde put on a Fair. Never having

Those Early Days.....

been to this old army post it was called "The Post" by local old timers, I just had to attend. Before reaching "The Post", I fell in with a troop of the 7th Cavalry. It was marching from Fort Apache, on the White Mountain Indian Reservation, to Phoenix, to take part in the Arizona State Fair. It camped at this old army post overnight. I believe this was the last Cavalry troop to visit this old "Post" that had been such an important part in helping to suppress the Indian and outlaw troubles in bygone days.

This Fair was a regular old timer's celebration. Many people were dressed in early day costumes. There were horse races, bronc ridings and other sports. In the evenings, a dance was held in one of the old adobe army barracks and was well attended. One of the exhibits that attracted my attention most was a big grizzly bear hide stretched on the side of one of the buildings. This bear had been killed by George Goswick, a well known hunter and trapper.

I took several pictures at this Fair with my little old Vest-pocket Kodak. One was of a fine gray team and new wagon owned and driven by George Casner, from the Casner Ranch, on Beaver Creek. Fifty years later I had enlargements made of this outfit. One was given to his daughter, Mrs. Butler, and another to the Fort Verde Museum, where it can be seen by museum visitors. That was in the buckboard, wagon and saddle horse days. Ranchers came from all directions and camped whereever it was convenient. An enjoyable time was had by all.

The springs of 1913 and 1914, I was detailed much to my disgust, to count the sheep on the Grief Hill driveway. This was down at old Beaver Head, as they drifted from the desert winter range to the summer range on the Coconino, Sitgraves and Apache National Forests. There were sheep by the thousands on the Forest ranges then.

I think it was the spring of 1915, a little German committed suicide, by drowning himself, in Oak Creek. He felt badly because Germany had started what we now know as World War I. He knew the United States was bound to get into it. A cook by profession, in hotels and restaurants, he took the job of cooking for the crew who were repairing the road from Sedona to Munds Park. Here he used Dutch-ovens and he was forever burning himself with them. Several thoughtless kids were in the crew, who continually teased him about the Reiser's war. All this brought on despondence and we found where he had sat and attempted to cut large arteries in his ankles. The odd part was a depression in the soil that looked as though it had been made by his chin. Later, it was found to be a heel mark instead of the chin. Lead by Joe Farley, who in his younger days, had been a hired trailer for the Texas Rangers, along the Rio Grande, he was trailed to a deep water hole in the creek. A ledge of rock protruded out over the opposite side and he had dived under that. Sheriff Bill Dickinson, was in the party and dived in and brought out the body. His remains were taken to what was known as "Chimney Flat" and buried near the center of this flat. The burial place is now lost and is covered by a residential section of Sedona.

Often times in going from Sedona to Munds Park, I rode up Oak Creek to Indian Gardens and then up what is known as "Thompson's Ladder". It was well named and did shorten the distance between these two places by several miles. I often wonder, now in 1966, if it is still used.

I liked the Munds Park-Sedona District and the people who lived there. Honest, hard working and honorable. I regretted leaving but one in U.S. Government Service is not free and is transferred elsewhere eventually. This happened to me.

I'll always remember that beautiful pine timber and red rock country and those fine folks who lived there. Many are now departed to the Great Beyond, but memory of them still remains with those of us who are still here.

Wouldn't it be wonderful if we could live these old days over - just as they were then! "Them was the days", as the old saying goes.

The above article was written at the request of Albert Thompson, of "Indian Gardens", Sedona, Arizona with the idea of reading it before the Westerners group of that place. Much more or less could have been written. However, this is an outline of duties and experiences of my days on the Munds Park-Sedona Ranger District. Times and conditions have changed so have Sedona and Munds Park, More people, better roads, and automobiles have replaced the buckboards, wagons and saddle and pack animals.

Albert was one of the pupils of the Sedona School. The teacher, who later became Mrs. Croxen, said, "I had a time to keep him occupied as he did his assigned studies so easily. I started him reading the encyclopedia and he read them through.

Those Early Days.....

## THE WINTER OF THE DEEP SNOW
### or The Schoolmarm's Dilemma
*by Edith Lamport Croxen*

The story that I have been asked to relate has to do with the big snowstorm during the Holiday Season of 1915 - 1916. At that time I was teaching the public school, at Sedona, Arizona, situated in the beautiful Red Rock and Oak Creek country. There were between thirty and thirty-five pupils attending and all grades from the first through the eighth were being taught in that one room. That did not leave time for much individual attention, so at times the pupils of the upper grades helped with the younger pupils. All were very busy so discipline was no problem.

As had been done the preceding year, we prepared and gave a long Christmas program at the schoolhouse with all the boys and girls taking their parts in plays and recitations. After all of these years, I recall with a great deal of pleasure how hard they worked and how proud their parents were of them.

Our beautiful Christmas tree was a tall spruce and was splendid in its tinsel and other decorations. We had all taken part in making it beautiful from the first grade to the eighth grade pupils. Candy, popcorn balls and gifts under the tree made eyes sparkle. Our Santa was one of the local fathers, all dressed in his red suit with white trimming, who talked to the youngsters and distributed their gifts in a way pleasing to all. My gift was a book to each child.

Of course, our program was followed by the usual dance in which every one took part. A variety of old-time dances were enjoyed by all. I still like the Varsouvian, or 'Tut Your Little Foot Down", Waltz and two steps. At mid-night a fine lunch was served. The coffee had been made in a five-gallon can, over an open fire outside. The musicians made music pleasing to all. These were of local talent, Frank Derrick, the left handed fiddler, Walter W. Van Deren, another fiddler, Jesse Purtymun, played the accordion and Albert Thompson played the accordion, too. There may have been others whose names have slipped my memory after these fifty long years. The program, dance and lunch, were enjoyed by all who were there.

After all the good time, which lasted until the wee small hours, the little ones who had been sleeping, were awakened by their fond parents. Then all departed for their separate homes, tired and happy. All agreed it was a fine Christmas party; in fact, one of the best.

My home was in Flagstaff, where I was born, and it was my desire to spend the Holidays there with my parents, brothers and sister. It was necessary that I take the train from Clarkdale, around by Drake and Ashfork to Flagstaff. A long, but restful ride. George W. Black, who with his fine wife, Stella, owned and operated the Sedona Hotel and fruit ranch, with whom I had room and board, took me to Clarkdale, on horse back. Being crowded for time, since trains fail to wait for schoolmarms, Mr. Black took a shortcut, or route, across the White Hills, to Clarkdale. He had ridden over the Red Rock and White Hills country since a boy and knew it like the palm of his hand. After seeing that I was safely aboard the train, he returned to Sedona, taking my horse back with him. (This horse was a very gentle animal, of good breeding. It had been purchased from Dr. Mack O. Dumas who owned the TV cattle outfit. The Doctor, now retired from dentistry, resides at Cottonwood, Arizona, with his wife, who at that time was, Miss Lenore Francis, Superintendant of Schools, of Coconino County.)

While vacationing with my family at Flagstaff, there came a three-day snowstorm, leaving a snow fall of sixty-four inches on the level. Then the sky cleared and the mercury went down to 25 degrees below zero. On the streets of Flagstaff, practically all transportation stopped. The Santa Fe Railroad was finally plowed open in time for me to leave for Clarkdale at the end of my vacation.

This unusual snowstorm left a snowfall of two feet on the level all over the Verde Valley. As a result practically all normal travel had to stop here the same as it had in the Flagstaff country, above the Mogollon Rim. As a result, the Sedona schoolmarm was taken in by "Grandma" Willard of Cottonwood for a stay of three days. Being young and conscientious and Sedona my first school, I was greatly worried about not returning on schedule.

Finally, a Mr. Worthington, learned of my plight. He said, "Your father, James A. Lamport, Coconino County Surveyor, once did me a muchly appreciated favor, at the Grand Canyon. This is a good time to return it. I have a team and buckboard and will take you to Sedona." The snow was still two feet deep and crusted. We started by the regular route across White Flat. After crossing the Verde River, at Bridgeport, the road was not to be seen. Mr. Worthington then said, "I do not know this country very well and with no roads to be seen, I do not feel we should take

## Those Early Days.....

the risk of getting off the regularly traveled road". He turned towards Cornville, Arizona, on lower Oak Creek and to the Johnny Hearst Ranch, whose family I had known in Flagstaff. This was indeed a favor to a conscientious stricken schoolmarm.

After waiting two or three days at the Hearst ranch, they loaned me a saddle horse. I rode on to Sedona, accompanying the mail carrier, Wallace Willard. This was indeed a long day. Much of the trail, or road, had not been opened and our horses had to flounder through this crusted snow, which was as deep there as it had been on the level, from Cottonwood to the Hearst ranch. To save the horses, we took turns breaking trail, first Mr. Willard taking the lead and then my horse and me. It was tough going.

We rode into Sedona at about 9:00 P.M., tired after this long and wearing day of approximately twenty (20) snow covered miles. To our surprise we saw lights at the schoolhouse. Riding to this lighted school, we found that the local Sedona folks had gotten together and a dance was in progress. They were really surprised to see us, as no one had been out of Sedona since the beginning of this big storm. Two other schoolmarms, who had come to Sedona, from Adamana, Arizona, for the Christmas Holidays, were still there and attending the dance. In a day or two they left with the mail carrier. I think Lloyd Van Deren, accompanied them, as one, or both, were guests at the Van Deren home. Then Lloyd brought the saddle horses back to the ranch.

This storm was a real experience, particularly that part from "Grandma" Willard's to the Hearst ranch and on up Oak Creek to Sedona. At the time, I was really worried all because of being unable to return to my school at a given time. Now - - after fifty (50) years have gone by, I look back on this as just another experience, and can smile at it.

Each and every one was so considerate of the young schoolmarm in her attempt to reach her snowed in school. Most of these kind friends have departed to their just Rewards, after these fifty years. I wish it were possible to again thank them at this time for being so kind and considerate of me, the Sedona schoolmarm, from 1914 to 1916.

## MORE ABOUT THE BIG SNOW STORM
*by Albert E. Thompson*

As I have a rather clear recollection of the Snowstorm that Mrs. Croxen has written about, I would like to make a few comments.

At the Thompson home at Indian Gardens the snow measured 37 inches on the level. I do not remember what the depth was in Sedona, but it must have been nearly 3 feet.

After the mail carrier, Wallace Willard, broke trail to Indian Gardens with his mule, I started out to walk to Sedona, so I would not miss any school. I was staying with my brother, Frank at the present Walter Jordan place. The old road followed around the foot of Steamboat Rock at that time. Where the mule had climbed up a slope, I had no trouble at all going down. Where the mule came down hill, I had to go uphill. The mule took mighty long steps coming downhill, and I just could not step that far in the deep snow. I had to almost crawl from one mule track to another. I made it but I was tired, putting it mildly.

As the Sedona post office was at Indian Gardens at that time, the mail carrier had to go that far. Mrs. Croxen tells of the trip from Lower Oak Creek to Sedona but the carrier had to go on another five miles. It was long after dark when he got near the house. The heavy snow had broken a lot of big limbs from the oak trees. These limbs blocked the road and broke the fence down. In the dark and deep snow, the mule got over on the wrong side of the fence and came to the house on the inside. Wallace did not know where he was but he trusted his mule. There was a log cross fence that the mule came to, but she was headed toward her supper and rest. She jumped the low fence and Wallace fell off in the snow. He got back on and came on to the house pretty excited. His mule brought him up to the yard, and Charley Thompson went out to get the mail. Wallace always talked in a very loud voice. We, in the house plainly heard him telling of his fall in the snow. He was so excited he yelled, "I jumped the fence and she fell off, and never did notice how he had said it. We kids thought that was pretty funny.

That big snow collapsed the movie theater in Flagstaff, and it smashed beams and hay sheds all over the Verde Valley and Oak Creek. I rather think it was the deepest fall of snow at one time since white folks have lived on Oak Creek. At least it was the deepest snow I ever saw here.

The following is the program of the Christmas entertainment

Those Early Days.....

the previous year of 1914. It was the same teacher who drilled and directed this mob of savages and had them almost letter perfect in their parts. There were a few changes in pupils in 1915 but was mostly the same gang.

Christmas Program:  Sedona School 1914

| | |
|---|---|
| SONG: Hark! The Herald Angels Sing | The School |
| The Mistletoe Bough | Linn Derrick |

Dialogue: CHRISTMAS GIFTS WE WILL GIVE

| | |
|---|---|
| Frances | Myrtle Taylor |
| Dorothy | Myrtle Nail |
| Estella | Minnie Farley |
| Gladys, (at home making ChristmasPresents) | Ethel Derrick |

RECITATIONS:

| | |
|---|---|
| My Dolly | Alice Bechtolt |
| Santa and the Mouse | Ethel Derrick |
| Piano Solo | Minnie Farley |
| Around the Christmas Tree | Greene Thompson |
| Song: Father Christmas | The School |

PLAY:  THE SUNSHINE SOCIETY

Scene one         Members of the Sunshine Society meet at Jennies' house
Scene two                    Mr. Grumps is at home as usual

Characters:

| | |
|---|---|
| Mr. Nathan Grump, a grumbler | Venn Derrick |
| Bridget, his servant girl | Pearl Guyton |
| Polly Filkins, who believes in Santa Clause | Iva Van Deren |
| Jennie, President of the society | Dolly Van Deren |

Committee on Christmas arrangements:

| | |
|---|---|
| Lucy | Ethel Derrick |
| Hattie | Lenore Hart |
| Mabel | Thelma Miller |

Willing workers in the good cause:

| | |
|---|---|
| Agnes | Ruth Miller |
| Tom | Greene Thompson |
| John | Linn Derrick |
| Henry | Earl Van Deren |

Recitations, Bennie Taylor

| | |
|---|---|
| The Stripped Stocking | Pearl Guyton |
| A Christmas Carol | Viola Taylor |
| Christmas day at the workhouse | Dolly Van Deren |
| Song: The Saviors Birthplace | The School |
| Dialogue | The Littlest Boy |
| The Burglar | Albert Thompson |
| The Littlest Boy | Joe Derrick |
| Big Brother | Linn Derrick |

Those Early Days.....

| | |
|---|---|
| Piano Solo | Mary Farley |
| Recitation, The Star of Bethlehem | Lenore Hart |
| Duet, Vocal | Dolly & Iva Van Deren |
| Santa's Assistant | Mabel Guyton |
| Santa Claus | Perry Van Deren |
| A Christmas Eve Thought | Alice Lay |
| Dialogue: | Poor Papa's Christmas Neckties |
|     Mama Keane | Iva Van Deren |
|     Papa Keane, a curious martyr | Linn Derrick |
|     Maude | Ruth Miller |
|     Ben & Dorothy, who love their father | Greene Thompson & Lenore Hart |
| Recitation | Mary Farley |
| Anna's and Willie's prayer | Iva Van Deren |
| Duet, Instrumental | Linn Derrick & Albert Thompson |

PLAY: GRANDPA'S CHRISTMAS STOCKING
Act 1. The Night Before Christmas
Act 2. Grandpa's Stocking is Filled
Act 3. Santa has come and all are happy
Characters:

| | |
|---|---|
|     Grandma & Grandpa, who have all of their grandchildren spending the holidays with them | Dolly Van Deren & Albert Thompson |
|     Phillip, their eldest grandson | Linn Derrick |
|     Elsie | Pearl Guyton |
|     Harry | Earl Van Deren |
|     May | Iva Van Deren |
|     Ted | Ted Guyton |
|     Bess, the smallest | Mabel Guyton |
|     I is Olive, whose other name is sweetheart | Mary Farley |
|     Jotham, who is willing to work | Venn Derrick |
| Just Before Christmas | Earl Van Deren |
| CHRISTMAS HYMN, Holy Night | By the School |
|     Santa and the Christmas Tree | |

Mrs. Croxen failed to mention that in 1915-16 school year she had along with her eight regular grades, a class of four 9th graders. I know because I was one of them.

Some few of these pupils have already crossed The Great Divide. Some who are still living are scattered far and wide, and a mere handful are still living in Sedona. In 1915 we did not have the Taylor children, nor the Farley children nor the Millers but, we gained the Smiths (Charley and Ira are still here) and we had the Blacks. Ed Black is still with us, and some others who were only temporary residents. Among them was the Fenstermaker family.

That has been quite a while ago, but I look back on those days with happy memories.

Those Early Days.....

## EARLY BUILDERS OF SEDONA
*by Inez Lay*

John Lay, his wife, America, known as "Aunt Mack", to her friends and neighbors, and their daughter Jennie, came to Lower Verde from Tennessee in the 1880s. Later a nephew, Dave Lay came to them.

Elijah Lay, Dave's father was never satisfied in Tennessee after Dave left home. As soon as he could gather his crops and sell his home the next year, he and his wife Mary and five children embarked on what was called an immigrant train from Jasper, Tennessee.

In those days an immigrant train would take your belongings right along with you.

They arrived in Prescott, Arizona, on March 22, 1892. They still had two days more to travel before reaching the Verde Valley. They found land to rent and were soon farming again in a new country to them. After two years they moved to Camp Verde and lived in part of the adobe buildings that are now the Fort Verde Museum.

After two more years they moved to Oak Creek and homesteaded 40 acres in the Cornville area. Later they sold that farm and bought another place up the creek a ways.

Joe Lay was a boy of eight years when the family came to Arizona. He soon decided that he wanted to be a cowboy. A neighbor gave him a "doggie" calf and when his father's cow had twin calves, his father gave them to him, together with a white heifer, so Joe was in the cattle business.

When the big snow of December 1898 came, Joe put his cattle in the cornfield and they all died from eating smut on the corn.

After losing his whole herd, Joe irrigated the alfalfa fields while his father worked away from home, and saved enough money to buy more cattle. His brand at that time was ⊼ and called T F open A. Soon afterward he had matrimonial ideas and had to sell his cattle to get money to build a house on the place his father had bought.

Later he bought the ℧ called Flying U Quarter Circle, brand from William Loy. I guess the daughter was included in the deal, for on December 23, 1906. Joe Lay and Inez Loy were married in the yard of their home.

In 1908, the family made another move, this time to Sedona. Elijah Lay homesteaded forty acres on the east side of the creek, south of the bridge and Joe took forty acres joining it farther down.

They built two houses on those homesteads.

The same year Charley Stemmer bought the Schnebly place and the Lays rented it from him. John Lay moved his wife to Sedona and Dave Lay also came. Aunt Mack suffered a stroke and she was moved into the Schnebly Hotel and a Mrs. Brown stayed with them to care for her and take care of the post office.

Dave and John Lay soon bought land and built the house where Mrs. L.E. Hart now lives. Soon Mrs. Brown got married and the post office was moved to the new house and the William Loy family came to take care of Aunt Mack and the post office. The mail came only twice a week and "Uncle Charley" Rutledge carried it in a saddle pouch on his saddle horse.

By this time there were getting to be so many families with children that a school was needed. After getting the district organized, the families that had wagons all got together and hauled enough lumber down from Flagstaff in one trip to build a one-room schoolhouse. The building was also built by the people.

The pupils of the first school in Sedona were Lloyd, Dolly and Iva Van Deren, Myron, Edward and Lindsay Loy, Henry and Lum Farley, Lewis Thompson and Frank Owenby. Miss Georgia Tomlinson was the first teacher. She was quite a young girl and it was too lonely for her and she soon resigned. Claude Thompson was the Forest Ranger in Sedona at that time and his wife, Olga, took over as teacher. Her baby was quite small and she had trouble getting someone to care for it so she had to give up teaching and Charley Stemmer had to finish the term.

Elijah and Joe Lay sold their homesteads to L.E. Hart and his son, Ed, about 1913, and sold the U Flying U cattle to Ira Hart. Soon afterwards they bought the 2 called Figure two Bar, cattle and the Clay Park ranch from Walt and Lee Van Deren. Clay Park was known later as Fox-borough ranch and later became Takaloma Lodge.

C.B. Wilson, an attorney in Flagstaff, said at the time, if it were not for the fellows south of town trading so much he would starve to death.

The Clay Park ranch was a wonderful place to live, but it had one problem. Joe Lay's daughter, Alice, was now old enough to go to school, so another house had to be built in Sedona, near the school. George Black leased us a building site across the creek below the bridge, for one dollar a year. Then we ran into another problem. The bridge was not completed yet and when the water was too high to cross on horseback, there was a cable

Those Early Days.....

*Pool Wagon roundup in 1914 at Clay Park, at present called Foxboro. Cowboys are branding calves. The two men in the foreground are; one on the right, Alf Dickenson, and the one on the left, Joe Lay.*

stretched between two trees across the creek and a wheelbarrow tied to pulleys that ran on the cable. The children would be pulled across that way. Imagine the anxiety of the parents seeing their children being suspended above the churning water!

In 1917 the Lay families sold their ranch and 2 Figure two cattle to Fred and Les Mickle, and the William Loy family sold their interest in the X L cattle and the two families bought adjoining farms at Cornville. The senior Loys and Lays spent the rest of their lives there.

After living on the Cornville ranch forty-five years and raising and educating seven children, the Joe Lays moved to Cottonwood, Arizona to a retirement home. On December 23, 1966, Joe and Inez Lay celebrated their sixtieth wedding anniversary.

We are very proud of our twenty-one grandchildren and nineteen great-grandchildren.

We still look back with pride at the part we were able to contribute to the building of Sedona, the place that is so well advertised as a place to live now.

## THEY WERE TOUGH IN THOSE DAYS
*by Albert E. Thompson*

In the 1890s and early 1900s there were lots of wild horses scattered over the ranges of the Verde Valley.

When the young cowboys of that time had some spare time they would chase wild horses for sport. Sometimes they could catch an unbranded young horse that could be tamed and broken and become a valued saddle horse.

One Sunday in wintertime, a neighbor boy, Lute Hart, came to the Dumas Ranch near Cornville, looking for diversion or merely something to pass the time. Lute Hart is an old time cowboy who is taking it easy in the Pioneer's home in Prescott, Ariz. now.

Dr. M.O. Dumas was a young fellow then about the same age that Lute was. Lute was riding an old horse that was past his prime in life. Dumas had a young horse that he had just broken, that was a top horse but he would still buck at every opportunity if not watched closely. He suggested that Lute turn his old horse into the barn lot and catch this horse and they would go up to the red rocks country north of the Windmill Ranch and chase wild horses.

The suggestion was taken. They made a long ride and ended up on the Black Mountain between the Windmill Ranch and the Verde River. They dismounted there to look the country over below them. Lute told Dumas that the horse was perfectly gentle and would not buck. Dumas agreed that the horse was gentle, but told Lute to watch him close. As they started to mount their horses again on the rocky hillside, Lute got careless. He did not watch the horse and before he got his seat in the saddle, the horse started bucking down the mountainside. He threw Lute over his head and Lute lit on his head and shoulders in the rocks.

Doc Dumas was concerned for fear that Lute had been hurt bad. When he helped him up he said, "Did it hurt you Lute?" Lute said, "No it did not hurt me any. I just drove the rocks into the ground a little farther."

Those Early Days.....

## ANOTHER OAK CREEK OLD TIMER
*Ambrosio Chavez as told to Albert E. Thompson*

Ambrosio Chavez first came to Upper Oak Creek seventy-two years ago, when he was only seven years old.

His father, Manuel Chavez grew up at Santa Fe, New Mexico. When the Apache wars were being waged in the Southwest in the 1860s and 1870s he joined the army as a scout and guide. He guided at least one detachment of New Mexico Volunteers to the army post of Fort Verde in the 1870s. He traveled over a lot of Northeastern Arizona as a scout and guide and liked Arizona as a place to live.

While he was still in the army service he married at Santa Fe and his first children were born there. At that time, St. Johns, Arizona was a Spanish American settlement named San Juan. Colonists of the L.D.S. Church, under Jacob Hamblin, later bought most of the land from the Spanish-speaking residents and Americanized the name. Manuel Chavez moved his family from Santa Fe to St. Johns, Arizona while it was still mostly a Spanish Speaking settlement. Ambrosio doesn't know whether his father was still in Government service at that time or not. He did state definitely that while his father had been sent to Camp Verde more than once he was never stationed there.

Ambrosio was born in St. Johns, Arizona in March 1888. While he was still a baby his father moved the family to Flagstaff, Arizona. They lived at that place almost seven years. Manuel Chavez worked in the logging camps with his teams, skidding and hauling logs.

Juan Armijo, who was a friend of the Chavez family had come to Oak Creek in the meantime and filed on a homestead. Armijo's son later married a daughter of Manuel Chavez. Three years after the Armijo family came to Oak Creek the Chavez family moved to Oak Creek also. Their first home was what is known now as the Bullard Ranch. It is the first homestead above the mouth of Dry Creek and the last homestead down the creek in the area that is generally thought of as Upper Oak Creek.

It was about 1895 when Mr. Chavez filed on that place. He had a patent to it by 1902 and he disposed of it to the husband of his oldest daughter, Juan Nuanez.

Ambrosio tells of going to school from their home there when the boys rode burros to the old Red Rock School District number 27. He and his two brothers rode to school there. He likes to tell of one morning when he had got almost to school and got a bad spill. He said that Erwin Schuerman had got to school ahead of him and hid in a patch of bushes. When Ambrosio rode around the bushes, Erwin jumped and scared his burro and it bucked him off in the rocks and skinned him up a bit and spilled his lunch. He jumped up and started for Erwin throwing rocks. Erwin ran into the schoolhouse and locked the door. He stayed there until the teacher got to school and by that time Ambrosio had had time to cool off so there was no battle.

Manuel Chavez had used his homestead rights on the place that he let Juan Nuanez have but he made a trade for the land where Ambrosio lives now. Dave James was squatting on the place. Chavez traded him an old wagon and a set of chain harness for his rights. The oldest son, Andrew, was old enough to homestead in a few years, but he married and moved to Flagstaff. The family lived on the place from 1902 until 1909 when Ambrosio was 21 years old and he homesteaded it.

Manuel Chavez drew an army pension from about 1902 until he died. Ambrosio tells of the trouble his father had trying to get the pension. At last the old man rode horseback from Oak Creek to St. Johns alone, after he was an old man to see a Spanish lawyer friend. His friend got the pension for him. Mr. Chavez was totally blind the last few years of his life.

Ambrosio had four sisters and two brothers. One sister, who was a widow, and his younger brother, Tommy, lived with the family on the ranch until after the father died, about 1912. The mother died in 1923.

Tommy was a cowboy and bronco rider. The Chavez family never had a very big bunch of cattle but Tommy punched cattle for other cattlemen and took care of the Chavez cattle as well. He was a good rider and he broke and trained horses for other cattlemen. When he was in the army in World War I he was in the remount service and put in all of his army service training horses for the army.

Ambrosio married Apolonia Peralta of Winslow, Arizona in 1918 while Tommy was still in the service. Tommy had taken a mountain homestead just before he went into the service. Ambrosio had to be cowboy in Tommy's place, while Tommy was gone and farmed his own place and Tommy's mountain ranch. He was a very busy man until his brother got home.

Ambrosio and his wife had two children. Ambrosio Jr., or Ambrose, lives in Phoenix. He was a soldier in World War II and served in Europe. He is married now and lives in Phoenix. They do not have any children. The daughter, Dora, is married and

## Those Early Days.....

lives in California. They have two children.

Ambrosio has sold part of his ranch for home sites, but still has enough left to keep a much younger man busy. His wife passed away a few years ago and he lives on the old place alone. He still farms and though his health is not so good, he still farms some. He says he wants to die in harness.

He and his brother, Andrew, who lives in California, are the only ones of the older generation of Chavez's who are still living.

## A TAPED INTERVIEW
*with Albert E. Thompson and Laura McBride*

"Uncle Albert what is the farthest back date you can remember?"

"It's kind of hard to tell what was the first thing that I remember, because there is no way to set the exact date of things I dimly recall. The farthest back date that I can remember is the 4th of July 1901. I got a finger nail mashed off and I rode a horse all by myself then. There was an all day picnic at the old log schoolhouse up the canyon and a dance that lasted till after sunup next morning. Frank Thompson and George Purtymun were in the schoolhouse sometime during the day, dancing together like big overgrown boys cut up sometimes. I was a little kid standing in the door watching them. I had a hand on each side of the doorway and they ran into the door and slammed it shut on my finger and mashed the nail off. I don't remember going to the picnic or anything else about the day. I don't remember anything about the dance. I suppose I slept through most of the night on a pallet bed someplace. I do remember coming home the next morning. Someone in the bunch had an old gray mare named Polly. She later belonged to Charley Rutledge, our first mail carrier to Sedona. He carried the mail on her for 8 years. Most of the folks must have wanted to walk coming home that morning, because they put me on the mare by myself and someone led her."

"What was the first town you remember going to?"

"The first trip I remember to any town was the fall of that same year, 1901, when I went to Jerome. I was four years old then and remember some parts of the trip quite clearly but other parts are a complete blank. The road was built up towards Indian Gardens as far as Wilson Canyon then and a wagon was kept there. Dad and Frank had packed a load of potatoes on packhorses out there the day before we started. They must have made several trips to get a wagonload for four horses out there. The wagon was loaded and already to go when Dad and Mom and Jim and Greene and I went out there early next morning. Frank went out that far to help us get started. He and Dad got the horses hitched up and we started, but our old pinto horse balked on the first hill we came to. They took the balky horse out and tied him to a tree and we started on with a three-horse spike team. We didn't go much farther till the wagon broke down. I don't know what part of it broke; a wheel or axle or what part but we had to stop. We had beds and camp outfits along but there was no water where the wagon

## Those Early Days.....

broke down.

    Frank was still with us and had his saddle horse, Rowdy, that he was going to ride back home. He rode back and got old Pinto and some saddles and we took the camp outfit and beds and went on to what is now Sedona. The Elijah Lay family was living on the ranch that the Schneblys had bought the spring before. They were the only people living there. We camped in their yard while Dad and Frank went back and fixed the wagon and brought it down. On the way down horseback, Mom was riding old Pinto sideways and carrying Greene in her arms. When we crossed Soldier Wash, just before we got to Lay's house, the saddle turned and dumped Mom and Greene on the ground. Greene was only about 18 months old then and he talked about "Old Pinto bucked in the creek" for months afterward. Mrs. Lay brought a big pot of bayou beans out to our camp because we were a little short on chuck.

    I don't remember anything else about the trip until we were in Jerome. We stayed all night at Munds' place, Mr. and Mrs. William Munds. Mr. Munds was the first Mayor of Jerome, and the father of John Munds who was Sheriff of Yavapai County at one time. Of course I did not know about any of them then. All that I remember was being in their house and that I liked Mr. Munds real well. The next morning we went to visit some friends named Irven or Irving. I don't know how the name was spelled. Anyway it was the Frank Irven family to me. They had a boy and a girl named Willie and Jessie. They were quite a lot older than we kids were. They took Jim on a trip to a store but the folks would not let me go. They said I was too little and I had to stay and play with Greene. I guess we did not have any more trouble of any kind coming home. I don't remember anything about the rest of the trip.

    My first trip to Flagstaff was in August 1903, two years after the Jerome trip. It was right after Clara and Ab got married; my sister and her husband Albert Purtymun. They were living at the old Pump House, the place the Pump House Canyon is named after. They came home one weekend. They came out to the top of Thompson Ladder Trail with a wagon and team. Ab unharnessed his team there and turned them loose to graze, and they walked down the trail. It was decided some time during the visit that Mom would take Greene and me and go back with them and spend a week. We got up early next morning and all of us walked up the trail. Ab went on ahead to hunt his horses and be all ready to go when we got on top. He didn't come in till noon and he did not have the horses then. We ate a lunch and he left again. It was 4 o'clock in the evening when he came in with the horses. I clearly remember that all of the open country on the mountain was covered with wild sunflowers and they were all in bloom. We did not get to the Pump House till long after dark. There came a pretty hard rain just before dark and we all got wet. One day while we were there, Ab took us all to Flagstaff. That was the first time I ever saw a railroad train. I don't remember much about what Flagstaff looked like then but I do remember being in Babbitt's store, and I remember that Mom bought an accordion. It was the one that I first learned to play a tune on".

"When did you first start to school and where was it?"

"I started to school in March 1902. I was about four and a half years old. The first two days I walked to the old log schoolhouse up the canyon from home. The Purtymun family had moved away from the creek by then and my folks decided to move the schoolhouse down closer to home. Frank and Dad started fixing up Frank's little log cabin. For two weeks we went to school in Grandma's tent. Frank's cabin was down near where Charley lives now. It was just a little bit of a cabin about 10 by 12 feet and had a dirt floor. We went the rest of the term in it and a short three months term there the next year. When we were going to school in the tent there came a snowstorm. I remember when we got out at noon to go home for dinner, Clara got me by one arm and Lizzie (my two sisters), got me by the other and they made a run for it. My feet touched the ground now and then. Miss Henrietta Dawson was the teacher."

"What was the weather like then? Was it any different than it is now?"

"The weather was just about the same then as it is now. Some years were dry with mild winters and others were very wet with lots of rain or snow. We had floods in the creek then at times the same as we do now. The main difference was that there were no bridges across any of the creeks or canyons. I remember one rainy winter - it must have been about 1901 or 1902, when the creek stayed up so long we ran out of flour. Dad and Frank started to go to Aultman, a little settlement at Middle Verde, where there was a store. It was on the east side of the river. They went down the east side of Oak Creek past present Sedona, but no one lived on the east side of the creek then. They went on out through Big Park. They were traveling horseback and had a packhorse to pack flour back on. They bogged some of the horses down in Big Park and when they got them out of the mud it was so late they decided to go over to Juan Armijo's place on Oak Creek and stay all night. They got a warm welcome from the

Those Early Days…..

*Front row left to right, Wm. Munds, Jim Thompson, Albert Thompson, Mrs. Thompson, Lizzie Thompson, Mrs. Munds, Jim Thompson, Charles Thompson, George Purtymun, Frank Thompson (standing), Fred Thompson is seated behind Albert and Clara Thompson is seated behind Mrs. Thompson.*

Armijo's and it happened that they had a good supply of flour on hand. Dad bought a hundred pounds of flour from them and they came home next day. We were all glad to see them back so soon. Mom had made a kind of bread while they were gone by taking a little flour and mixing a lot of eggs with it. I guess we had plenty of eggs and most other groceries except flour.

While we are talking about the weather I would like to put in my two cents worth about what the real old timers had to say about it. Some of them tell about the big snows every winter on the mountains and good summer rains every year and lots of good grass on the range. Then others tell of the awful dry spells when all of the springs and lakes on the mountain dried up and stockmen built trails to Oak Creek to water their stock. I think some of them just remembered dry years and others just remembered wet ones. I believe it was just about the same as it is now. We have dry cycles and wet ones.

There is one thing that I can see a big change in, ever since I can remember. That is the pine forests on the mountain. The National Forests or Forest Reserves as they were called at first, were just a few years old when I can first remember the mountain country. There had never been any fire control at all up to the time of the first Forest Reserves. There was not much fire hazard because there was not much to burn. The forests looked like well kept parks, mostly just big trees with grass sod all underneath and very little undergrowth. There were fires some place on the forest every year but they did not do much harm. They just burned off the dry grass and the few pine needles and went out by themselves. Now the young pines are so thick you can't even crawl through them in places. I have seen them so thick and tall that the winter's snows mashed them flat like a field of grain. In places there is no grass sod left and there is a mat of pine straw on the ground a foot deep. When that gets on fire it kills everything."

"Did you have many dances when you were little?"

"We always had a dance on the 4th of July. Before the road was finished to the ranch, the fellows used to haul a load of lumber out to the top of Thompson Ladder trail. Then they would nail 5 or 6 planks together and put a chain around one end of them and drag them down the trail with horses. The outside boards got roughed up some but the inside was still slick enough to dance on. They would build a platform out under the trees and the 4th of July dances always lasted till after sunup next morning. On the 4th of July 1905, I have heard Mom say that there were 75 people at the house for midnight supper. There were always lots of firecrackers popping all day long the 4th, and big shots of dynamite now and then through the day, especially just at the break of day. Dad liked to celebrate the 4th and he had lots of help. Of course that was long before I was big enough to play for dances but there was always music of some kind. Mr. Dumas played the fiddle for many a dance. John James or Jess Purtymun played the accordion if they were around. Some of the summer fishermen were musicians. When the summer people came to camp and fish we had dances most every weekend. There was always a dance somewhere around at Christmas time. Some of them were so far away not many of the family attended them."

"Did you always attend summer school?"

"No, the last summer school when I was a kid was in 1906. We lost the district because there were not enough kids to keep it going. We missed all of 1907 and in the late fall of 1908 we moved to Red Rock to go to school. We went three terms or parts of terms there. Five months was the longest we ever went to school there and the last year was only three months. Six months was a full school year then. The Sedona School was started in 1910, the last year we went to Red Rock. Jim and Greene and I went to Sedona

Those Early Days.....

School a few months in 1911 and in 1912. The first year we drove a buggy from Indian Gardens and the next year we went horseback. We had to quit by the middle of January because of high water or bad weather. I was in the second grade for three years and when I finally got to the third grade I went right on to the sixth grade that same year. It depended a lot on what kind of a teacher I had."

"When was your first job away from home?"

"I believe that was in 1913; I was about 15 and a half years old. I worked four days for Dan Purtymun, up at the old Purtymun ranch. That's the present Junipine Ranch. I got paid with a second hand camera and developing outfit to make pictures. That was all agreed on before I started to work and I was satisfied with the deal. I never did learn to use the outfit so it was useless to me but it made me feel important to own it. I still have the camera but it is so out of date it is worthless except for a souvenir."

"When did you first stay away from home?"

"After my sisters were married I used to stay with them a lot to keep them company when their husbands would be gone from home. Ab and Clara Purtymun lived at Junipine from 1906 until sometime in 1909. I stayed with Clara several times when Ab had to be gone. I remember in the fall of 1906 Ab came to our place to borrow a horse and got me to stay with Clara while he made a trip to Flagstaff. We went up the Thompson Ladder to where there was a wagon. He hitched his horse and the borrowed one to the wagon and drove over to the top of the Purtymun Trail. He left the wagon there and we took the horses down the trail to his place. He stayed all night at home and next morning he took the horses back up the trail and made his trip to town. I stayed with Clara while he was gone."

## FROM TRAIL DUST TO JET TRAILS
*by Allen L. Bristow*

I have heard a good deal of discussion about the difference between Pioneers and Old Timers. I am not a Pioneer, as the dictionary defines a pioneer as one who does something first; settles a new country, plows virgin soil, etc. The Astronauts of today are certainly Pioneers. I am an Old Timer.

My grandfather, J.C. (Parson) Bristow was a Pioneer. He and his family, together with the Buffords, Dickinsons, Hawkins', the Letts, Davidsons, Hutchinsons, Tom Smiths, James Humans, and Pleasant Bristows left Missouri in nine wagons, drawn by oxen, on April 25, 1875. Some three months later, after many hardships but no Indian attacks, they reached the Verde Valley. I believe they came in to the Verde byway of Chino Valley and over the hills north of Clarkdale. They had to make their own roads in places and let their wagons down over some of the steep hills with ropes.

On October 3, 1875 Grandfather preached the first Baptist sermon in Arizona under a big cottonwood tree across the river from his first place at Middle Verde. And for many years thereafter, commemorative services were held under the old tree on the first Sunday in October, known as "The Old Tree Meetings". The sermon on October 3, 1920 was Grandfather's last, as he went to his reward soon after.

Grandfather first settled on a place on the west side of the river at Middle Verde, which is now the Cloverleaf Ranch. They lived there about two years when my Aunt Teedie and husband, John Will Ralston came from Missouri. Grandfather turned the place over to them and he moved across the river and took up a farm that is now owned by A.J. Mackey.

The first few years, the pioneer's lived mostly off the land. Game was plentiful and the grass on the mesas was high and thick enough that they cut it with a scythe and sold it at the Post for hay.

Grandmother made all the clothes by hand using whatever material was available. Flour sacks were the most popular, and my father told how he hated the pants she made from canvas wagon cover. He called them "Shotgun Pants". (I wonder if this is where they got the idea for the white jeans of today).

After my father had finished what little schooling was available in the Valley, he decided to be a Cowboy. He learned his trade from some of the early day cowhands and Mexican

Those Early Days.....

Vaqueros. Among them was Juan Villa and his half brother "Poncho". My father learned his trade well and could throw a fifty-foot riata with the best of them. It was about this time that the big cow outfits were organized; one of them was the Diamond S. operated by the Eamons'. My father was their range boss for several years. He was a Pioneer cowboy.

My mother, Calista A. Woods, was a Pioneer School Teacher. She had just finished Normal School at Topeka, Kansas at the age of seventeen and was looking for a teaching position. Her sister, Lola was teaching in the little railroad town of Flagstaff, Arizona and heard that the Territory had started a school in a mining camp in the Aqua Fria District. My mother applied for the job and was accepted. So in the fall of 1887, she packed her valise and set out alone for the Wild West. The Santa Fe Railroad had recently been completed to the west coast, so my mother enjoyed the luxury of train travel to Ash Fork, thence to Aqua Fria via stagecoach where she got lodging in the only place there. It was a hotel in the true frontier tradition, catering to the needs and desires of the miners and cowboys. However, the landlady took my mother under her wing and did a good job of shielding her from the rougher element and my mother pretended she didn't know what went on upstairs.

The one-roomed school consisted of all eight grades, although most of the pupils were in the first grade with ages ranging from five to twenty-five. Needless to say the new schoolmarm had some problems; one of which some of these first graders would get drunk during noon hour but with the aid of the other big boys, things were kept under control.

Mother's next school was the Squaw Peak on the lower Verde. She arrived here by way of Ash Creek and Copper Canyon on a stage driven by one of the feudin' Grahams. He really gave her a wild ride. After a term or two at Squaw Peak School, my mother taught at the Clear Creek School and also several terms at Camp Verde.

During her stay in the Verde Valley, she boarded with a newlywed couple, Charles and Lulu Harbeson. During the several years she was with the Harbesons', their oldest daughter Edna, was born and when she began to talk she couldn't say Calista, so she called her Aunt "Dit", the moniker stuck and she was known as Aunt Dit to many of the old timers in the Verde Valley the rest of her life.

In true Western tradition, the schoolmarm and the cowboy fell in love and were married in Prescott, January 27th, 1897. A year later, my sister Marie was born. Not long after this, my father bought a few acres of ground with a two-room house and a barn on it, located on upper Clear Creek about where the present road to Fossil Creek crosses. On May 27th, 1900 I was born amid the usual flurry and excitement plus an added incident. My father had hired Jim Gilbert, a young tenderfoot from Michigan, to help with the chores and farm work. Along in the afternoon, my mother felt her time was near so my father ran out in the field and told Jim to saddle up old Smokey and go to Camp Verde for Dr. Ketcherside. Jim lost no time in catching a horse and tore out at a dead run for Camp Verde and in a very short time he was back with the doctor, accomplishing the sixteen mile round trip in record time. When Father saw Jim ride into the yard, he exclaimed "good Lord almighty" and gently took the reins telling Jim to get off real easy as he had ridden "Old Wall Eye", the out-law, informing Jim that he was the only man ever to ride him. When Jim recovered from the shock, he said, "He never bucked a jump but he sure could run".

You know, even though I was there, I can't remember whether anyone else ever rode "Old Wall Eye".

My earliest memories are when we came back from California. My parents had decided to try their fortunes there but gave up in less than a year, mainly because of the unfriendly attitude of the people there. We stayed with grandpa and grandma Bristow at Middle Verde. She was a wonderful person. I remember her kindness to me especially since I felt pretty much neglected as my brother, Elwood, born in California, was a blue baby and took most of mothers' time. When I felt blue or got into trouble, grandma would give me one of her soda 'biskits' spread with homemade jam. Those 'biskits' had a very special taste all their own; Grandma and Aunt Teedie Ralston were the only ones I ever knew who made them. While living at Middle Verde, I fell in the irrigation canal that ran in front of the house. Luckily Uncle Charley pulled me out before I had a chance to try out my ability to swim. This was the first of many, many falls in irrigation ditches, creeks and the river (the length of the Verde Valley), probably because it gave me an excuse to take a swim while my clothes dried.

We had not lived at Middle Verde very long until my folks bought the H bar Y ⍭ cattle from Mr. Heath and we moved to a little board house in the shade of Squaw Peak on the Lower Verde. The H bar Y range was in the upper Clear Creek area south to Fossil Creek. Father would be gone for a week or more

## Those Early Days.....

at a time in this rough area looking after the cattle. Mother had her hands full taking care of us kids, doing chores, milking a couple of half-wild cows, and doing the family washing. Washing clothes in those days was a little more than turning on a switch. First you had to chop wood then, build a fire under a big kettle filled with water, which was drawn from the well which was ninety feet deep. This was done with a bucket attached to a rope that ran over a pulley. Shavings from homemade soap were added to the water and after a melting time, clothes were placed in this kettle and boiled to save rubbing time. Rubbing of the clothes was done by hand on a washboard made of galvanized iron or brass. In those days, many women made their own soap by using one can of lye to five pounds of cracklings (or four pounds of pure grease) to each ten pound bucket of water. While cooking this in a kettle, it was continually stirred with a large wooden paddle. Extra water was kept boiling in another kettle for adding to this mixture, It was usually added by a bucket at a time. After a while, a small amount was taken out of the kettle and cooled. If it did not harden, more water was added and the cooking continued. When done, it was allowed to stand until cool then, it was cut into bars. Soap was usually made in the fall at hog-killing time, but many women made it when their supply got low.

    I suppose I added to Mothers' worries with the little exploration trips I liked to take. I always wanted to see what was on the other side of the mountain. I had been told that California and the Pacific Ocean were over the mountains to the West. Imagine my surprise when, several years later, we visited Dewey and there was another range of mountains on the other side of the Black Hills and another range beyond that.

    In August 1905 my brother, Frank, was born at Lower Verde. Father got us kids a billy goat for a pet, hopeful that it would keep us out of mischief and relieve Mother of some of the responsibility. This did not work out, as Billy got into more mischief than we did. One of his favorite stunts was to jump up on the well casing and walk around the one-inch boards of the casing. Father made a lid for the well, so ole' Billy turned to other sports; one of which was butting people and things. No one would dare stoop over when Billy was within striking distance. Mother had one of the local Indian squaws to help with the washing each week; Ole' Billy got her as she bent over the washtub. Us kids had a hard time keeping her from making a stew out of him in the wash boiler, then and there.

    Father made a set of harness and a small cart for Billy to

pull and we had lots of fun riding this around the yard. One day, my sister and I hooked up Billy and went down to Hoppers'. Maud Hopper joined us and we went up the ridge to where the Indians were having a pow-wow. Billy was reluctant to go, so it took both the girls (one was pushing and the other pulling) to get him up the ridge. I was riding in the cart. Eva (Ebbie) Quail saw us coming and ran down and told us to go home as fast as we could because some of the braves were getting mean. They had a tub of "tiswin", a brew made from mesquite beans and were feeling pretty high; so we turned ole' Billy around and he took off down over the hillside. About half way down, we hit some boulders and the cart disintegrated, spilling me out into the mesquite and cactus. The girls picked me up and we made it home where Mother patched me up with arnica salve and strips of an old bed sheet. The Indians had a big fight that night and three of them were carved up pretty bad.

I started school at Squaw Peak, which was about a mile below where we lived, and not as far to walk as some of the other students. Miss Weatherford was the teacher at that time. She later became Mrs. C.C. Calloway.

In the summer of 1906, Father sold the H bar Y's back to Mr. Heath and bought a small farm on the other side of the river between the Len Maxwell and Frank Wingfield places. We went to the Clear Creek School, later called Rutherford. No school buses, so Father got us a jinni burro to ride; we would saddle her up and kick and beat her to school. She was staked out until school was dismissed, then she was saddled up, we climbed on and Jinni would tear out for home. A burro can really run when they want to. After a while at a dead run, Jinni would bury her front feet, throw down her head and unload kids, saddle, bridle and all; then trot on home. Marie and I would carry the gear the rest of the way. After several such experiences, we began walking to school.
Early in 1909, we sold the farm to Len Maxwell and bought the Billie Stevens place on the lane south of Camp Verde, across the road from Charlie Harbeson. We went to school in the old two-room building about where the present school is now.

Though we were poor and there was much work to be done on the farm we had plenty to eat. I always had a lot of fun swimming, hunting, fishing and just roaming around in the hills with as good a group of friends as anyone ever had. My cousin, George Jordan, who lived at the upper end of the Valley, and I used to visit each other and ride our bicycles over the rocky roads. These visits were something special.

Those Early Days.....

My youngest brother, John W. was born in October 1909. He now lives in Oakland, California. My sister, Marie, lives in Alameda, California. We are the only three members of the family remaining. Father passed away in 1934, Mother in 1942, Woody and Frank in 1946.

One of the highlights of my youth was the trip, by covered wagon, to the Arizona State Fair at Phoenix in 1913. There were five wagons; Uncle John Will Ralston and family, Jim and John Ralston and wives. C.B. Coulson and family, the Cooks and our family. We camped the first night at Cordes thence via the old Woolsey Trail to Rock Springs. From there to New River by noon the second day, and after some repairs to wagons damaged as a result from letting them down with ropes over a washed out section, we were able to get to the Arizona Canal for a late camp the third night. From there we headed for the Five Points, just south of the Fair Grounds where we camped on a vacant lot that belonged to one of Father's relatives. (Conway Bristow, I think).

Uncle John Will kept us in fresh game on the way, with his eight-gauge shotgun; he got seventeen quail with one shot at Rock Springs. After a week of seeing all the wonders of the fair and the big city, we set out for home via Wickenburg, Kirkland Valley and Prescott. It took seven days; there was a washout between Wickenburg and Congress Junction and it took several hours to head the wash so it was late at night when we camped at Congress (it takes less than twenty minutes now by auto).

In 1913, Father, Uncle Will Jordan and cousins, Jim and John Ralston, formed the Pioneer Cattle Company and bought the 'Bar J H' cattle. Their range was in the Black Hills from Squaw Peak to Mingus Mountain.

I had a go at being a cowboy. I learned to ride pretty good and to bulldog calves but didn't do so well as a roper though my father, who was an expert roper, did his best to teach me. There are two ways to rope an animal; one is by skill and the other is by patience where you run him until he is so tired that he slows to a walk, then you lay the loop on him or lay it on the ground and let him walk into it. I used the latter method. In 1915 they sold the Bar JH cattle to Fred Back, Dave Murdock and Mose Hazeltine and dissolved the Pioneer Cattle Company; however, Father and the Ralstons still ran the JM Bar Cattle on the same range until 1921. One of the things we bought with the money from the cattle was an automobile, a 1915 Maxwell.

Along about this time, an incident happened that had a

great deal of influence on my life. Some tourists were driving through in a Velie automobile and stripped the timing gears. Jake Webber, the local blacksmith, took the gears out; there were five of them, it being a "T" head, and he had Arthur Hendee in Prescott make another set. Jake put it together, then cranked and cranked, all the farmers and cow punchers in the valley took turns cranking the car but it would not start. They pulled it around with horses, still no luck. Then someone came up with the idea that the gears had to be put on just right so that the valves and magneto would do the right things at the right time, so Jake tore it down and moved the gears one tooth and put it together again; still no results so he tore it down and moved the gears another tooth, etc. for about a week, when the school teacher told him that unless he was very lucky it would take over a million years to set all the gears right, so Jake gave up. The timing marks that were on the teeth, had been stripped off.

The Velie was almost forgotten when a young man by the name of Homer Cummings showed up and said he had come to fix the Velie. Many of the folks were very skeptical and when Homer opened a book and began reading, there were some salty remarks and everyone drifted away except me. He asked me if I wanted to help and I was tickled to death.

He took the timing case off and had me crank it over while he found dead center with a rod down the spark plug hole on number one cylinder, then, explaining as he went along, he set the magneto to fire number one, then set the number four exhaust valve to be just closed and number four intake valve to begin to open. He had me turn it over slowly several times to double check, then put it back together, poured some ether into the priming cups, set the gas and spark levers, gave the crank a spin and away she went. People came running from all directions and stood around in awe.

Homer Cummings was a Genius. Then everyone had a ride around town in the Velie. There were quite a few automobiles in the valley by that time so Homer started a garage in Camp Verde.

After I finished the two years of high school at Camp Verde, I worked at various odd jobs as a cowboy, farming, etc. I hung around Homer Cummings' garage a good deal so Homer suggested to my father that I take an apprentice-ship with him to be an auto mechanic. I started the apprenticeship in the spring of 1917. I got so dirty wallowing around in the grease on the dirt floor that my mother "bowed up" on the auto mechanic business and sent me to the Normal School in Flagstaff, which is now NAU. Summer

Those Early Days.....

*Allen Bristow in Grasshopper Flats in 1922 standing beside a 1920 Maxwell that belonged to his father, John Bristow of Camp Verde.*

school was just starting. I went to school in Flagstaff the summer of 1917 and the winter of 1917-18 and started the term in 1918. There had been a change in Administration, I couldn't get along with them so quit and went home. My cousin, Nettie Gilbert, was visiting from California and she suggested that I come to Riverside and stay with them to finish school at Poly High, which I did and graduated in the spring of 1919.

Nettie's husband was Jim Gilbert, the one who rode Old Wall Eye to get the doctor. He was a General Foreman for the Pacific Electric Railway and after I finished school, I applied for a job there. I got the job in August 1919 and started my forty-five year career in Transportation Maintenance; from grease monkey, to car repairer, auto mechanic and up to Division Superintendent when I retired in 1965.

In 1921, I met a pretty little blue-eyed girl, Stella Garrett, just fresh out of the Ozarks in Missouri. We were married September 24th, 1922 and spent our honeymoon in the Verde Valley.

One day we drove the folks' Maxwell over the rough road to Sedona and spent a very happy day in the solitude of the Red Rocks. We had a picnic and I took a picture of the bride sitting on a rock along Oak Creek just south of Sedona where the bridge is now located. This was the first of many vacations we spent in the Red Rocks.

We have two sons, Kenneth G., who is an architect and lives in Chicago and John D. is a designer for 3M Company in Camarillo, California. Both are married and John has one son and a daughter.

*Stella Bristow on her honeymoon in Oak Creek Canyon in Sept. 1922. This was taken about where the present bridge crosses the creek on highway 179.*

When my cousin, George Jordan, subdivided their property west of the water tower in Sedona we bought a lot and our son, Ken, designed a house for us. When I retired in 1965, we sold out in California and had Wes Thompson build the house for us. We moved into it on January 1st, 1966. We like the scenery and climate here but we especially like the friendly people.

## YOU DON'T NEED A SADDLE
*by Albert E. Thompson*

Joe Lay lived in Sedona from 1908 until 1915. He sometimes had to buy hay to feed his saddle horses through the winter.

One time in the winter he had gone to Beaver Creek with a wagon and a pair of mules to get a load of hay. He had his wagon loaded with baled hay stacked pretty high and tied down with "lass ropes".

On his way home he came through Big Park and by Bell Rock. Just after he passed Bell Rock, a small bunch of gentle cattle crossed the road in front of him. In the bunch was a big unbranded calf. So big in fact it was already weaned and was not following its mother. That was too much a temptation for Joe. He had to have that calf even if he did not have a horse and saddle.

He stopped his team right there and unhitched his mules. He took the harness off one of his mules, all but the collar and bridle. He untied his load of hay and got a rope. He tied the rope to the horse collar on his mule and mounted the mule barebacked. He followed the cattle up and caught the big calf and managed to get it tied to a tree. He came back to is wagon and hitched his team up again and brought his load of hay on home. Next morning he went back on horseback and branded the calf.

## A REMARKABLE WOMAN OF THE EARLY WEST
*by Lenore Dumas*

Margaret Ann Martin was born in Greenfield, Nelson County, Virginia on January 20th, 1834. Her parents were Hudson Martin and Nancy Thorpe. Hudson Martin was born in Virginia in 1765. At the close of the Revolutionary War, Giddeon Martin, his father moved to Kentucky. Giddeon Martin had fought for seven years in the Revolution under General George Washington.

Hudson Martin and Nancy Thorpe were married March 22nd, 1824. The following children were born to this union: John, their only son, and daughters Jane, Mahalley, Margaret Ann, Nancy and Jennie. They were raised in Virginia.

Margaret Ann's mother died in 1859, and her father in 1861.

Margaret Ann was married to Andrew Jackson on December 16th, 1858. They lived in Broxton County, West Virginia. Andrew Jackson was a nephew of General Stonewall Jackson.

In April 1861, Margaret Ann's husband, Andrew Jackson, joined with the Confederate Army and was made Captain of Company B-19th Virginia Cavalry.

Mrs. Jackson was ordered north in the fall of 1863. All of her possessions and property were confiscated and she was allowed to take only two saddlebags of clothing, approximately sixty pounds of baggage. She was carried on horseback, under a flag of truce through the Confederate lines to her house in Virginia.

During his four years of service in the army, Captain Jackson came home to visit his wife three times. On one visit, he only had time for dinner with her and had been gone but about fifteen minutes when the house was surrounded by soldiers. Once he came for a visit overnight and at another time for nine days.

At the close of war, Capt. and Mrs. Jackson moved to South Carolina on June 7th, 1865. They remained here in Greenfield, South Carolina for two years and in the fall of 1867 they started west by ox teams, stopping in Bandera County, Texas, where they remained until 1873. Mr. Jackson was running a sawmill here.

They left Texas, May 1873 with three wagons and ox teams, driving five yoke of oxen to one wagon and four yoke each to the other two wagons. They averaged from twenty to twenty-five miles per day. At night, when camped, two oxen were necked together and belled.

They spent that winter in Trinidad, Colorado, where they could have good range for the cattle, remaining here until May

1874 when they started north on the third leg of their journey, going out by Larma City, Pueblo, Denver and down to the great Salt Lake, hence to Corrine into Idaho, down le Snake River to Munds Ferry, then out over the Powder Range into taker City, Oregon. From here they traveled into Grand Round Valley, crossed the Blue Mountains into Walla-Walla and continued up the Columbia River, crossing it October 13, 1874, coming into Yakama County, Washington. They arrived at Kittitas Valley, November 2nd, 1874. Mr. Jackson was a stock and horse trader so in the spring he decided to go to Puget Sound where he sold his oxen for $250.00 a team, realizing some 3,250.00. He then bought two teams of horses, four head, and one team of mules with wagon. They lived in Washington for a few years, logging and working in a sawmill but he soon became restless and wanted to go South, through Oregon, Klamath Lake, Tule Lake and out into California, they crossed the Sacramento River at Red Bluffs into Sacramento City, and continued on into San Joaquin Valley, coming through to San Bernardino, California. After some short rest and many needed repairs, the wagon rain started across the desert to Hardyville, hence on into Arizona. They arrived in Prescott, January 1st, 1876. They drove out to Chino Valley and lived there for three months in a house owned by Mr. Hall.

While speculating and trading around, Mr. Jackson made up his mind to move to Oak Creek. Here, they were the first white settlers or ranchers on the lower creek until late in the fall of 1876. Mrs. Jackson was the first white woman to live on Lower Oak Creek. Living among the warring Apaches, she saw many fierce out-breaks and raids.

Mr. Jackson was a stoic, carefree and dominating man. He traded and handled stock, traveling about the country for many miles, leaving his wife alone in their cabin on the creek. Mrs. Jackson tended the stock and did all the ranch chores alone. She related that many a time she saw and heard the yelling Indians ride by the place on the surrounding hills, but he was never molested and remained secluded in her small cabin. The Jackson's only had one child and it passed away in infancy.

While living here on lower Oak Creek, Mrs. Jackson named House Mtn. U this time, there was a tall rock chimney at one end of the mountain for-nation, which was later destroyed by a bolt of lightning.

Captain Jackson died on February 22nd, 1892, and was buried at diddle Verde Cemetery, near Camp Verde.

Three years after the death of Captain Jackson, Mrs. Jackson became the wife of David E. Dumas, being married on October 13th, 1895. They continue to live on the lower Oak Creek ranch and it was here in 1896 that Mack Oliver Dumas, son of David Dumas came west from Texas o make his home with his Dad and new Mother. Mother Dumas loved her acquired son most dearly, just as if he were her own. She gave a very good home to this wandering boy of sixteen years.

In 1905 the family moved to the Red Rock Country on a ranch at the foot of Court House Rock, adjoining the old Schuerman Ranch.

One of Mother Dumas' closest and dearest friends was Mrs. James Thompson, mother of Charles and Albert Thompson. Their friendship was long and lasting, their visits extended over three or four days at a time, as they were so far apart and it was not too convenient to make many trips by wagon and team.

The Schuerman's and Dumas' were always close friends, and raised much fruit, which included peaches, apples, apricots and plums in addition to large gardens.

Dad and Mother Dumas were known throughout the valley for their warm hospitality and sincere welcome, which they extended to everyone in the valley, also Jerome and Camp Verde. Never was a person refused a meal or bed at the Dumas Ranch. Often they would retire alone at night and would awaken next morning with a house full of hungry people, ready to eat hot biscuits, bacon and eggs with good strong coffee. Mother Dumas would never allow a single (lone) biscuit to be thrown out after a meal. She always said, "Someone will come along before morning and just might need a bite to eat".

Dad Dumas made one trip to town a year, buying all the staples and supplies for the family, which together with garden and orchard produce would take care of the family and visitors for the months ahead. Vegetables were canned, as were many of the fruits, which also were dried. David Dumas was a charter member of the Masonic Lodge in Jerome. He acted as Deputy Assessor of Yavapai County in 1887 and 1888. He was appointed by the Supervisors at this time because they could not get anyone brave enough to ride into Pleasant Valley Country, where the Tewkesbury and Graham Feud was in full operation. Dad Dumas volunteered to take on the duty of riding into the valley to collect the taxes. He rode a buckskin horse with canvas saddlebags on each side of his saddle. Word was sent ahead to these people that the tax assessor would be riding through their valley. The

Those Early Days…..

above description was given of Dad Dumas on the buckskin horse.

Many times riding down a trail, someone would come out of hiding to stop him and pay their taxes, telling him where they lived and that only the women folks would be home but that if he would go down and tell them who he was, they would make him welcome to spend the night and he would find feed there for his horse. He was never accosted or given trouble in any way, while all this bloody fighting was going on.

Dad and Mother Dumas lived many happy long years at the old Dumas Ranch, now known as Crescent Moon Ranch.

In the summer of 1920, Dad Dumas became ill and passed away in Flagstaff where he was buried.

Occupying the ranch at this time was Dr. M.O. Dumas and his wife, Lenore. The ranch was used as winter range for his cattle outfit while during the summer months he drove them up to Timber Draw in Munds Park.

Mother Dumas lived to enjoy two grandchildren here and was a very dear member of the stepson's household. Her health began to fail in 1924 and she passed away January 24th, 1925 at the age of ninety-one years. She was buried beside Capt. Jackson in Middle Verde Cemetery.

Mother Dumas had the most remarkable memory. She could repeat historical dates, deaths, marriages or birthdays of persons in the Verde Valley. She was reminiscent of her past years as a young girl, and told of dancing on the Puncheon floor. The dance was opened by a person calling, "Every man to his puncheon". She described that a Puncheon floor was made by splitting a log length-wise and then was planed down with a foot-adze to make them smooth.

When she went to church she always went with oxen team and wagon, hitched with a lynchpin.

With her death in 1925, passed a most well-loved and remarkable woman of the early west.

## HOW TO SLAUGHTER A BEEF
*by Albert E. Thompson*

This is a story Roy Owenby told on Hank Stuinkle. Henry (Hank) Stuinkle was a German, born in St. Louis, but he talked with more of a German accent than many people who came here from Germany.

Hank came to Arizona when he was a young man and found work on a cow ranch. He was a very good hand with stock though he was not noted as a wild cowboy or bronco rider.

Sometime before 1908, the roundup wagon was camped on what was known more recently as the Fred Hart ranch in Sedona. It was vacant land at that time. The roundup boss had had some of the men tie a calf to a tree near camp to be butchered for camp meat later in the day.

Late in the afternoon, Roy Owenby and Hank Stuinkle were delegated to go to camp ahead of the rest of the crew and butcher the calf. Someone had been to the Schuerman ranch at Red Rock and brought a few bottles of wine to the roundup. Henry Schuerman Sr. made wine for sale. (It was legal to do so at that time.) Hank had got his share of the wine. When he and Roy rode near to where the calf was tied, Hank was in the lead. He either could not find the camp ax to knock the calf in the head, or was in too much of a hurry to look for it. Roy said that Hank jumped off of his horse and picked up a rock about the size of his two fists and said, "Kill him to death mit a rock" and proceeded to knock the calf down with the rock and cut its throat.

Those Early Days.....

## HOW CARL RICHARDS CAME TO SEDONA
*as told to Sedona Westerners Book Committee*

Carl Richards, long time auto garage operator, now blacksmith and machinist, leaned back in a lawn chair in front of his comfortable red sandstone house in Sedona, and recalled events leading to his arrival here in 1922. Carl is the only resident here who came to the State and to Sedona on horseback.

I had not planned to come here, hadn't even heard of the place before leaving my native Rome, Missouri, where I was born in 1903. When I first saw Sedona I was tired, hungry and disgusted. But all of that did not keep me from staying in business in Sedona for more than 33 years, and I appreciate being a member of the community.

After World War I, my doctor told me that my asthma was so bad I would have to get out of the damp climate of Missouri if I expected to live and keep from getting tuberculosis. I'd always wanted to be a cowboy, so I hopped a freight train and started west. I hoboed over a good part of Iowa, Nebraska, Oklahoma, Texas, South Dakota, and Wyoming. I worked as a harvest hand in several places, but I still wanted a job on a cattle ranch. In Wyoming I got my first chance. I was not a top hand there, most likely, but I was getting experience.

From there I rode freight trains to Colorado. I got a job for the winter near Colorado Springs. That was a cold, snowy winter, and when spring came I started lookin' for a lower elevation. I took short ranch jobs through the summer. In the fall of 1921, I left a freight train at Rifle, Colorado and paid a driver of a Model T Ford truck a dollar for a ride to Meeker, Colorado, where I got a job at the Cross-L Ranch.

Meeker was named for Nathan Meeker, who was killed by Ute Indians along with all of the agency workers in the 1870s. Meeker was the agent who wanted to make farmers out of the wild Utes. When he plowed up their racetrack and planted oats they got mad and killed him. My boss at the Cross-L told me to tear Meeker's house down. I thought it should be saved as a place of historic interest, but the boss said, "Tear it down", so I tore it down. Soon after that I and my boss agreed to disagree and I saddled my horse and rode on to see new country and find another job.

I drifted into Utah's Uinta Basin, by the way of Jenson and Vernal. I rode the chuck line through the basin till I heard of Preston Nutter's Double O ranch in Nine Mile Canyon in the Uinta Mountains. I always headed for the biggest cattle ranches, because there's a better chance to get a job. When I left Meeker, Colorado, I was riding my own saddle horse and had quit riding freight trains. It was a good thing I had as there were no railroads in many a mile of where I was traveling on horseback.

After leaving the Double O outfit, I wanted to explore the breaks near Green River, as I had heard that there was a trail down that way to near Lee's Ferry, Arizona. Some one or more persons didn't welcome strangers in the area. Every time I got near the river and asked directions of someone they would steer me back away from the river. The longest ride I made between water holes was 65 miles. By starting in the evening and riding all night I got through without any hardships. From Utah's Castle Valley, I crossed the Divide to the Sevier River Valley.

I didn't follow roads, as trails were generally shorter. After I got over the mountain, I met a trail herd being driven to Marysvale, Utah to be shipped out by rail. They could use another hand, so I got a job. I continued to meet herds going to the railroad as I drifted on South. I got work with most of them and they paid better wages than was paid for ranch work. I ended up near the Utah - Arizona border in the vicinity of Johnson, Utah. Johnson is a ghost town now, but there were cattle ranches there then.

I heard of a big round up and trail drive that was getting ready to start. I rode out to one of the wagons that was camped a good ways from water. The crews of two wagons were there but the other wagon had not showed up yet. I fell in with the bunch and was promised work as soon as the other wagon got there. The double crew, living on the chuck that was meant for half as many men, soon threw them all on short rations. There was plenty of flour and coffee left and they could always kill a beef, so they made out all right. Their main problem was water. Water had to be hauled quite a distance, so they had to be mighty saving with it. They finally quite washin' dishes, and as the chuck got down to bread, beef, and coffee, they didn't even use dishes - except coffee cups. After a wait of several days they learned that the other chuck wagon was broke down and the drive would not start for weeks. By that time I heard about a big drive by the old Grand Canyon Cattle Company's Bar-Z ranch in House Rock Valley of Arizona to Flagstaff.

The boss was gone to find out about cars for shipping when I got to the roundup in the North Kaibab. They furnished me with saddle horses and I rode with the crew while I waited for the boss. When the boss did get in, he said there would be a delay of a month or more before they could start, because there were no stock cars for shipping. He told me I could stay on and work for

Those Early Days…..

*Carl "Slim" Richards at the age of 19. This was taken shortly after arriving in the West.*

my board until the drive started, but I didn't think much of the offer.

I saddled my private horse again and headed for Lee's Ferry. When I got there the Southern California Edison Company had a camp there making a survey for a dam near where the present Glen Canyon Dam is. They gave me the same treatment the Bar-Z cattle outfit had - I could work for my board. Well, I stayed a few days and rested my horse and then I started on for Flagstaff. To give an idea how bad the roads were at that time, I met a truck of the Edison Company a few miles south of Lee's Ferry. They invited me to have supper with them that evening at Cedar Ridge in the direction I was headed. They went on to Lee's Ferry and unloaded and got back to Cedar Ridge about the time I got there and I had supper with them. The truck had traveled only 14 miles farther in a day than I had traveled on horseback.

Stopping for the night at Cameron, I met James Giddings, "Ole' Rimmy Jim", whose ranch was a little off the road between Cameron and Flagstaff. Rimmy Jim warned me by saying that, "I'm the crankiest man in these parts", but offered me work. I worked for Giddings two or three weeks, but because he also was having trouble getting cars to ship cattle, I moved on to Flagstaff.

I don't know how I came to miss Babbitt's C O Bar outfit but I came on to Flagstaff from Cameron and went to work for the D K's Coconino Cattle Company. Their summer quarters was at Rogers Lake a few miles southwest of Flagstaff, and the winter quarters at Windmill Ranch, southwest of Sedona. It was pretty late in the fall when I went to work, and there had been a snow that fall of a foot and a half. My job was hauling hay to the roundup camps, as they were moving the cattle to the valley for the winter.

After a few months work with the D K's, I went on to Prescott and went to work for Cecil W. Pardee. "Doc Pardee" was the spark plug and master of ceremonies of Prescott's Frontier days Rodeo for a good many years. He had a livery stable and feed corrals at the time I worked for him. Pardee had some horses at Jerome Junction that he wanted brought to Prescott. He took me, and my saddle out there in a car and came back and left me to bring the horses in. There had been some horses stolen from Prescott just before I started out with the Pardee horses. Sheriff George Ruffner was out lookin' for the horse thieves and met me drivin' a bunch of horses. The sheriff asked me where I was from and I said, "Prescott". Ruffner said, "Where from before that, and what are you doing with the horses?" I explained that I was workin' for Pardee and the sheriff said he guessed he was after the wrong man.

I should explain here that I had been followed and watched by Sheriffs Officers all the way from Meeker, Colorado. Just a few days after I left my job at the Cross-L Ranch at Meeker, some young

## Those Early Days.....

fellows that I knew stole a bunch of horses and left that part of the country. When the Sheriffs party started huntin' them they struck my trail first. They could see that I did not have any horses, but they expected I would lead them to the rest of the gang. Part of the thieves were killed by officers in the North Kaibab of Arizona, and two got away. I was not given a clean bill until after I talked with Sheriff Ruffner of Prescott.

I came back to the Verde Valley and worked for the Coconino Cattle Company again. In the fall after a 4-inch snowfall at Rogers Lake, the company watchman who was supposed to look out for the ranch at Rogers Lake, caught a logging train going to Flagstaff and left the job. The boss told me I would have to hold job down for a few days. They left me there pretty near all winter. When I did start out with 4 horses and two wagons for the Windmill Ranch, by way of Schnebly Hill and Sedona, I was told I would be there on the second day. Coming down Schnebly Hill I had to take the lead team off, and in getting around some of the curves I had to hitch them to the trail wagon and drag it sideways to get around the turns. I was so long on the road I had used practically all of my groceries before I got to Sedona. There had been a little store in a shake building, but it was closed at that time. That is why I got such a poor impression of Sedona the first time I saw it. I drove on toward the Windmill Ranch and got there about midnight, but I never took anyone's word again about how far it was to some place, and I always took groceries enough for a week when I started out on a trip.

I worked for the Forest Service as a "Smoke Chaser", fireguard through the fire season a few years and trapped coyotes in the winter. Not much money in it, but I had lots of fun.
Sometime in 1927, I started a little blacksmith shop in Flagstaff and a year or so later - - I don't know just when - - I noticed a good-looking girl that would walk by the shop once in a while.

My old cowboy friends around there got to kidding me about my good looking girl. After 2 or 3 years - - I don't know just when - - an old feller I had done some work for, came into the shop one time - - his car had broke down. Well, he lived out in Dead Man Flat. So I went out to fix his car. I found my girl there and I found out who she was: Vela Meredith, daughter of Charley Meredith.

So after that I got out to Dead Man Flat fairly regular. Sometimes the snow would get deep and drifted. Pd get stuck in the snow and sometimes wait all day for the snow plow to get me out. But I got there sometime in the day or night. And that went on until - - come leap year - - January 30, in 1932. I went out and got her and took her to town with me, and we were married. So I didn't have to go through that snow anymore!

Sometime in 1933, my lease ran out where I rented my shop, so me and my wife - we got in the car and started to try to find something better. We got into Sedona and found a little place there and a snowstorm covered us again. So we just took that little place and went back to Flagstaff for our things and didn't look for anything any better. So, we've been in Sedona ever since then. In October 1933, I started as a garage man and blacksmith in Sedona and have been in Sedona ever since.

I always carried a gun in my wandering days. I did not know that a six-shooter was not supposed to kill big animals, and I killed everything I needed to kill from quail to a 2,000 pound bull with my old .45. A rifle or other long gun is a problem to carry on horseback. I could stick a six-shooter in my pocket and forget about it. I have used various calibers of guns, but now I have a .38-40. I beat 2 fellows with rifles at a turkey shoot, and could shoot up to 200 yards with my 6-gun.

About the only changes I would make, if I had my life to live over, would be to stay a little longer along the trail and see a little more of it.

I learned the blacksmith trade because I grew up in a blacksmith shop in Missouri. Both of my granddads were blacksmiths. One was a blacksmith in the army in the Civil War. I have a little Bible my granddad carried in the Civil War. That was my father's dad.

The accompanying photo of me of those days show the reason for the various nicknames I was known by at times. Slim was a natural, and my name was Carl and I came here from Utah, so "Utah" or "Utah Carl" was another natural, because almost all of the cowboys were familiar with the song "Utah Carl". It was just by chance that I was called "Tex" some places.

When workin' at cowboying, I would sometimes curl up and sleep afternoons till 3 o'clock and then work till dark or later. While travelin' horseback, housing accommodations were simple. I just coiled up in my saddle blanket and slicker and went to sleep.

I have made lots of stamp branding irons, as well as spurs, and bridle bits. In common with most cowboys, I have shod lots of horses and even shod some since coming to Sedona.

I believe that we have waited too long to start gathering the colorful history of Sedona. I think we should do all we can to preserve what we can of it now.

Those Early Days.....

## A LOAF OF BREAD FOR A NICKEL
*by M.O. Dumas*

Around the turn of the century, and for some years later, a person could buy a loaf of bread for a nickel. The price of almost every other commodity has advanced accordingly. For example: a pair of Levi's cost about ninety cents; one hundred pounds of flour cost $1.50. We did not have ground coffee at the time and the most often bought brand was the old Arbuckle Bros, coffee which came in one pound paper packages and sold for twenty cents a pound. Some people preferred to buy green coffee, which they parched in the oven of the old kitchen wood stove. This, of course, cost even less.

What I notice the most in these times are all of the old liberties, which we have had to give up. Years ago everything in the land was free to use. One could go into the timberlands and help himself to timber to meet his needs and all that he wanted. The same could be said about hunting and fishing and many other such things. If a person had a horse or a cow or even many more animals, he could turn them out on the open range and no questions were ever asked of him.

Now what of today?

Taxes are one item that have soared and are still being raised to meet the many needs each year. In the olden days, I was running a herd of 1500 head of cattle on the open range. There were no fences, and as well as I can remember, my taxes were less than $100.00 and I am sure this is a very conservative estimate. We never knew of a Federal tax then, but this did not last long.

Around about this time you were requested to secure a permit to run stock on the range but there was no charge for the permit. A few years later you were assessed ten cents per head. At a later date it was raised to twenty-five cents, then up to fifty cents, then up to a dollar a head and so on. I knew of some yearlong permits for $5.00 per head. There may have been some a little higher.

Our Territorial and County taxes were about one-fifth of what they are now. You also had a road and poll tax to pay; the road tax was $3.00 a year. You could pay this or work on the road for two days and get a receipt for some from the road boss. Every district had such a boss who was appointed by the County Supervisors. I think the poll tax was collected and earmarked for the schools. You had to pay this in order to have the right to vote in general elections. If you worked for a corporation, this was deducted from your paycheck.

***Dr. M.O. Dumas standing by a tree near an ancient Cliff Dwellers home on Lost Mountain, which can be reached from Hart Well Canyon, on headwaters of Spring Creek. The limbs of the tree were cut off with a stone axe by primitive people.***

In 1898 when I was eighteen years of age, I was working in Jerome. They deducted this said poll tax and I protested saying I was only eighteen but the clerk said I looked the age. As I had no birth certificate, I had to pay on my looks and still could not vote. In place of being born thirty years too soon, a great many of you were born fifty years too late to enjoy a fine country. At that time about the only thing we had to get a permit or license for was to get married. Of course I realize that conditions have to change as our population increases. But what will our privileges be in another fifty years? You will probably have to have a college degree to secure a license to drive your own car. At the start of this century our population was probably less than 40,000 in our home Territory of Arizona.

Sometimes I envy the old Indians and the freedom they enjoyed. They had very few rules to abide; no taxes, no schools, no courts or law suits or fines to pay, and to get married they only crossed two sticks. They had no divorces and few family troubles as the bucks rode the horses and the squaws walked, chopped wood, made camp and cooked the meals. Then there seemed no danger of over population as there is today. They had very few medical problems or medical science. They had a Medicine Man but all was based on superstition and the use of roots, herbs or leaves made into tea for relief of pain.

They lived off the land and at times it was a very tough problem too but most of them undoubtedly were a very happy and carefree people.

## SOME MEMORIES IN PICTURES
*by Don Willard*

I would like to show you some pictures. I won't be able to use slides, projector or screen, since they were not recorded by camera, sketch or painting. So you will have figuratively to close your eyes to see them. The scenes are intended to be depicted in word pictures if possible, showing some phases of life, as it was in these Verde and Red Rock areas in early days.

Since there were certain features of living in those times that have not been given as much attention in some of the stories told as has been devoted to the personal and historical facts, it may be interesting to look more closely at a few, more or less forgotten experiences and conditions of that period. This is intended deliberately to provoke nostalgia and revive memories. One of the most elementary needs then as it is now, being the matter of food, both in its preparation and its use; some of our most vivid recollections are grouped naturally in that relation.

The home of my grandfather, David Scott, was at the edge of the Verde River and near the Cottonwood ditch. He had built a gristmill using waterpower from that ditch to grind meal. His idea of breakfast was cornmeal mush, meat and eggs and fresh ground Arbuckle's coffee. A waking sound each morning was my grandmother turning the coffee mill at the kitchen door. Convenient to the back door was the covered well with its bucket on the end of a rope running over a pulley. At one side stood the rock and adobe milk-house covered with ivy. It was always cool enough to keep milk fresh until the cream could rise to be skimmed for making butter in the old hand churn. Of course, there was plenty of sour milk for clabber to make schmier kase (cottage cheese), the memory of which brings only fond regret when compared with today's cottage cheese. After the butter was pressed in a wooden mould it was wrapped and lowered to water level in the well to keep it firm. The buttermilk was real, not cultured, and went just right with grandmother's corn bread.

Another building my grandfather had constructed was the smoke house for curing hams and bacon after hog killing time in the fall. Fresh meats were homegrown or sometimes hunted. Did you ever eat a quail mulligan? This was made with green chili, dumplings, etc., and was quite a dish. I remember shooting many quail in the mesquite thickets where you now find the streets of Cottonwood.

Calories were unknown and a balanced diet was vaguely

## Those Early Days.....

thought to mean always eating plenty of vegetables from the kitchen garden, being sure to have plenty of homemade bread to go with the meat, and never to eat preserves or jelly without bread, which children are inclined to do.

Fruit canning was a very important summer job, and shelves lined with fruit jars, jams and jellies was a matter of pride. Wild grape jelly was one special treat, probably because picking them and preparing the jelly was such an adventure.

Many ranchers hated to leave their work in fields at noon until they were called. This was often done by a triangle, shaped from a steel bar. Believe me, it was real music to the ears of a hungry man or boy.

Holidays sometimes meant not enough table and seating room, and this required the use of a very unpopular arrangement known as the "second table", where the younger generation were inclined to feel there just might be something missing, especially as to a favorite piece of chicken or pie and cake. A famous summertime institution was the ice cream social - a neighborhood get-together where a five-gallon freezer turned by hand produced another treat worth going miles to enjoy. Then there were the box suppers, a social activity still continued in certain rural areas.

Some food supplies had to be purchased, such as sugar, coffee, white flour and miscellaneous minor items. Trips to a store could be spaced at long intervals and sometimes it was possible to take in for exchange such things as butter, eggs and other farm produce. There were always enough tasks to sharpen a boy's appetite; drawing water from the well, turning the grindstone, picking fruit or carrying firewood.

Shifting the scene now, we come to some pictures on the subject of transportation. Roads were quite primitive and frequently difficult, or even hazardous to traverse. The saddle horse was the primary method, of course. But after that came vehicles, ranging from buggy, carriage, buckboard, spring wagon, and finally for heavy hauling, to "dead-ex" wagons, sometimes with high wheels and deep boxes. If you have never seen a teamster handle eight or ten, sometimes riding a wheel horse and guiding the leaders with a "jerk-line", you have missed something. Do you remember the livery rigs the town folks used to drive out from Jerome, or group riding "Talley-ho?"

One wagon trip I experienced was with 'Dolph Willard from his place on Lower Oak Creek near Page Spring with a load of fruit. Starting at noon we reached the ranger station at Sedona to camp for the night. Breaking camp before daylight we undertook the climb up Schnebly Hill. To lighten the load a little I left the wagon below the "Merry-go-round" rock and clambered to the rim where the old right hand switchback topped out. From there I watched the wagon for over two hours as it seemed slowly to inch ahead, stopping to rest the horses at short intervals. At about eleven o'clock after the wagon reached the top we proceeded through Clay Park (now Foxboro), Munds Park and on toward Flagstaff. Near sundown and just past the "Pump House", we encountered an automobile. Ranchers hated them. My uncle was no exception. When they stopped in the deep wheel tracks in front of us, he reached for my rifle, which was behind us under the seat blankets. Raising it in their general direction, he suggested with a few words they could understand that they should turn out. They did so. He drove ahead saying, for their ears to hear, it would be a very long time before he would turn aside for a blank automobile. This was 1914 and will illustrate one problem faced by early autoists in some parts of our country.

A real thrill to kids in those days was a chance to ride the train from Jerome to Prescott. Leaving Jerome on the narrow gauge in an accommodation coach attached to a string of freights, and creeping around the mountain to Jerome Junction in Chino Valley, a distance of twenty-six miles, took two hours and a quarter. At that point there was a change into the luxury of a Santa Fe coach on the "Pea Vine" (Prescott and Phoenix) line.

The mail was usually carried by stage from Camp Verde to Prescott on one route and to Jerome on another. Passengers were allowed to avail themselves of this special transportation; it was an all-day trip with stops to change horses. Passengers could carry lunches or obtain meals family style at these places.

We should not overlook the really considerable part played by the lowly burro around the mines for prospectors and others. I have a vivid memory of the packsaddle burro trains carrying wood for the cook stoves of Jerome from all directions on the surrounding hills.

Also, I remember riding the only bicycle, as far as I knew, in the entire valley at that time, and having to dismount and stand at the side of he road to avoid frightening neighbors' horses as they passed. My range of useable road was limited to only a few miles around Cottonwood, and even that was too much to suit those neighbors.

The next category of early day scenes was the school and activities connected with it. Mine was not an unusual experience.

## Those Early Days.....

When I was old enough to go to school, we were in a mining camp where there was no school. My mother got schoolbooks and had taught me up to third grade before I had the opportunity to attend. After we moved to Camp Verde, I went to the old two-room schoolhouse. Later I attended the one-room school at Cottonwood with all eight grades, one teacher and an average of sixteen or eighteen pupils. Boys were required to carry wood for the big stove and bring drinking water from the well on a nearby farm. This was kept on a shelf in an open bucket with one dipper hanging beside for all to use. In those days, we walked to school and carried our lunch in a pail, which was sometimes an emptied tobacco tin.

Strange as it may seem, we had teachers who were able to get across to those who were willing to learn, not only covering the subjects in our ext books but I believe also many of the lessons of life. As I look back I tm glad we did not realize we were underprivileged.

Some of my special memories are connected with the old brick house till standing in the north side of Cottonwood, where I was born; living or a time on old Mt. Vernon Street in Prescott, then later at Ox Yoke Spring in the foothills of Mingus Mountain, and again in the army residence once occupied by Captain Charles King at Camp Verde, where my brother and I played with Indian youngsters, attending the first Indian School just started there. It was located in the army building now known as the Fort Verde Museum.

We even enjoyed the thrill of 'going to town' to help celebrate the 4th of July and hearing a band play and the oratory as the flag waved. In those days a march or parade meant pride, not protest and our dreams were of hope, not fear.

With all our progress and material advantages, there is something to be said for the "good ole days". While we were short on paved roads and prosperity, we were not yet threatened with extinction by the problems of traffic peril, pollution, and the population explosion.

## BEAVER HEAD STAGE STATION
*by Albert E. Thompson*

The old Beaver Head stage station, on Highway 179, below the bridge on Dry Beaver Creek, is a spot of historic interest. It should be marked by a historic marker. The Sedona Westerners group have taken a great interest in this project. They have made several attempts to get either State or Federal recognition of this worthwhile project but have not had much success as yet. However they have not given up the fight.

There seems to have been very little written about this station or the Star Mail Route that used the station. In the book, "Pioneer Stories of Arizona's Verde Valley", Ed Peplow states in his introduction, that a military route from Santa Fe, New Mexico, through this area and by present Prescott, to Fort Yuma, was opened, prior to the settlement of Prescott. he gives no reference of where he got the information.

In H.F. "Tack" Gaddis' story in the above-mentioned book, he states hat his family came to the Verde Valley in 1875. He makes mention of topping at Pine Springs and that it was a mail station and that the mail vas carried on horseback.

I talked with "Uncle Tack" some years before he wrote his story. He said that the mail station on Beaver Creek when he came here was at present McGuireville. I asked him where the next station from there on the mountain was and he said it was Pine Springs. To the best of my knowledge the Pine Springs station has all been destroyed and the location is almost impossible to find. Pine Springs became a post office in 1879 and vas discontinued in 1882. Tack Gaddis wrote that, Wales Arnold was station keeper at the lower Beaver Creek station in 1875, and that his (Tack's) brother, Will got a job of herding horses that belonged to the mail line. He also stated that the station was a division point on the mail route, and hat Charley Dickinson was the mail carrier from there to Prescott and hat the mail was carried on horseback. Tack Gaddis stated that a new station was built at Beaver Head in 1876.

In Martha Summerhays' book, "Vanished Arizona", she described a trip from Fort Apache to Fort Whipple by the way of Beaver Head in 1875. They camped overnight at Dry Beaver Creek and she said her ambulance river called the place Beaver Springs. There was no stage station there at that time.

There is some confusion about the name of the road and about when it was first used. There is no doubt that it was used

Those Early Days.....

as a military road but there is no record of who used it first. It was no doubt an Indian Trail and might have been used by prospectors or trappers.

I have been unable to find any record of when the mail route was discontinued. The station was very likely abandoned as a mail station when the route was discontinued. My mother's folks came to lower Oak Creek in the spring of 1878 and there were a few Indian scares after that. I have heard her tell of going with the family to Beaver Head to fort up during an Indian scare soon after arriving on Oak Creek.

It is the general belief locally that the mail route was discontinued shortly after the Atlantic and Pacific Railroad was built across northern Arizona. To bear that out, I will refer to the book "Arizona Post offices and Postmasters", by John and Lillian Theobald. Said book gives the opening date of Pine Springs post office as March 20, 1879 and the closing date as July 27, 1882. Further on in said book is this note: date 1882, James Stuart advertised a stage line from Prescott to Williams, Arizona connecting with the Atlantic and Pacific Railroad at Williams.

If there was a mail stage from Williams to Prescott, Arizona in 1882 and the Pine Springs office was closed that year there is no doubt about the mail route from the Little Colorado River by way of Chavez Pass, Pine Springs, Stoneman Lake and Beaver Head to Camp Verde was discontinued in 1882 also.

The first reference to that mail route in the Theobald book is a news item taken from the Daily Arizona Miner, and dated 1866. It states, Santa Fe Stage, operated from Prescott to Santa Fe and on to Denver and Kansas City. Stage carries mail, passengers and express. Leaves Kansas City every Friday for Denver and Santa Fe. The next news item in said book is dated 1875. It is from the Arizona Sentinel. It states, Santa Fe and Prescott mail lines buckboards leave Prescott for Santa Fe every Wednesday and Saturday morning, carrying U.S. mail and passengers. Connects with Randlesville on the Colorado Chiquita with buckboards for Fort Apache. Fare to Santa Fe $75.00, time 7½ days - distance 500 miles.

Apparently this mail line had a lot of difficulties from Indians and crooked employees, as well as financial troubles. It changed hands several times in the 17 year period that I can find records that it was operated.

I will again quote from the newspaper items in the Theobald book, Weekly Arizona Miner, 1879. Star Line Transportation Co., Prescott to Santa Fe, connected with railroad at Ortero, New

Mexico. Carried mail by way of Camp Verde, Beaver Head, Pine Springs, Brigham City, St. Joseph, Little Colorado Horsehead Crossing, Fort Wingate, and to intermediate points. This was Route Number 40,101. Prescott-Santa Fe stage lines or Santa Fe-Prescott Mail Lines, both being the same mail line, carried passengers and express from Prescott to Santa Fe in four days. Route claimed to be two days faster and $50.00 cheaper to the East than any other line. Distance was 507 miles. Route was stocked with 230 mules, 18 wagons, good stations, etc. Sub-contractor, J.A. Walsh on the Prescott and Santa Fe Mail Route telegraphs to Postmaster Otis (Prescott) from Santa Fe that he is just starting out over the route. He proposes to carry the mails on time and in good style-not withstanding the failure of the McDonnough Co., Weekly Arizona Miner, Jan. 3, 1879.

Next item-Weekly Arizona Miner, Jan. 17, 1879—Mr. Fiske, agent for John A. Walsh, sub-contractor of Prescott and Santa Fe route-Suit brought against Fisher Stage Lines, lately carrying mails on that route and taking Company property by attachment—makes it impossible to produce buck-boards for use between Prescott and Beaver Head-but mail will be carried regularly by horse until buckboards can be shipped from the East.

Weekly Arizona Miner, Jan. 10, 1879-Prescott to Santa Fe mail route is in a demoralized state. The employees have taken all the company's stock. There has been no mail in 10 days. The mail sacks are scattered all along the line. The stock is all driven off between Santa Fe and Fort Ningate. Daily Arizona Miner, Verde date line-1875-The New Mexico nail driver, Ben Baker, has just arrived on foot. He reports that the Indians have driven off all the stock on the Little Colorado River.

In the Sept. and Oct. issues of the Arizona Miner, 1879, the editor lobbied for better service of existing lines and extension of mail service to new areas. In the Jan. 13, 1880 issues he speaks his mind. The people of Smithville, Cherry Creek District, almost 100 in number, have to come to Prescott, 40 miles for their mail. The people of Upper Verde and Oak Creek have to go from 15 to 25 miles to Camp Verde for their mail. There should be a post office at Stemmer's on Ash Creek, one at Captain Jackson's on Oak Creek and another at Beaver Head.

## A ROLLING STONE
*by Charles Smith*

My father, Abraham L. (Link) Smith left Humansville, Missouri in May, 1877 with his thirteen year old brother, Grant and an older half brother. They arrived at Beaver Creek Ranger Station on August 3, 1877 by mule train. In 1878, Grant was killed by a horse at Beaver Creek, while wrangling horses for Bob Baker. Shortly afterward, Dad moved to the small Mormon settlement of Mesa, Arizona where he homesteaded 160 acres.

In 1891, he married Addie C. Fenstermaker and in 1892 Roerick (Roe) was born, followed by Jimmy in 1894, who died at age four from pneumonia. I was born in 1897, and in 1900, Nellie came along.

In 1901 Dad sold his 160-acre homestead for $350.00 because of the illness of Mother and Nellie, who was one year old. Dad wanted to get them into the mountains where he thought they might breathe better.

On the first day of our journey we reached New River where we made night camp. The second night we camped at Cordes Junction and the third night at the Schroder Place at Beaver Creek where we stayed over for a few days to let the team rest. We headed for Flagstaff by way of the old stage road, which was the only route then and we got as far as Rattlesnake Tanks the first day out from Beaver Creek. I believe we were on the road about ten days from Mesa to Flagstaff excluding layovers.

Flagstaff was just a small railroad town. We camped near where the underpass is now located, and which was just a big pine timber area at that time with nothing south of the railroad track. We did not stay long in Flagstaff, as Roe was school age. So we came to Camp Verde and Roe started to school in the fall of 1901. Dad rented a house near where the Fort Verde Museum now stands and Roe went to school that winter of 1901 and 1902. His teacher was Ellsworth Schnebly, an uncle to Ellsworth Schnebly here in Sedona. Dad took on the job of hauling water for Camp Verde that winter from a spring on Wet Beaver Creek with wagon and team for .25$ per barrel. He would make from two to three trips a day, crossing the Verde River at the point where it comes into Beaver Creek.

In the spring of 1902, we moved to Cornville and rented a place from Frank Derrick and started truck farming. Dad hauled the produce to Jerome, Camp Verde and Flagstaff. There was no town of Cottonwood then. Jerome and Camp Verde was only a day's drive by borrowing part of the night, but Flagstaff was from five to six days for the round trip, if you were lucky. I went along several times that summer. I recall one trip when we got as far as Mormon Lake and sold out everything to the logging camp and went back home. In the fall of this same year, Frank Derrick took the place back and we moved again. We only moved about one mile away to a place owned by Ed Grives and Dad went to work for him. We lived in a big tent overlooking Oak Creek, and Roe went to school at Cornville.

In the spring of 1903, we moved across the creek and Dad worked for J.H. Jack, grubbing mesquite stumps. In August that year Ira was born.

In 1904 we moved off under the hill where the Mulcaire place is now, which was only a short distance from the Cornville Post Office, where Uncle Sammie Dickinson was postmaster.

Still a vivid picture in my mind was an incident that happened while we were living here. My sister Nellie and I were having dinner at Grandma Dickinson's one day, and while we were eating, grandma took her teeth out and placed them on the table. That night, I did not mention anything about this to mama, but the next day I was working at my teeth with my fingers when she noticed me and said, "What are you doing, Charles?" I told her that I was trying to take my teeth out, and she wanted to know why I wanted to take them out. Then I told her Grandma Dickinson had taken her teeth out, and mama told me that they were false teeth. That was he first time I had ever seen or heard of false teeth.

In the fall of 1904 I started to school and had trouble the very first day. I wanted to get a drink of water and the teacher, Miss Black, told me that I must say "please", and I did without a drink of water because of my refusal to be polite. From that time on, I applied better manners and got along pretty well.

We lived here until 1906 when Dad filed on 40 acres of land next to he Jim Page property and we moved up there that fall. There was a log house on the place. The logs were up and down like a picket corral. That was the same year of the San Francisco earthquake, which really scared everyone. We thought it would tear the house down. I did not go to school much that winter because of the big snowstorm and Oak Creek was up or a long time. We had no bridges then.

It was in the spring of 1907 that I got my pants warmed up. There were a few fruit trees on the place along the ditch and Dad was pruning. I was wading in the ditch and mama told me

Those Early Days.....

to get out of the water. I didn't hear her. She told me a second time, and I still did not hear her. At her third request (which I heard), I told her I would not. She picked up a long plum sprout, which she wore out on the seat of my pants. Well I got out alright, and stayed out. I believe that was the last time I ever talked back to mama.

Later in the spring, Dad got a house near where the Page Spring Store is now. It was here that same year that Delia, another sister came along. Roe was old enough to help in the hay fields, and what time they were not busy working in the hay, they were building a new house on the place. The new house was being built across the creek from the old house so that we would not have to cross the creek to go to school. We moved to the new house in the spring of 1908 and Dad went to work for Mrs. Gates, while Roe and I took care of our garden and young orchard we had planted.

We got along pretty good then and had a better chance to attend school even if we did walk three miles. There was no such thing as a school bus, in those days you just had to do the best you could.

Everything was fine until the winter of 1911 when Dad traded the place for a larger one and took over the debt that was on the place. We lived here for one year when Dad saw that he couldn't pay out so he traded the place for a house and lot in Jerome. But we didn't move to Jerome, we just moved out in a tent that fall and winter.

I reached the age of sixteen that fall of 1913 and Roe had become of age and wanted to take up a homestead. I can't remember how the deal came about or how it was worked. But anyway Jack Lay, a cousin of Joe Lay, had a homestead on the mountain south of Flagstaff. Somehow they got together and Dad traded the house and lot in Jerome for the place on the mountain. Jack turned the papers over to Roe, who was to complete improvements on the homestead. In the spring of 1914, we moved to the mountain and on to Flagstaff where Dad worked that summer. Another sister, Ella was born while we lived in Flagstaff. That fall we moved to Red Rock to go to school.

In the summer of 1915 we built a house here in Sedona near where Ed Wright's place is in Soldier Wash and that was my first encounter with the beautiful red rocks of Sedona. I started to school that fall in Sedona, the teacher was Miss Edith Lamport (now Mrs. Fred Croxen). We lived in Sedona until 1918 when we sold out and moved to Beaver Creek. We just kept moving around, up to the mountain in the spring and back down to the valley in the fall. Roe was in the army and stationed in France. I got my draft call for the army that September and was examined on November 7, 1918. The Armistice was signed November 11th and I did not hear any more about going to war.

In 1920, I worked all summer on the cut off road from Pump House Canyon to the head of Oak Creek Canyon. I was on the bridge crew.

In 1921, Roe had returned from the war and rented what is now the Poco Diablo Golf Course and Restaurant. I built a log house there where the old fireplace still stands.

In 1922 we moved up to Fred Hart's place where the Oak Creek Trailer Court is now located. From this time on until 1925, I worked mostly for Coconino County.

In 1925 I met Ivy Thomas in Oak Creek Canyon at a dance and we were married on October 8,1927 in Jerome. We went to the Grand Canyon on our honeymoon. Our first child, Charles Albert Smith was born here in Sedona on April 2, 1929. I was working for Dad Hart before we were married and continued to work for him until the winter of 1929 when we moved to Clemenceau where I went to work in the U.V.X. Smelter and worked there until 1936.

Bad luck struck us in January 1932 when I fell down and broke a leg, and in February of the same year we lost our baby. In 1933 another baby came along in July but died at birth.

The smelter shut down in July 1936, so we sold out and went to Oregon where we stayed all summer. We returned to Sedona that fall and I worked at anything I could find until 1938. I went to work on the W.P.A. and put in two years at 'starve to death' wages.

In the fall of 1940, I went to work for the Cottonwood School as janitor. After school was out in the spring of 1943, I worked for the Forest Service at Lee Springs, on the mountain. I was terminated by them in August 1943. We moved to Clarkdale and I got a job as janitor at the high school.

In October 1944, our son Marvin was born in Flagstaff. I left the school in 1945 and went back to Oregon where my wife's folks were living. We returned to Sedona that winter and I went to work the following spring for Mrs. Baldwin at Red Rock. In the summer of 1947, our house burned down. In September we went to Texas with Frank Wallen, where we stayed until January 1948. I didn't like that country at all and we again returned to God's Country and the Red Rocks. I worked for George Jordan until 1950. Then we moved to Cottonwood and tried farming but could

Those Early Days…..

not make a go of it, so we came back to Sedona and I went to work for Mrs. Delia Hart until 1955 when I went to work for building contractors taking on various tasks connected with the trade.

In 1957 I took the lock trade as I was looking forward to my retirement, knowing I would need a less strenuous job and my trade has been most interesting and rewarding. I am now 70 years old and my trade keeps me busier all the time. In addition to this, I sharpen tools and implements with hand file during my free time. Even though I am retired, I still look after our very dear friend, Mrs. Delia Hart known by many as Aunt Delia.

I love it here in Sedona and the Red Rock Country and believe that my moving days have come to an end.

Just a moment please!

My wife Ivy has a few words about her earlier days.

My family came to Arizona in 1919 from Rodeo, New Mexico when I was ten years old. My father drove the big wagon, which was loaded with all the household belongings and Mother drove the spring wagon with eight children, the youngest being one month old. My two older brothers rode the two burros. The number of children totaled ten.

We arrived in Clarkdale, Arizona, which was not much of a town then. We camped there for about three months. My father started to work building houses in Clarkdale, as he was a carpenter.

We left Clarkdale and moved to the mouth of Oak Creek where we met a lady named Mrs. Matthew who asked us to move across the river to her place. We were there for a short time when my folks decided it was time to find a place to settle so we could attend school. We came first to Sedona, then on to Flagstaff and back down to the place that is now called Hidden Valley Ranch. We bought the ranch from Mr. O.A. Benedict. There was no dwelling of any kind on it and nothing else was on it. My folks built an underground house first, covering it over with poles and dirt. Later they built a little rock house on which they toiled endlessly it seemed, to make it ready for moving in. The next project they undertook was the digging of a ditch to irrigate a garden. The first two or three years there, they raised some of the finest produce in the valley, then, next they put in an orchard. Mother and the older brothers cultivated the garden using a plow with a burro hitched to it. We also had a grape vineyard and a bee apiary, which I disliked very much. I was stung by one of those blasted honey makers every time I looked around. I do believe that a bee knows a coward; I was also a coward toward many other insects.

We started to school that fall; our teacher was Mrs. Wyncoop and school was held in the front room of her home. After about three years, a new schoolhouse was built and we had several different teachers after Mrs. Wyncoop.

My folks worked very hard on the ranch and three more children were born making a dozen and one.

In 1925 I went to a dance up Oak Creek Canyon with my oldest sister and her date (later became her husband). Here is where I met Charles Smith and two years later in October, we were married.

You have just read about our life from there on written by Charlie.

## A FALSE ALARM
*by Albert E. Thompson*

This is a story about my dad, Jim Thompson, that I never heard him tell, but Roy Owenby told me that he heard Dad tell the story to his father. It was when Roy was small and he was kind of hazy on details, as he did not ask any questions.

As near as I can figure it out from what Roy told me, the occurrence took place in 1876, the year that Dad came to Prescott, and before he came over to Oak Creek.

It seems there was a report that came in to Ft. Whipple of Indian depredations to the north of Prescott, near present Seligman. Dad apparently took a job as packer and night herder for the soldiers' mules on the campaign to investigate.

The soldiers made camp for the night a long day's ride north of Ft. Whipple. After the evening meal Dad drove the army mules over a low ridge out of sight of camp where there was good grass. After a while he gathered some sticks and built a small fire. He tied his saddle horse and lay down to take a nap. As he turned around and around the fire to keep warm he spilled some cartridges out of his pocket near the fire. Just at the break of day he woke up cold and began to rake the charred ends of sticks and grass onto the embers to kindle his fire again. In the dark he got two or three of the cartridges into the hot coals. Of course they exploded. The noise was heard at the main camp. Right away he heard a bugle blowing. He quickly jumped on his horse and rounded up the mules and started toward camp. He met the guards before he got there. They asked if he had heard the shooting. Yes he had heard it, but had not seen anyone. They quickly saddled up and searched the area thoroughly but could not find any sign of Indians or anyone else. Dad kept a straight face and never did tell them what the shooting was.

## A LOST RETREAT (Poem)
*by Lee B. Woodcock, introduction by Mildred Johnson*

This poem was written years ago by the late Dr. Lee B. Woodcock, who presented it as a gift to his dear friend Bea Willard, mother of Don Willard.

A Pennsylvania physician who was also a musician and had trained in both fields in Pennsylvania and later in Vienna, Dr. Woodcock, retired to Sedona in the mid-thirties. He was a friend to man and a protector of animals and for his words of wisdom was lovingly called "The Sage of Sedona". In a then doctor less community he served the sick as a layman, counseling those who called on him either to seek medical aid or to curb neurotic fears. In his new found home, out of very limited retirement means, he helped many people who were beset by financial difficulties.

Music was the other half of Dr. Woodcock's life. Evenings he would be at his piano, composing, playing, singing. In earlier Sedona days, he held simple concerts in the old schoolhouse whenever successful singers, once pupils of his in the east, came to visit the old maestro. He gave of himself always. His life ended in October of nineteen fifty-eight.

> Where can one hide away today,
>     Away from civilization,
> Its turmoil, crimes and perfidies,
>     Its wars of extermination?
> A lone retreat I found one day,
>     And not so many years ago,
> Remote, and free from sordid world,
>     With much to set the heart aglow;
> With Nature, smiling undefiled,
>     Her lofty mountains, rocks and trees,
> A lovely virgin canyon stream
>     That rippled with each gentle breeze;
> And, oh, the silences I found!
>     So eloquent for those who feel
> The soulful things that move within,
>     That make one somehow wish to kneel
> And render thanks unto some force
>     Beneficient, unseen, though real.
> But now, my dream of happiness
>     And lone retreat are gone for aye.
> Since progress robbed me of the twain
>     With heavy heart I go my way.

Those Early Days.....

## AN OLD TIME SEDONA FAMILY
*by Minnie Farley Steele*

My Father, Joseph T. Farley, was born near Del Rio, Texas in 1873. He was working in a store in Del Rio by the time he was 13 years old. In the early 1890s an older brother, John Farley, had come out to Phoenix, Arizona. Not long afterward my father came out to join him. Father rode horseback from Texas to Phoenix. He did not like it in Phoenix, so he did not stay there long. He kept on riding. He came up through the Verde Valley and Sedona area but did not stop here at that time. He rode right on into Nevada to the mining camps where things were booming. He no doubt worked in the mines a while and learned how to use dynamite and other explosives. He was powder man on a ditch job many years later.

He did not stay many years in Nevada, because he was in Jerome, Arizona in the late 1890s when Jerome was a wild and wooly mining camp. He did not work in the mines there, but started a little store. At that time, Mother's brother, Dave Lay, also had a store in Jerome. My mother, Jane Lay, was visiting her brother Dave in Jerome when she and Father first met.

Mother was born in Tennessee, on April 18, 1877. My aunt, Mrs. Inez Lay has written the story of how the Lay family came to the Verde Valley, so I will not repeat.

Father and Mother went to Prescott on the old narrow gauge railroad and were married in 1900. They did not keep the store long after that but went down to the Verde River near present Clarkdale and Father worked for W.A. (Bill) Jordan. Next he took a homestead that would be in the present town of Clarkdale. While they were living on the Verde, I was born in Jerome in 1903.

Times were hard and money was scarce, so they left the homestead and moved to the old Pfau Mine, near the present road to Cherry Creek. Mother's sister and family, the Derricks were living there at that time. Our family did not stay there long either. The next move was to Dewey and then to the old Iron King Mine on Mingus Mountain, west of Dewey. My sister, Mary was born there in 1906. By the end of 1907, Father was back on Oak Creek, and he made application to homestead the place where I am now living, that year.

My grandfather and grandmother Lay got a house built on their homestead, a short ways down the creek, before we had one on our place. Mother and we girls lived with the Lays while Father was getting a house on our place. He hauled a small house from the Iron King Mine over to Sedona and put it together for our first home here. By the latter part of 1908 we were living in our own house. Father got water on part of the land that year and made a garden on the low land. By 1910, we moved back to Lower Oak Creek for a while and Father was powder man on a ditch that Mrs. Gates was having built. He did all of the blasting on that job. He had to be back on the homestead however after a few months, so we were not gone long.

Not long after that he got the irrigation ditch finished on the higher part of our place and planted fruit trees and put out a good sized patch of strawberries.

I attended the Sedona School until the spring of 1915, when Father got interested in oil properties near Sanderson, Texas. He sold the Sedona place that year and we moved to Texas. We did not get rich in the oil business but we lived. I finished school there. About 1918, we came back to Arizona and lived in Jerome for a few months, but went back to Texas again.

In the early 1920's I was working in a store in Sanderson, Texas when I met a young man named W.C. (Will) Steele. He was running a water pump for the railroad company at that time. Will Steele was born in Glasgow, Scotland in 1888. He came to this country when he was 19 years old. He was on the East coast for a while, and later came to the Mid West. He had been in Texas about two years when we met. We were married in 1922.

In 1924, Father and Mother got word that their old home in Sedona was for sale again. They came to see Will and me to see if we would come to Arizona with them. They said they would not make the move unless Will and I would come also. We all came back to look at the place, and Will liked it. Of course I was glad to get back on Oak Creek. Father and Mother and sister Mary, moved back here that same year but Will and I did not come until 1925. Father did not ride horseback on that trip like he did on the first one, but drove a Model T Ford touring car. He kept that car almost all the rest of his life. He did not drive much and he took good care of the car. He drove it in the first parade that the Coconino Sheriffs Posse put on in Sedona.

For a while after we moved to Sedona, Will was a Fuller Brush salesman and traveled all over Northern Arizona. I went with him part of the time. Later we grew fruit and vegetables and sold them all over Northern Arizona.

All three of my children were born in Arizona, at Flagstaff. They are my two sons, Will and Raymond and my daughter

Those Early Days.....

Minnie, who is married to Robert Willard and lives at Las Vegas, Nevada.

We had not been in Sedona very long when a vacancy occurred on the school board. Jesse Bushnell, the local Forest Ranger, came over to Will to see if he would consent to be appointed to finish out the term. Will agreed and the people of Sedona continued to vote him in on the school board until just before Sedona District #11, was consolidated with the Flagstaff district, in the 1940s. In the late 1930s the Forest Service had a shallow well dug near the creek, and put in a pump and pipeline to a high knoll back of the schoolhouse, where they built a large storage tank. It was all built so there would be running water at the Sedona Ranger. Station. Will Steele got permission from the local ranger to tap that water line to have running water to the schoolhouse. He put in drinking fountains, washrooms and flush toilets. Up to that time, all water for the school had to be carried in buckets.

Sedona had never had a full time deputy sheriff until about 1940. There had been special deputies for a short time but no full time deputy. In 1940, Sylvester McDowell was appointed full time deputy. McDowell only lived a few months after being deputized, and after his death, Will Steele, was appointed to take his place. Will served as deputy sheriff all of the rest of his life. Part of that time he was also deputy stock inspector. Will passed away on January 14, 1951. Our son, Will J. Steele was appointed to take his father's place and he is still holding the job of deputy at the present time.

After Will passed away, I got young Will to help me set up a trailer court, on our place here. I manage to keep pretty well occupied managing the court.

Father and mother built a house on the part of our land that extended across the creek to the west side. They started a little business on Main Street of Sedona. As they grew older they sold the property. Father lived until 10 years ago. He died on December 17, 1957. Mother moved back over here with us and is still living at age 90.

## EARLY SEDONA FRUIT GROWERS
*by Helen Jordan*

George W. Jordan came to Sedona in 1926 to help farm the ranch his father, William A. Jordan, bought from Claude Black. This place was originally homesteaded by the Owenby family, and had been used to raise alfalfa. The old stone house was in an abandoned state, with weeds growing in profusion everywhere. Orchards were planted, and, until the trees began to produce fruit, strawberries and vegetables were grown between the rows. I came to Sedona after we were married in 1927, and we bought the ranch several years later.

George bought a second-hand Hudson touring car, and converted it into a truck after installing an International truck rear end. It served for years, and as things wore out, they were replaced with other parts, until it had a Chevrolet truck cab, a Lincoln Zephyr motor, and extra gears of various sorts; we couldn't afford a new truck.

We painted the dark red mud walls of the house with calcimine, replaced broken window panes and screens, planted a lawn, and George installed a water powered electric plant.

Very few families lived here, and the school, at that time, had one teacher. The school building was used for entertainments, meetings, dances, and also as a meeting place for the little American Union Sunday School which is now Wayside Chapel.

One teacher organized the "Sedona Literary Society" which met once a month in the schoolhouse, and anyone who could carry a tune, play an instrument, or give a reading, would perform. Real corny, but everyone had a great time.

To market the fruit and vegetables, it was necessary to travel very narrow dirt roads. The old Schnebly road to Flagstaff was unsurfaced, so there was lots of dust in summer, and mud up to the fenders when it stormed, and the canyon road was little more than a trail. It followed Jordan Road north around Steamboat Rock, and was a real one-way road. The road to Cottonwood was surfaced, but melting snow or a rainstorm could cause Spring Creek and Dry Creek to become rivers, and sometimes it took a long time for the flood stage to subside enough for a car to be able to ford the streams.

George wasn't afraid of hard work, and being very ambitious and determined to make a success of the ranch, he worked early and late. In order to get to Flagstaff by the time the stores opened, he would leave long before daylight, taking along spare parts, such as connecting rods, pinion gears, axles, etc., in case of a breakdown and this often happened.

One time his sister Alice, and her husband, Bill Gray, came to stay all night with us. We had a lot of ripe tomatoes, which had to be packed and loaded on the truck, so we worked long after dark out in the yard under a big light, with my brother helping us. Next day, Bill, who loved to tease and joke, said to Dad Hart, "Sure don't take long to stay all night at the Jordan's. About midnight Helen went to bed, and at one Paul came in. Then at two, George came in, took off his pants, shook them, put them back on and went to Flagstaff."

*The overshot water wheel built by George W. Jordan on his fruit ranch in Sedona.*

During the depression, the prices of farm produce reached a new low, and with each farmer trying to compete with his neighbor you could hardly give it away, so they decided to form a cooperative. They brought their fruit to our packing shed where we packed it uniformly, and George did the marketing for everyone. He made regular trips each week to Cottonwood, Clarkdale, Jerome and

Prescott, and also to Flagstaff, Williams and Ash-fork, and even to Winslow and Holbrook, each time taking orders for the next trip. He would get home late, and we would work till midnight, and after, getting the truck loaded for an early start next morning. This brought about a much better market, but it was hard and grueling.

Our water supply came from the creek down the irrigation ditch, and a hydraulic ram pumped it directly to the kitchen faucet, which made it bad when the ditch was being cleaned, or the creek was muddy.

We cleared more land and planted a large orchard above the ditch, and in order to irrigate it, George decided to build a water wheel to pump the water to a large open reservoir above the orchard, and also to a large storage tank for the house.

He built an overshot wheel, 20 feet in diameter, which was powered by the ditch water. He cut the buckets for the wheel, and riveted them by hand. This water wheel worked perfectly for many years, and was a favorite subject for photographers.

We found that Sedona had the perfect climate for the fruit grower, and our trees produced so much fruit that we needed a packing house other than the canvas sided shed we had been using. We also needed a cold storage to take care of the fruit properly. George hauled lumber with which to build the packing house from a mill near Mormon Lake. This was during the depression, and the mill owner offered the lumber at a very low price, otherwise we could not have bought it. The old truck would be loaded to capacity for each trip, and stones piled on the running boards and fenders kept the front end on the ground, and, with the help of two carpenters, one being Jim Farley, the packing house, now the Sedona Art Barn, was built.

*This picture is of the George Jordan farm in Oak Creek in 1928, one half mile above the Sedona Post Office. The barn is where Wayside*

Those Early Days.....

*Chapel now stands. The old stone house is still there by the Art Barn.*

We eventually got good roads, and more people came to Sedona and wanted to live here, but the town needed a good water supply in order to grow, so George was persuaded to dig a well and start a water system for the community. This well provided pure water, and was approved by the health department, but it was a difficult task to get the pipelines to the scattered settlement through the very rocky terrain, and even hard to find good pipe during the wartime. As more and more people came, and subdivisions were developed, the pipeline was extended across the creek and on down to the Broken Arrow Subdivision. This was the beginning of the Sedona Water System, which is now the Arizona Water Company.

The busy years flew by, filled with lots of work, and also lots of good times. George enjoyed having fun and was usually the life of every party with his jokes and musical talents. Our big lawn was the scene of many, many picnics and gatherings through the years.

People came from everywhere to buy our fruit, and, so that it would be more convenient for fruit buyers and give us more much needed cold storage space, we built the market building along the highway.

George was handicapped by painful and crippling rheumatoid arthritis for many years, but he kept going in spite of it. In the summer of 1958, when his health grew much worse, we sold the water system. The next spring we sold part of the ranch and moved from the old place, and later into a new home which we built on the rim of Mormon Canyon overlooking the creek, and also our old place, and giving us a wonderful view of Wilson Mountain.

George passed away in April 1964, having accomplished much, but not nearly all he had planned. In recent years he said to me, "You know, when I think back on all the hard work I did, and remember all the hardships we had, I shudder, and wonder how I managed, but at the time I didn't mind at all."

## THE TORTURE ROD
*by Fletch Fairchild*

In the month of July 1914, a beautiful morning dawned in Flagstaff, Arizona and we were ready for it. The spanking new, shiny, red and black "Chevrolet Baby Grand" touring car reposing in front of our house also looked ready. This "Chevy" was the first ever purchased in Flagstaff and this was the first year of its manufacture.

Our party consisted of two of my sisters, my brother-in-law Carl Anderson and myself. I'm sure all of us were experiencing the same feeling as Charles A. Lindberg experienced several years later as he and "The Spirit of St. Louis" poised at a New York airport awaiting weather conditions to begin their now-famous Trans-Atlantic flight. Our destination was just Sedona, Arizona.

Our proposed adventure was, indeed, not as phenomenal as Lindberg's but to us - in its own way-was quite as adventuresome. Our destination was to be achieved via Schnebly Hill. I had traversed this route many times with team or teams and wagons and had often wondered when and if an automobile-such as they were; and such as the so-called road was, in those days, would ever make the trip and how soon this might become a reality; and how soon I could get behind the wheel of one and try it.

Having learned to drive an automobile in the year 1911 and, in the meantime, I had lived in Oak Creek Canyon much of the interim; one might imagine as I plodded along in a slow, rough lumber wagon during the heat, rain and cold how the thought of slithering along up and down this same route in a sleek automobile became more and more intriguing to me.

In the wagon days it was necessary to stop frequently and let the horses blow, (as we referred to letting them catch their breath). This entailed chocking rocks behind the wagon wheels at each stop to avoid the loss of any precious footage gained while ascending the steep grade. This operation was especially true on the steepest part known as Glasgow Pitch.

Glasgow Pitch was the east and west portion of the road slightly on the Sedona side of the famous portion known as the Merry-Go-Round. Remains of this treacherous stretch may still be seen from the present Schnebly Hill. To view this little beauty today, one should stop just before arriving at the old Merry-Go-Round, going up the hill, then look back toward Sedona. It would make a nice hike-out of rattlesnake season. However, I think I hiked it enough in the old days to last me from now on.

Those Early Days.....

Our anticipation was at the breaking point at take-off time and the Chevrolet Baby Grand (the nickname "Chevy" had not yet been applied at that time-just in passing) purred sweetly as we passed through the school section, five miles south of Flagstaff, the case being the same as we slid past the Pump House, Newman Tank, Munds Park, John Loy's Ranch, the Price place and Clay Park as well.

Upon our arrival at the top of Schnebly I shall never forget the expressions of Carl as we stopped at the vantage point as he viewed for the first time the awesome spectacle of the valley below. The rest of us knew exactly what he was experiencing as we had all experienced the same mixed feelings at our first glimpse of this magnificent perspective. I must admit I still thrill deeply each time I gaze over this most beautiful panorama.

This time-to me-things were slightly different. I was secretly wondering could we really make it in this magic of all machines? I had reassured the rest of the party, time and again, there was nothing to it; but I must admit when I looked into the valley this particular day, it looked very much bigger and a great deal more defiant than I had ever noticed before. These thoughts, I kept very much to myself.

Down the rough hill we started, easing along over Kinsey Canyons and rocks. (A Kinsey Canyon was sort of a ditch thrown up across the road at strategic intervals to avoid the rains and runoff from washing out the road). My step-granddad, L.E. (Dad) Hart used to say as he and I traveled over this terrain so many times in wagons, "You just go off of one rock onto two, and that the road went up hill, in places just in order to get to go down". So we were on our way down and never a statement bore more truth than Dad's.

The farther down we went, the steeper it seemed to me and I was just certain it had changed since my last wagon trip; especially when I could take an occasional look back and wonder if this bright, beautiful machine was really going to take us back up as anxiously as it was taking us down. Anxiously it was too. I used engine compression, brakes and what have you and several times I wished I had a pole dragging under the wheels as we sometimes did with heavily loaded wagons.

With the above exceptions we finally arrived, uneventfully, at Ed Hart's ranch. This is the first ranch to the right after crossing the bridge on Highway 179 going south from Sedona. Our intentions upon leaving Flagstaff were to go down to our lower ranch on Oak Creek, which was down below the old

Schuerman ranch and is close to where the Cup of Gold estate is today. Our better judgment dissuaded us of this, however, and we were content to just stay with Ed and Sarah Hart for a few days and let the few natives of the Sedona area come and admire the beautiful red and black monster as we fondly polished her in our leisure moments.

All too soon the time arrived when we decided to make our departure and head back toward Flagstaff; that turned out to be exactly what it was-head toward Flagstaff.

All went fine until we tackled Glasgow Pitch with its surface of loose dirt. With wheels slipping and barely moving, with all power on, a noise broke loose under the back of the car which sounded like all the chariots of Troy traveling over the cobble-stone pavements of Hoboken.

We quickly stopped, and not of our own accord. We were out of the car in a flash peering under the car like crazy. Then we discovered it. The Torsion Rod was broken squarely in two, this being the brace that held the rear axle housing and differential in place. Of course, with this vital organ gone the drive shaft and rear universal joint were beating against the floorboards of the rear seat—no wonder all the racket. My two sisters who were riding in the rear seat at the time said later: "They were just sure the thing was blowing up".

The whole thing reminded me of a story I once heard when one man asked the other: "Which would you rather be in, a ship wreck or a train wreck?" The other replied, "Why a train wreck, of course, cause if you are in a ship wreck, where in the heck are you; but if you are in a train wreck, there you are". So there we were smack in the middle of Glasgow Pitch with what seemed like doom staring us squarely in the face, and the sun bearing down on us more and more.

Luckily, Carl had considerable mechanical knowledge plus ingenuity of no small degree as a few years prior he had earned a degree in mechanical engineering from a large eastern university. I was also quite adept as I had helped shoe a couple of horses in my time.

Those days were not like the present when one may call a tow car and the thing will be there before you have time to relax and light a smoke. So we got out the kit of tools from under the seat. These consisted of a pair of pliers, a monkey wrench, screwdriver, hubcap wrench and I think, a tire iron. We then set to work removing the Torsion Rod which we immediately renamed Torture Rod.

Those Early Days.....

After removing this beautiful, black painted part we found it to be made of tubular steel (or iron of some nature). We held an autopsy and figured if we could get it back down to Ed Hart's ranch we might-just might be able to fix it, by possibly slipping a piece of pipe over the broken place and riveting same.

We considered the disdainful walk back to the ranch in ever-increasing heat with worse than an utter lack of enthusiasm; I wonder why? Just as we were ready to call upon "Shanks Mares" we heard the rumble of a wagon bouncing over the rocky road in the direction of Sedona. We just couldn't be this lucky, but sure enough we were. The wagon turned out to be that of Johnnie Hearst, a fruit rancher from lower Oak Creek. Johnnie had been to Flagstaff with a load of fruit and was returning. I have seen a lot of sights in my time, but none more welcome than this.

My sisters climbed up on the seat with Johnnie while Carl and I loaded the Torture Rod, then made ourselves as comfortable as anyone could atop a load of empty fruit boxes in the back of a wagon.

We arrived back at the ranch shortly after noon; our dismay sinking to a very low level, once more, when we found Ed Hart had suddenly decided to take his team and wagon to the lower ranch to help out with some work pending there. So, here went our transportation back up the hill, even though, we might get the Torture Rod fixed so it might hold.

After a fine repast prepared by Sarah Hart our spirits and ambitions were restored and we set to work on the Torture Rod. All seemed to fall in place on the mending job and we concluded it might be stronger than it was in its original make-up.

We had the job finished by about 4:00 P.M. and were so enthused about our, now, good fortune we decided we would wait till late evening and coolness, walk back to the car, sleep in the nice, comfortable leather seats and at the crack of dawn start replacing the Torture Rod and return for my sisters and then give Schnebly Hill another go at it.

As planned, we started hoofing it up the hill about dusk with the Torture Rod. Carl was from the east and I doubt very much if he had ever spent a night out before, unless it might have been in a well protected, secluded summer camp in his native environment. We were taking our time and soon a bright moon was shining. We took turns carrying the Torture Rod; it wasn't too heavy but cumbersome. As we approached the depths of Bear Wallow, some three or four miles from Sedona, I was carrying the rod nonchalantly, marveling the cool, fresh air and serenity of our surroundings.

Carl was enjoying the hike also and had just made a remark confirming the fact when the air was rent with the most ungodly scream imaginable. We both froze in our tracks but not until I had, unknowingly, brought the Torture Rod to be ready; and Carl had exclaimed in a shaky, hollow voice: "What on earth was that?" After slight recovery, there I stood, the Torture Rod poised over my shoulder, not unlike a major league baseball player ready to hit the winning home run of a world's series. Carl was babbling something about the unprecedented noise sounding like the scream of a woman in distress or much more so.

I had heard such a sound before and knew it was the scream of a panther (a more romantic name for a mountain lion or cougar), these animals being quite common in this area in those days. However, the scream occurring as this one did, when least expected, curdled the blood in my veins as it had Carl's.

After an unknown period of recovery we proceeded, cautiously on toward the Chevrolet Baby Grand. During the rest of the hike I used my conversation in trying to reassure Carl (as well as myself) that the panther had probably been as startled by our approach as we were of hearing its scream and was, by this time, twenty miles away. Secretly I hoped I was correct.

Without further incident we arrived at the car, approaching it with apprehension, lest the panther had availed himself of the back seat.

This Chevrolet had an outstanding innovation, for its time, this being a trouble light with a long cord wound around a spring roller, which could be pulled out of the dash and carried any place around the car, in case one had trouble in the dark. The light was fed off the battery under the front seat. Most cars of this vintage, that were equipped with batteries, used the battery for starting the motor and when the motor had been started, it was then necessary to switch to a magneto for running. The Chevrolet had added the trouble light, which this night served Carl in good stead, as he was in trouble after hearing the cat scream. The consequence was that Carl stretched the trouble light into the back seat and read magazines the rest of the night. I was glad also that the light was on, but I did sleep fitfully in the front seat.

As morning light broke over the top of Schnebly we were munching sandwiches prepared for us by the good Sarah Hart. Then came the installation of the Torture Rod; in this we had

## Those Early Days.....

good luck and it looked as if it would hold and did.

The car was turned around and within a short time we were back in Sedona. After partaking of some more of Sarah's good food we took off to tackle Schnebly once more, with some forebodings. Schnebly, at that time, had all the significance of the Matterhorn, or so it seemed to me. I'm sure the others felt the same.

Arriving at Glasgow Pitch we stopped and did some road work; smoothing, packing brush into places we had dug when the rod had broken. When finished I backed up where I could get a good run at the Pitch. After getting out and studying the topography a bit, and telling the passengers to hang on for dear life, I hit old Glasgow with every ounce the Baby Grand had in all her four cylinders. We made it. Eureka!

There was no stopping now, this precious momentum must be kept alive till, and if, we reached the top. None had time to even look back at Glasgow Pitch. I was too busy dodging rocks, high centers, and jumping Kinsey Canyons. The rest watching the road and wondering if we were going to stay in the right place; for in those days, had a car gone off the road, in certain spots, the birds would have built a nest in the back seat before it reached bottom.

Arriving at the top of Schnebly we stopped and checked the Baby Grand. With the exception of being quite warm, she seemed to be shipshape, with Torture Rod as good as new or perhaps a little better, and I thought the beautiful valley spread before us had never looked more beautiful; since we and the Chevrolet were sitting on top of Schnebly and the Baby Grand had conquered her objective.

What an automobile for her time. I don't know exactly what her serial number was but it was somewhere between one and number 6,243. These numbers came from an old automobile bluebook, one of my prized possessions. That first year of manufacture of the Chevrolet, only 6,743 cars were built by the company then, headquartered in New York City.

Now 53 years later, I have a Chevrolet pick-up purchased in 1964, just 50 years after this incident; and its serial number is 4C144H126282. I have no idea about what these numbers mean but it appears likely the company has been a success.

The Baby Grand was traded in later on a brand new Hupmobile and both of their bones-might very well be today an integral part of some one's bright new sports car or something.

What a transfiguration - not only in automobiles, but of highways and things too numerous to mention even by me. Very remarkable - this progress - and I love it. I don't have to repair Torture Rods any more because cars of today are not equipped with them. I don't have to listen to panther screams in Bear Wallow either, because these are practically extinct. And I don't have to walk up Schnebly Hill any more.

Today's transportation is just too much for good old Schnebly Hill.

Those Early Days.....

## FROM KEROSENE TO KILOWATTS
*by Wilma Dallas*

Inevitably there came a transition from the period of the early settlers and old-timers to this modern era of conveniences, good highways, tourism, and retirement. It might be interesting to consider this transition in the Verde Valley and Oak Creek as being marked by the "phasing out" of the kerosene lamp when electricity was being made available.

Last summer Mr. Sam Hosier conducted a Sedona Westerners hiking group to the Childs Power Plant near Verde Hot Springs and the mouth of Fossil Creek, where they learned about that plant and also the one at Irving where the road to Pine and Payson from Camp Verde crosses Fossil Creek. He is still sure very few people living here have any knowledge that these hydroelectric generating systems are in existence.

The story of the early development at Childs, one of the first sources of power for Prescott and Jerome, is one of great difficulties that had to be overcome on account of the nearly inaccessible terrain. Several years were spent in establishing water rights, engineering studies, and financing and organization planning. This took from 1902 until 1907.

First, 50 miles of road construction was necessary. Then came a temporary power turbine for producing power to operate rock crushers, compressors, drills, illumination, tunnel fans, machine and blacksmith shops, etc. Faced with the proposed 12-month construction schedule, there were employed 600 men, 400 mules, and 150 wagons. To deliver Fossil Creek water from springs and creek to a reservoir high above the plant, required eleven more miles of road, thousands of feet of pipe line, concrete and wooden flumes, tunnels, siphons, and steel supporting bridges. Below Stehr Lake reservoir came the high-pressure steel pipe to the power plant penstock, the generators, and transformers. To all of this must be added 75 miles of transmission line, substations, houses, stables, camps, and warehouses. Mules transported materials, equipment and supplies from the nearest railroad at Mayer.

It was in 1909 that the construction begun in 1907 reached the point that the first electric energy was being delivered at Jerome. In a few short years after that, new smelters in the Valley brought about the starting of the towns of Clarkdale, Clemenceau and Cottonwood and thus led to continuous spread of electric lines until now the use of kerosene has practically ceased in the entire area.

The Childs and Irving plants first were part of the Arizona Power Company, Prescott; later merging with the Central Arizona Light and Power Co., Phoenix; and at the present time the nearly statewide Arizona Public Service Co.

Now we go back to our guide, Mr. Sam Hosier. It was in 1906 that Sam, age 22, arrived in Winslow, Arizona. He had left Pennsylvania at the age of 17 when he began working on railroads across the country, landing in Winslow while working on the Santa Fe as an engineer. Meanwhile, Martha Guthrie had accompanied her father to Winslow on a business trip from Ohio as she frequently did. Her father set up water and sewer systems throughout the country for American Light and Power Company out of Kansas City, Missouri. At that time Arizona was still a territory, becoming a state in 1912. Martha and Sam married in 1910 in Martha's hometown of Coshocton, Ohio, and returned to Winslow where Sam kept his job on the Santa Fe. In 1911 Martha got a pass on the train and went home to mother, where their first child, a son Odyth was born.

In 1912 a group of eight railroaders left Winslow by wagon to attend the snake dance held on the first mesa of the Hopi villages. Martha recalls that there were only two automobiles in Winslow at that time. The Hosiers were among the eight who made the trip to Walpi in a covered wagon; each with his own bed roll. The four women squatted on the floor of the wagon during the day and played cards; two men rode on the front seat of the wagon and two rode ponies. Their cooking was done in dutch ovens. The group camped out three nights along the way; the round trip took about one week. President Theodore Roosevelt and two sons were also camped at the base of the mesa. They, too, had made the trip to see the Hopi Snake Ceremony. The President was a guest of Don Lorenzo Hubbell, famous Indian trader, two-term Sheriff of Apache County, and member of the Senate in the territorial legislative assembly from 1893 to 1912.

Hosiers lived for a while in Ohio where their daughter Sylvia was born in 1923. But it seemed that Arizona was calling them and they moved back to Winslow. It was in 1942 that Sam, employed by the old Arizona Power Company, became superintendent of Arizona's first hydroelectric plants at Fossil Creek and agent of a newer generating plant at Tapco near Clarkdale.

Sam and Martha lived at Childs in company housing, where neatly kept lawns, trees and flowers still make an attractive setting. At that time the population also included a chief operator, relief

Those Early Days.....

operator, a machinist, a roustabout, and a patrolman who rode horseback to patrol the lines.

Sam retired from the Arizona Public Service Company in 1952 and retired to Sedona, where he and Martha now live. These early Arizona folks celebrated their 57th wedding anniversary Sept. 14, 1967. Their story spans a period of great change from wagons and railroads to automobiles and, from kerosene to kilowatts.

## THE NARROW GAUGE
*by Don Willard*

To old-timers in the Verde Valley and Oak Creek for a period of about twenty years, one of the greatest means of contact with the outside world was the unforgettable "narrow gauge" railroad connecting Jerome with the Santa Fe "Pea Vine", or Ash Fork, Prescott and Phoenix branch in Chino Valley. Nearly all supplies for the mine, smelter, and town of Jerome were shipped in by this facility, and the result was that Jerome became a trading center for most of the valley. It was once the fifth largest town in the state. For fuller facts as to its hey-day, it is suggested that one refer to Mr. H.V. Young's "Ghosts of Cleopatra Hill".

The "Narrow Gauge" wore the imposing title of "The United Verde and Pacific Railway. Probably the chief item of freight was coke for firing the smelter furnaces, and next was hauling the copper "matte" out to be transferred to the Santa Fe for transport to the refinery in the East. "Accommodation" coaches were attached to the end of the "string" of freight cars. Passenger traffic was usually quite important as roads were primitive and afforded no service with equal convenience. The run to or from the "Junction", 26 miles, usually took about two hours and

*Time - 1905. Occasion - - Mixed train about to start from "Narrow Gauge" station, which overlooked old smelter at Jerome, on holiday "excursion" to Prescott. Frank Nail, father of Mrs. Myrtle Smith of Sedona, at left in dark suit. Engineer, George Haskins, with mustache, father of James Haskins of Phoenix Cement Co., at Clarkdale, who generously furnished this photo.*

a quarter longer, if necessary to let a "hot box" cool off (when a

Those Early Days…..

wheel bearing over-heated on its axle).

The depot was located above the old smelter, which was several hundred feet higher than Main Street in Jerome. That site has been completely excavated and is now the "Pit". It was necessary to build a new more modem smelter at Clarkdale and a great portion of the ore body was found to be immediately under the old smelter.

The "Narrow Gauge" had to give way to a Santa Fe branch into Clarkdale by way of Perkinsville and the Verde River. Two other railroads once operating in the area were the V T & S or Verde Tunnel and Smelter line from Jerome and the big mine to the smelter at Clarkdale, and the U V Ex connecting the United Verde Extension mine below Jerome with its smelter at Clemenceau and with Clarkdale. These three abandoned lines are now marked only by traces of their roadbeds, which have to be pointed out for identification to visitors or new residents.

We old-timers cannot forget the "Narrow Gauge" which so often served us well on those occasions when it provided access to an outlet from the valley so much more satisfactorily than the limited alternatives of those days.

## AS TIME DRAWS ON
*by Wilma Dallas*

In 1927 Henry Elmer Cook homesteaded 160 acres extending from the foot of Table Mountain to the southwest in Grasshopper Flat. He lived here until his death at almost age 90. Henry and wife, Effie were parents of eight girls and two boys now widely scattered throughout the country. In 1911, their oldest daughter, Bessie Cook married Frank Gibson in Oklahoma. They lived near Seminole and times were very rough.

In 1930 Bessie's' father wrote to them that this Red Rock area would be a good place to live and even though times were rough, homesteading was no problem here. That same year the Gibson's arrived in Sedona with their four children; Lucille, Wade, Darlene and Paul.

They homesteaded 160 acres, grew fruit and vegetables and built a one-room shack on the 160 acres adding a room to it as often as they could. Frank got quite a bit of work from the movie industry when many films were made in this area.

Bessie was sick much of the time. She recalls the kindness of "Aunt" Delia Hart who sent vegetables and fruit to her from their store during winter months.

Frank hauled four to six barrels of water at a time with a team and wagon. He had to come all the way to Oak Creek where he filled the barrels from a ditch that was parallel with the creek, by using a pipe and siphon. Bessie said they were never short of water. At that time, she says there were only two houses along 89A from their home near Settler's Rest into Sedona.

Bessie's brother Fred Cook and Frank would make trips to California during watermelon season and buy a truck load which they sold on their return trip realizing a small profit, which in those days was better than no profit.

For a while, the Gibson's owned the Rainbow's End where they operated a service station and store. One of their first acquaintances was Charles and Avis Thompson whom they visited often.

Their number of children had increased to six, Peggy and Billie Rae were born in Sedona. They spent many happy days roaming over the vast countryside while being protected by their long time and faithful lifeguard, a shepherd dog named Troubles. Bessie fell in March 1966 and broke her hip, after which she made a remarkable recovery. The thing she enjoys most is having all the children and grandchildren visit them at their usual family gatherings. She feels very fortunate to have them all nearby. Mrs. Peggy Dickison and Mrs. Lucille Newton live in Sedona while Mrs. Billie Rae Bowman and Wade Gibson live in Phoenix. Paul lives in Cottonwood and Mrs. Darlene Pirtle in Cornville. This enables the frequent gatherings, which are so popular at the Gibson home.

Bessie celebrated her 73rd birthday on July 4, 1967. She is quite active despite her recent injury and has just finished a batch of jelly made from their own vineyard. She puts up pickles, other vegetables and fruits.

Frank at 76 has a fine sense of humor and likes also to keep busy. He is kept busy with caring for their fruit trees and garden, staking his tomatoes, poling beans, etc.

As Bessie and Frank look back over their 56 years of marriage, they admit that those 'bad years' weren't really so bad after all.

## OLD ROADS
*by Virginia Finnie Webb*

This is a postscript to Albert Thompson's excellent chapter on, "Early Roads of the Sedona Area," and covers memories and impressions of early Verde Valley roads when I was a child and young girl.

The mountains surrounding the Verde Valley and the hills within the valley and between the creeks tributary to the Verde River, made it difficult of access by wheeled vehicles until the pioneers built by hand, with the aid of pick and shovel, the rough old roads we remember. A visiting minister, they called his book selling type a colporteur, on arriving by buckboard at my parents' home on Beaver Creek in the eighteen nineties said, "Brother Finnie, your roads are macadamized with boulders the size of a man's head."

The Verde River enters its valley through a narrow deep canyon and departs the same way. This made access to the valley over high mountain ranges bordering the narrow valley on either side the only feasible routes for pioneers to build roads into it.

There is a fascination in following the old roads across the Verde Valley, and imagining all the variety of characters who passed over them in former times. You can easily visualize the big old army ambulances with their mule teams and accompanying mounted soldiers, as they bumped and swayed along the rough old road running from Fort Whipple at Prescott to Camp Verde; thence across the valley over the Mogollon Plateau past Stoneman Lake through the divide between Hutch Mountain and Mahan Mountain, through Sunset Pass to the Little Colorado River and east to Fort Wingate or southeast to Fort Apache. One of the way stations along this lonely route was the Beaver Head Station on Dry Beaver Creek, midway between Beaver Creek and Oak Creek. My father, Robert Finnie, said he received mail at Beaver Head brought in by the army when he first settled at our ranch on Wet Beaver Creek. This must have been about 1881. There were mail routes under private contracts, but because of their constant difficulties the army also carried mail both by vehicle and horseback.

I can recall the old stage station and its rock chimney, though today only a pile of rocks marks the spot. However, the road on the west side of the creek and the road ascending the rim on the east are easily followed by foot or horseback. At a later date, when stock raising was at its zenith in this area, the sheep trail running from Cordes into the Verde Valley and on to Beaver Head, saw

Those Early Days.....

thousands of sheep pass in spring north to summer grass and in fall returning to the desert for winter pasture. The old sheep trail came by Rattlesnake Tanks and on to Beaver Head, crossing the Verde River near the mouth of Oak Creek, and going west north of Grief Hill on to Cordes.

Another sheep trail from the Mud Tanks range ran across Lower Verde and over the north slope of Squaw Peak below Camp Verde. An early memory is of bright lights high on Squaw Peak across the valley and the cowboys always saying they were campfires on the sheep trail. The old road on Grief Hill is well known for the massacre, which occurred there and for at least two engagements between the soldiers and Indians in 1866 and 1869. Grief Hill was a very early wagon road coming into the Verde Valley from the west. Large corrals were built at Beaver Head for counting the sheep by the Forest Service ranger as they went north, and the remains of these cedar corrals were picturesque for our city guests to photograph and paint in the 1930's.

The pool of water at Beaver Head made it a campsite for sheepherders and for cowboys working that range, and later was a favorite ride and picnic spot for the dude ranches on Beaver Creek. My parents occasionally mentioned the names of people who lived in the old station but the only one I recall is Mitch Burch and by the time I first remember it was a deserted station of another era. Some years ago Lloyd Linn, son of the then Beaver Creek District ranger, found on the old army road between Hutch Mountain and Schell Spring an old U.S. Cavalry spur some long ago soldier lost along that old road.

There are traces of an old road that ran from Beaver Head south to the Wales Arnold farm below Montezuma Well and on down the ridge to cross Beaver Creek just above its junction with Dry Beaver Creek. The Beaver Creek end of this road ran into Camp Verde and was a main wagon road until a few ranchers, including my father and brother and Jack Blome, decided to build a road along the hills where the Black Canyon Highway now runs between McGuireville and the turn off to Montezuma Castle, thus avoiding creek crossings that were often impassable for cars and sometimes for horses during flood periods.

The old adobe ranch house Uncle Wales Arnold built on the land below Montezuma Well was a little fortress with portholes and an inside well, and there was some mail delivery service there before the Beaver Head Station was built. This sturdy old adobe house stood until recent years when it was dozed over - a real historical loss. Uncle Wales' partner in this farm was killed by the Apaches across the creek from the house. Early pioneers of Beaver Creek fled to this fortress house during Indian scares.

When General Crook became commanding officer in the Arizona Territory he laid out a shorter route along the Tonto Rim between Fort Apache and Camp Verde. It was a rough direct route and was called "The Crook Trail."

Mrs. Summerhayes in her book, "Vanished Arizona," relates her journey over the Crook Trail and after her husband's service at Fort Apache tells of their return trip by the Little Colorado River, Stoneman Lake and Beaver Head. After all these years a highway is being built along the old Crook Trail. To pioneers the only acceptable name for the new highway is its historic title Crook Trail. Over it the energetic and remarkable General Crook and his indefatigable saddle mule traveled in his successful efforts to bring safety to our early settlers. See Bourke's, "On the Border with Crook."

All the early horse-drawn travel from the Verde Valley to the Mogollon Plateau and Flagstaff used the pioneer and army road from Beaver Head. At Rattlesnake Tanks a fork turned directly north to Flagstaff via Pine Springs (not to be confused with Pine Mountain and Spring on the army road between Stoneman Lake and Sunset Pass), Woods Ranch and Munds Park. My father and Lyman Drum, Mr. Price and others decided to build a more direct road up the mountain from their winter homes on Wet Beaver Creek. They looked over what later became the Blue Grade, but were forced to build a mile or so parallel to it up Hog Tanks Wash because they were only a few men with picks and shovels. In 1912, Yavapai County did build along Little Dry Creek Canyon a spectacular narrow road up the mountain to intercept the old army road from Beaver Head.

This road was surfaced with blue rock chips and gravel, thus the name Blue Grade, and it served as the main road from Camp Verde and Beaver Creek to the northeast until the Black Canyon Highway was built. The county established a large camp at the foot of this Blue Grade for the many men who worked on the road with hand tools, blasting the mountainside and preparing the way for teams and Fresno scrapers. My brother and I took fruit and vegetables to this big, busy camp where engineers, white men and a large camp of Apache Indians in wigwams were eager customers and we were happy kids to take home a pocket full of money. Gail Gardner, who was a friend of ours, was there that summer.

The country people were delighted with the new road as it had a gradual grade and made climbing the mountain much easier. Later automobiles used the road and town tourists considered it an

Those Early Days.....

eyebrow road. I recall the first summer I drove a car, a Wills St. Clair, I took my father on some business up the Blue Grade and met Frank Walroup coming down with the T Bar S chuck wagon loaded high with food and beds. I was petrified at the thought of passing on the outside rim of the road this big wagon and teams. Frank continued toward us until there was a sight slope on the wall side of the road where he expertly put his lead team up on the hillside and drew the wheelers and wagon close in and beckoned for me to come on. Years later the county sent in a crew to widen the old Blue Grade road.

On Oak Creek the ranchers in that area built a direct road up the mountain known as Schnebly Hill Road to make a shorter haul to Flagstaff, and years later a very picturesque road was built up Oak Creek Canyon, a few remnants of which can be seen from the present Oak Creek Canyon road. These old roads were replete with startlingly beautiful views and hair-raising grades. My mother told me of the beautiful little lodges in Oak Creek Canyon and the beauty of the isolated canyon when it was accessible only by trail. Oak Creek Lodge belonged to Mrs. Thomas and Lolomai Lodge to Mrs. Sisson, both prominent women of Flagstaff in the late 19th century.

My mother, Flora Weatherford, was a young teacher in Flagstaff and her trip to Oak Creek Lodge must have been in the early eighteen nineties. She said they went in carriages and horseback to the rim of the canyon and there packed the horses and walked down to the lodge. The lodges were built of hewn logs cut on the land and were very attractive. The Oak Creek Lodge living room shows the good hand worked logs today.

I recall meeting Mrs. Thomas in Pasadena, California. Mrs. E.S. Gosney invited my mother to a luncheon she gave for Mrs. Thomas and I attended also. My memory of Mrs. Thomas is of a very gracious elderly lady dressed in black taffeta and interested in Flora's little girl, no doubt the reason I remembered her so clearly.

On the west side of the valley the route to Prescott was through Copper Canyon, on to the Cienega, Ash Creek, across Lonesome Valley, Lynx Creek and into Prescott past the cavalry post at Fort Whipple. Such fun for us children to see a troop of cavalry dashing down the hills in practice formation! A small streetcar ran from Prescott to old Fort Whipple and was another exciting sight. My aunt, Mrs. Dave Finnie, took me for my first ride on it when I was five years old.

*Until 1927, vehicles passed through this tunnel, south of Encinoso Camp Grounds, on Highway 89A. The white cliff was blasted off and hauled far away. Notice the boulder, which the traveler had to move before he could proceed.*

From the Black Canyon Highway the old Copper Canyon wagon road can be seen following the tiny stream along the bottom of the canyon past the old Durfee goat ranch and climbing out at the head of the canyon on a short steep grade. There were "thank you ma'ams" as water breaks on this grade where we could rest the heaving animals. Remembering the wagons seeming to pitch on the horse's rumps and the old brake blocks screaming as we descended, I smile now when I see the highway sign "check your brakes," at the head of Copper Canyon.

On a long ago trip to Prescott my father bought a new wagon and towed it home behind the wagon he was driving. He told my mother she would have to brake the second wagon, but en route Mr. L.B. Bell of Camp Verde and his son Roy overtook us in a light vehicle and, good neighbor that he was, he offered to have Roy, who was about twelve years of age, take mother's place on the wagon and let mother ride in his easier conveyance. As Mr. Bell and mother went ahead of us they saw a bird flying frantically around a bush some eight feet high. A closer view revealed a large rattlesnake ascending the bush to the bird's nest. Mr. Bell killed the snake but the bird appeared to be having a nervous breakdown from so much excitement.

Old roads were hard work for the horses and mules that by animal power pulled heavy loads over the rough country, and tiring to the pioneers who rode the swaying, bouncing wagon seats, but for children it was adventure and delight. The wagon sheet

Those Early Days.....

covered the bows over the wagon and the bed had hay a foot deep for padding the loads and feeding the teams, all of which made a fine place for a child to nap after runs along the road for exercise. There were exciting things to see, squirrels, prairie dog towns, large swift brilliantly green lizards standing high on stiff legs to look at us, occasional deer and antelope and my father to draw our attention to the marvels of nature around us. As we passed slate hill we always ran ahead and found ourselves two or three new slates to take home and on Lynx Creek hurriedly searched for a gold nugget.

The Copper Canyon road was little used after Yavapai County graded and improved the old Cherry Creek wagon road. It became the only road going west out of the valley suitable for automobiles. It passed through the little Cherry Creek Valley with its gardens and orchards; until autos replaced it, a horse drawn stage ran from Dewey to Camp Verde with a stop for a meal and change of teams in Cherry Creek.

The arrival of the stage with mail and passengers in Camp Verde at the old Wingfield store was an event. The adobe and wooden store, remnant of the army's Sutler store, had the usual open southwestern porch and here gathered the picturesque population of that time: Apache Indians, cowboys, ranch families and at-ease cow ponies, rein-trained to stand, teams, wagons, buckboards and buggies.

The Cherry Creek Road coming from Dewey crossed Ash Creek at the John Scissorilla ranch where Mary Rust provided beds for travelers not equipped with camp material. The little houses were very clean and had exceptionally steep roofs. My father explained that John and his cousin, Mary, were from Switzerland and accustomed to heavy snow.

Predating the overnight stops at the Scissorilla Ranch on Ash Creek was, a short distance down the creek, a home site and stage stop. John Stemmer established this busy station during army days supplying food, horse feed and supplies, and the Hudson family also ran it at one time. My mother remembered her first overnight there, as unusual and interesting. There were large cottonwood trees and a stone corral high enough to protect the goats that the family herded daytime in the surrounding hills, and brought in at night to foil the coyotes. Before arrival my father told my mother it was said the parents lived there with their several children, but had not spoken to each other for twelve years. Mother said the parents sat at either end of a long table and communication seemed to be through the children.

After leaving Ash Creek the road ran along Hackberry Wash and over the summit down through wild cherry trees and evergreens into Cherry Creek. This road is still in use and offers several fine views of the Verde Valley and the San Francisco peaks.

On the old Cherry Creek road we occasionally met ore wagons with teams driven by jerk line. The driver had a long line that extended to the lead team and their reaction to it was miraculous to observe.

To pass our wagon on the narrow road the driver communicated by his line that the lead team take to the roadside, and they quickly left the road with the following teams, except the wheelers, jumping their pull chain that was attached to the stretchers and swinging the wheelers and wagon off to one side of the road for us to pass. With the same skill the driver, directing by his jerk line, had the teams cross back over the center chain into pulling position. Six or eight teams or more were hitched to one or two heavily loaded wagons in a long line. The wheelers hitched to the doubletree next to the wagon, then the team called the pointers preceded by the other teams. A chain from the end of the wagon tongue ran to the lead team and was called a pull chain, king chain or fifth chain. It could be added to or shortened depending on the number of teams in use. The teams ahead of the wheelers were hitched, each animal, to a single-tree and the single-trees attached to a strong but lighter made double-tree called a stretcher that was rendered maneuverable by the clevis which attached it to the pull chain.

This maneuverability was a key factor in pulling the heavy freight wagons with twelve to sixteen mules or horses over narrow and sharply curved mountain roads. One long single line ran from the hand of the driver riding the near wheeler through a ring on the mane of the left hand animal of each team to the bit of the left animal on the lead team. A small hardwood stick about three (3) feet long with a snap at each end, one end snapped to the hame of the jerk line animal and the other end snapped into the snaffle-bit of the off-animal of the lead team, making it possible for the jerk-line animal to push the off animal to the right or pull it to the left.

One of the remarkable old roads that brought electricity to the Verde Valley and Prescott was the one from Dugas down into the Verde River Canyon to the power plant at Childs. All the machinery and necessary building materials plus necessities for the workmen came in by wagon and pack trains to that isolated spot. Also it crossed the river and went up the other side of the canyon to Irving on Fossil Creek, and carried the pipe for the amazing big siphon line that goes over a mountain and drops the once lovely water of Fossil Spring and Creek to the Verde River level of the Childs Power Plant. At the time

Those Early Days.....

this activity was in progress there was no road connecting Camp Verde to Irving and on up the mountain to Strawberry Valley and Pine. Travel along that route was by pack animal and horseback.

Giles Goswick freighted on this old road as a very young man and he said after an innocent enough beginning, it dropped off over an extremely steep road to the river. He mentioned that larger wagons and heavier built draft teams brought the materials to the rim of the canyon and there they were reloaded onto the wagons pulled with jerk-line teams, such as he drove, for the ten miles on down to Childs. He mentioned a metal device called a rough check they put on the front wheels of the rear wagon to act as brakes, and on ascending the steep grade a heavy six by six notched block for the wheel to settle into was dragged behind the rear wagon to hold the wagons when they stopped on the grade to give the teams a chance to rest. Giles mentioned a wheel horse he was riding falling as they descended over rocky ledges and he dared not leap off as his right hand was pulling the brake rope so he pulled up his legs and rode the fallen animal as it was dragged along to the bottom of a dip in the road where the outfit could be stopped. He also mentioned how maneuverable his jerk-line teams had to be to get the wagons around the sharp curves.

Nettie Goddard Peach told me she remembers going down this old road with her parents in a Nash car and her mother was so frightened she kept the car door open. I said, "Nettie, was it as bad as the steep old road going from Lake Stehr to the river on the east side? Oh!" she exclaimed, "That was a boulevard compared to the road on the west side of the canyon."

Bessie Hopkins Walker remembers that when she was a child living in Strawberry Valley her father and his uncle James Hopkins had goats in Fossil Creek Canyon and they took the mohair out over the old Childs road to Dugas. They also had cattle above the Rim and they were trailed to shipping points. She remembers her father brought in a cook stove for Irving Power Plant on a pack animal

My mother often recalled a ride she and my father made from Beaver Creek over the Fossil Creek Trail to Strawberry Valley to spend Christmas with her sister, Virginia Weatherford (later Mrs. C.C. Calloway) who was teaching there in the historic little log schoolhouse. With other young people in Strawberry they rode to the Pine Natural Bridge where the old Scotchman, Mr. Gowan, told them he was anticipating the arrival of his nephew, Mr. Goodfellow and family, from Scotland who in turn owned and lived at Tonto Natural Bridge many years. This entire journey was for my mother on a good horse and sidesaddle.

Later the mining town of Jerome and the smelter towns of

Clarkdale and Clemenceau increased in business and population. Their business necessitated many trips to Prescott, the county seat of Yavapai County, and the only road west out of the valley usable by automobiles was over Cherry Creek far south of Jerome. After a period of ignored requests for an improved road directly from Jerome to Prescott the report was that Major Midgely, the Verde Valley representative on the Yavapai County Board of Supervisors, banged his fist on the table and said, "Gentlemen, I represent the area having over eighty per cent of the assessed valuation of this county and we are in a position to form a new county if we do not get this road." The beautiful road over Mingus Mountain resulted and is certainly one of the most scenic in our state.

*The old bridge, a short distance below Slide Rock, used until replaced by the present bridge near Pendley's orchard.*

At various points can be seen the old ore road used by the United Verde Copper Company, before the narrow gauge railroad was built, where teams pulled the heavily loaded wagons of smelted copper over the mountains to Jerome Junction on the Prescott to Ashfork railroad. My father told me he was glad to see the ore transported by rail as the mules sweat blood on that steep old wagon road.

A wagon road went north from Jerome to Perkinsville in use on or before 1912 and in about 1930 was improved into a road suitable for automobiles to traverse.

A road I recall with pleasure was the narrow gauge railroad

from Jerome Junction terminating above Jerome with the finish of the trip in hacks down a steep descent into town. The little railroad was a toy of a thing with a fat little engine puffing away, squat little ore cars, baggage cars and at the end a doll of a chair car, so tiny there was a single row of wicker chairs cretonne-covered on either side of a narrow carpet running down the aisle. I rode it on return from boarding school and thought it looked like something out of Alice in Wonderland. The conductor on this train was Martha (Mattie) Lyle's father, Mr. G. Thomas Jacobs. Two eastern women on one trip were amazed at the little railroad with the track running along the rim and curves so sharp you could see the engine and cars curving around you, and frightened by the drive down into the town. On inquiring where I lived I gleefully told them thirty miles from Jerome and that my brother would meet me with saddle horses and we would ride to my ranch home next day. They were impressed with the rigors of the West! When the Verde Mix Railroad was built down the Verde River to Clarkdale the Narrow Gauge was abandoned and I heard it was sold to China. I would like to go to China just to ride it again.

  The Verde Mix running from Drake to Clarkdale was also an adventure in scenery along the Verde River. Dr. Carlson at the Jerome Hospital told me that when he came to Arizona, not well and discouraged at leaving an assured position behind, the job he got was doctor to the railroad gang building the line for the Verde Mix down the Verde River Canyon. Since there was no road he had to ride horseback to attend to the health of the crews of men. He disliked horseback riding and I remember he thought my enthusiasm for riding bordered on the suicidal. Dr. Carlson mentioned a hazardous trip he made driving a buckboard from Perkinsville to Prescott in a snowstorm to get a Mexican, ill with pneumonia, to an oxygen tank. He had doubts as to whether he or the patient would arrive in Prescott alive. Both survived.

  In later years a favorite outing for the Dude Ranches on Beaver Creek was a picnic at the mouth of Sycamore Canyon. The train of ore cars, chair and baggage car could have everything from fruit trees to trays of baby chicks on it and this obligingly mixed train would stop and let us off with lunch baskets and cameras. On the afternoon as it returned to Clarkdale it stopped to let us on again. Letters from city guests still reminisce about the joys of the Verde Valley's old roads, horseback trails and the Verde Mix.

*Clear Creek School, 1892-93*

Back to cliff-house, home ranch or camp.
Over them passed time, color, warrior, renegade, saint,
Burros, cattle, horses, game — all to leave their stamp;
Along with this throng
Goes a cheery song
Since the padre's first cross sign,
Greetings to you, friend, whatever the trail may wind.
Trails across the open range
Run winding far and wide,
Some were worn by moccasin tread
And some by the cowboy's ride,
All lead out to canyon, mountain and waterhole

Those Early Days.....

## HOW THE SEDONA COUNTRY HOOKED ME
*by Dixon Faberberg, Jr.*

What does it take to be an Arizona old-timer? It depends on when you came along. Strictly speaking, only a member of the Walker party (1863) can be considered a true pioneer. From that viewpoint, only a pre-1880 settler could be classified as a pioneer; one who came in the 1880's would be a tenderfoot; in the 1890's, a greenhorn; and one from 1900 to statehood, a rather second-rate Johnny-come-lately.

On this standard, my own credentials as an old-timer are embarrassingly anemic. The best I could do was to arrive, by natural means, at the tender age of zero, in Prescott, Territory of Arizona on March 20, 1909.

In harmony with these extremely weak qualifications, I have many misgivings in deigning to render an account of my own particular advent to these parts.

Anyhow, at the grave risk of being expelled from the Sedona Westerners by the true old-timers still in the membership, I'll take the chance and attempt to narrate how Sedona happened to get to this Johnny-come-lately and finally locked him up.

The key dates in the wondrous tale, I might say, are 1921, 1956 and 1971.

### 1921

When I became 12 years old I promptly joined the Boy Scouts. We Prescott scouts did a lot of hiking in the Granite Dells, Thumb Butte, and Bradshaw Mountains. Then one day there was an exciting announcement. In June there was to be a one-week camp-out in Oak Creek Canyon near Sedona in company with boys from Jerome and Clarkdale. But where was Sedona? We had never heard of it.

Memory is too hazy to attempt a round-by-round account of all that happened that week. The durable impressions, however, were four in number. One was what an arduous journey it was - the breathtaking descent down through Jerome, the deep ruts in the dirt roads after leaving Bridgeport, the several breakdowns experienced by the erratic Essex, several flat tires and recurring doubts whether we would ever "make it." The second vivid recollection was the red rocks and, more especially, the clouds of dust that infiltrated our clothes, our gear, our bedrolls - our mothers claimed it took four weeks of washings to eliminate the last remnants of that "red Sedona dirt." The third is easy to guess: the creek itself, with its swirls and tumblings, its grasses and wildflowers and foliage, and, under the old bridge, the best natural swimmin' hole in all Christendom. The fourth indelible memory was of the versatile beauty of the landscape regardless of angle or distance — looking up, down or sideways, and focusing at 15, 50, or 500 feet or 1, 5, 15 or 50 miles. All in all, Sedona was unforgettable. A Shangri-La! Something to dream about! But, of course, unattainable in this life.

## 1956

So it remained for 25 years. In adult life I had become a CPA with Phoenix as my headquarters. Then in 1945 I learned to fly and thereafter used my airplane to get around the state to serve my clients, including some in the Flagstaff area. Now the numerous flights to Flagstaff (215 of them) took me over Munds Mountain so I became once again an admirer and student of the magnificent terrain between Humphreys Peak and the Verde River. Then one day I noticed something from the air I couldn't believe. A 2,600-foot strip was apparently being cleared and graded on the flat top just west of Sedona. Could it be used as a runway?

I allowed a few weeks to pass and then set aside a full day to check out the situation. Sure enough, the dirt strip was intended for airplanes and my logbook records that I first landed on the Sedona "flat-top" on October 29, 1955. (Next to Joe Moser, who operated the new airport, this may have been the first landing there.) Once landed, my first impulse was to hoof it to Oak Creek. So I headed down the long ridge, then down an arroyo, and wound up at the ranch of Ambrosio Chavez. Two unexpected pleasures there awaited me. Meeting Mr. and Mrs. Chavez was the first, and learning that they were starting to sell a few one-acre parcels was the second. To make a long story short, after several investigative camping trips with my wife, Mary, we bought one of the lots. For, after all, there were only 15 years to go before retirement.

As a direct consequence of the purchase, my logbook shows 259 landings at Sedona airport from October 29, 1955 to June 30, 1971. At first there was no gasoline and no tie-down facilities, so I used ropes weighted down with big malapai boulders. One time after a hard rain, the caliche was literally converted into glue. The airplane was "stuck" and I had to catch a bus back to Phoenix. Accordingly I maintain that the mud on Sedona's airport hill is the stickiest to be found in all the annals of geology.

Shortly after buying the Chavez lot we decided to build a log cabin weekend retreat. Our congenial neighbors were Aaron McCreary, the immortal Lumberjack "coach," and his wife Elsie.

# Those Early Days.....

Although a digression, I think it fitting to say a little right here about that old-timer I became so fond of, Ambrosio Chavez. He came to mean many things to me. Farm wise, he was my "maestro" and taught me the art of "setting" (not planting) a fruit tree, the do's and don'ts of irrigation, and the tricks of putting up a barb wire fence. Moreover, as a firsthand historian he often told of the old days, going clear back to the time when his father was an Indian scout who escorted parties between Santa Fe and the Verde Valley (Chavez Pass was named for his father). But perhaps more than anything else, Mr. Chavez seemed to enjoy having someone to sit and talk and smoke a pipe with after supper. He had strong views, strongly expressed; and most of them were rooted in his own experience. Like all of us, he of course had certain favorite topics. Early in the game he told me all about his two horses Mollie and Brownie. Another time he spoke glowingly of Pal, his little black watchdog, and how reliable Pal was in meeting his responsibilities, especially when raccoons sneaked into the corn patch. To him, Pal was a real person, one who had made his mark in the world and deserved a lot of credit for it. Of course, as with all farmers, a topic never omitted was the weather, particularly the winter weather and how it would probably affect the oncoming fruit crop. I noticed that, for the most part, Mr. Chavez thought that the weather around here is no longer as good as it used to be. For example, when the great flood came in 1968 he said it wasn't as big as the one in 1918 or 1936. Even so, since it demonstrated what Oak Creek's full potential might be, I gathered that Mr. Chavez was actually rather proud of the 1968 flood.

Usually in the course of these recurring evening conversations the talk would touch at some point on the subject of bad road maintenance and high taxes and then would finally trail off into the spacious realm of national politics, international economics, farm prices, government interference - the whole bit. At length, after considering the vicissitudes and repercussions, and amid many a puff of the pipe, Mr. Chavez would invariably conclude the discussion by biting his pipe stem hard, look very serious, and say "Well, I guess we'll just have to take it as it comes." He was right. How else we might attempt to take it I, for one, have never quite been able to figure out.

## 1971

Influenced by the refreshing weekends at our cabin on Oak Creek, we knew as early as 1961 that the town of Sedona was to be our permanent retirement home. Even with that issue settled, we still faced the two questions familiar to all who look forward to retirement: (1) will we be able to survive the countdown, and (2) what about the adjustments? Above all, what about making new friends?

As it turned out the answer to the last question exceeded our most optimistic expectations, thanks largely to the clan known as the Sedona Westerners. It's a most unusual organization because, in an easygoing, outdoors, openhanded way it guides the newcomer into the paths of friendship, of acquaintance with the choice scenic areas hereabouts at the same time that it encourages him to rebuild that lost leg power and to savor the history of the genuine frontiersmen who blazed the trail before us. So, with due apologies to Pepsi company, whose bottles and cans we often pick up in the course of our hikes, I think the Sedona Westerners can truthfully proclaim to all Sedona newcomers, "You've got a lot to live - and we've got a lot to give!"

In conclusion I would like to explain that if, back in 1921, I had known this "assignment" was coming up, I would have jotted down some authentic field notes and made a better story. Anyway, such as it is, this is more or less how it came about that the Sedona country hooked me. I'm sure glad it did.

Those Early Days…..

*Montezuma Castle in November 1901 when the painters' ladders were not anchored on the ledges, from T.C. Schnebly collection*

## THE OLD ADOBE

This house now free from worry
And fretting cares of feeble man
Still stands, a monument to the vision
And dreams of a man long gone.
The roof is only partly there,
And the walls are crumbling
Where the plaster has fallen and left them bare.
The man has gone whose home was here;
Yet, if you should look closely
You would see that the old adobe
Can still be a home for God's other little families.
The rusty lizard runs over the wall —
The snake glides across the floor,
And in the corner there
An old coyote has made her lair.
In the falling roof above, a wren's nest is giving life —
While the mice in the niche of the wall
Drop seeds of grass on the suckling coyotes below.
Yet, still more life the old adobe gives
For the happy drumming of a woodpecker
Comes from the sagging beam and a wasp's nest,
As big as you will ever see
Is tied to a corner there
Where the old tree used to be.
An ant trail leads you to a hole in the wall,
Where a ground squirrel is peering out to see
What happened to the rest of his family.
Yes, the old adobe stands alone in the desert now —
A living monument to old Jose.

                                              Vic Sterzing

Those Early Days.....

## AUNT DIT, THE PIONEER SCHOOL TEACHER
*by Allen L. Bristow*

Soon after the Pioneers settled in an area and the immediate needs were taken care of they would get together and build a school house out of the materials at hand, generally a one-room affair, with crude benches for the children to sit on, a wood stove in one end for heating and a barrel on a low table with a couple of tin dippers hanging on the side for drinking water; two out houses in the back completed the set up. Then they would advertise for a teacher. My Mother, Calista A. Woods, was one who answered the call.

Mother was born in eastern Kansas in 1868, the youngest of six children. When she was a small child they moved to western Kansas and homesteaded a piece of prairie land. They suffered many hardships, as they had to live in a sod house until Grandfather could build a better one. There were Indians in the area but they were not warlike. They would walk right in the house, sit on the floor and point to their open mouths to say they wanted food. Grandmother would give them some of whatever there was to eat. They weren't particular. After a while they would leave. Grandmother was really afraid of them, but they never did any worse than steal a little corn.

In spite of a lot of hardship and poverty my Grandparents managed to send Mother through Normal School at Topeka, Kansas. When she got her teachers' certificate, Mother set about finding a school. Her sister Lola Woods, also a pioneer school teacher, was teaching school at Flagstaff, Arizona, at the time and told Mother that they were going to start a school on the Aqua Fria east of Prescott.

Mother applied for the school and was accepted, so in the fall of 1887 she packed her valise and headed for the Wild West. She was 19 at the time. Aunt Lola accompanied her to Flagstaff and Mother continued on to Ash Fork then, took a stagecoach to Prescott and another to Aqua Fria. Aqua Fria was a little mining town located between where Dewey and Humboldt are now, neither of which had been established at that time.

The only place to stay in Aqua Fria was a rough looking boarding house run by Grandma Hildebrandt. Though she was capable of running such an establishment in a rough and tumble frontier mining town, Mrs. Hildebrandt had a heart of gold and took the young School Ma'am under her wing, gave her the best room down stairs and watched over her as a mother hen does a bunch of ducklings.

The schoolhouse was a typical one-room affair, very crude even to western Kansas standards and the dozen or so pupils who showed up weren't like the children at Topeka Normal. They ranged from 5 to 25 years of age. It helped that most of them were in the first grade.

Mother was responsible for everything connected with the school including the janitor work. One of her worst problems was drunkenness among the first graders. Some of the older boys (men) would go to the saloon across the street during noon hour and drink their lunch. However, with the help of some of the older students Mother was able to maintain a semblance of control and toughed it out for that term.

Mother heard they were starting another school in the Verde Valley by Squaw Peak and being assured that the children were smaller and tamer and that there weren't any saloons near-by she took the Squaw Peak School for the next term.

When Mother came into the Verde Valley the next fall she took the stage from Prescott by way of Ash Creek and Copper Canyon. The driver let it be known that he was one of the feudin' Grahams of Pleasant Valley and proceeded to give the School Ma'am a wild ride that nearly scared her to death, after which he let her sit for an hour, in the heat and flies, while he fortified himself in the Horn saloon, at the mouth of Copper Canyon, before continuing to Camp Verde.

Mother taught two terms at Squaw Peak; then two at Clear Creek and four at Camp Verde.

When she was teaching at Camp Verde, Mother boarded with a young couple there, Charles and Lulu Harbeson, whose daughter Edna was just learning to talk and couldn't say "Calista," Mother told her that her folks called her "Dit" when she was a little girl, so Edna called her Aunt Dit. The older folks took it up and called Mother Aunt Dit, or just Dit and she was known by that name by some of the Old Timers the rest of her life.

When Grandmother Woods died Mother went back to Kansas with the intention of staying there, but after a month or so she found that she had fallen in love with the Verde Valley and the people there, or maybe it was the handsome cowboy who wrote in her memory book, "When you are old and cannot see put on your specs and think of me".

Those Early Days…..

*Camp Verde School 1895, Miss Calista Woods [AuntDit] Teacher, Children, front row left to right: Minnie Wingfield, Bessie Norwood, Mason Norwood, Ohio Rush, Fern Munds, Pete Davis, Frank Hanna, Charley Ryall, Clarence Davis, Charley Norwood, Sylvester Durfee, Joe Norwood, Fred Munds and Ben Ryall Back row: May Norwood, Sophia Munds, Etta Mahuran, Bertha Hanna, Lena Munds, Vinnie Hanna, Ella Bristow, Alex Wieben, Wilson See, Ross Bristow, Oscar Rush, Howard Ceose and Herbert Hanna.*

Mother accepted another term at Camp Verde and came back to Arizona. She and my father, John Bristow, were married at Prescott in January 1897. Mother finished that term before they settled down, raised a family and lived the rest of their lives in the Verde Valley.

*Camp Verde Schoolhouse, 1890's*

## THE "LONER"
*by Don Willard*

Where he came from no one knew. He had no family and had nothing to tell as to his past. My father had worked with him in a little mining camp in Nevada in the early 1880's. He seemed to have no friends, and that was by his own choice.

When Jerome, Arizona, started to "boom" as a big copper producer, and by the mid 90's had a smelter and narrow-gauge railroad, it attracted the "loner," Ed Hurley. However, since this period in mining history was to be the era of the great "prospector" with his dream of "striking it rich," Hurley was to work for the "Company" only long enough for a "grubstake." As soon as he was ready to strike out on his own he "headed for the hills," out of Jerome where scores of others were "staking claims" in all directions.

In those days the Black Hills of which Mingus Mountain forms a part, were covered with forest and heavy underbrush. There were numerous springs and water holes, and a prospector was often able to select a claim where he could have his own spring water supply. One very choice area was about ten miles south of Jerome in a deeply wooded canyon with a small stream and many large oak trees. It came to be known as "Little Oak Creek" for the reasons indicated.

Hurley selected his claim, built a small cabin and settled down. He was required by mining law to do a specified amount of "assessment" work each year. Annually, a new filing had to be made. To mark the beginning corner of a claim a "monument" was erected, consisting of a pile of stones usually three or four feet high. The claim holder would place his dated notice of filing, describing his claim, in a tin can somewhere in the face of the rocks, protected from the weather. Of course, he could also record his filing officially at the county seat. This situation led to a practice known as "claim jumping," made possible when the prospector may have happened to neglect doing his assessment work or re-filing by the last hour of his year. My father once lost a claim by less than a day, when another man got to the monument just ahead of him.

Hurley stuck with his claim and worked it for several years. A few dollars could supply beans, bacon, coffee, flour, etc. for a month, so he was able to supply his needs from time to time by intervals of work at the "big mine." He became more than ever a recluse as time passed, eventually distrusting any who

Those Early Days.....

approached his premises. Every prospector tends to convince himself that his claim is a potential bonanza, and that he has enemies who are determined to do him out of it. This obsession in Hurley's case was to lead to a tragedy.

Adjoining Hurley's claim and next above in the canyon, another prospector had established his claim. He had also built a cabin where he lived with his wife and four children. Their access was almost impossible except by following the bottom of the canyon up its course, which was across the bounds of Hurley's claim. As part of the Conrey Family's support they kept a small herd of goats, which grazed the hillsides on and around their claim. This led to no problem or objection except on the part of Hurley. Ill feeling and quarreling increased. Hurley warned and threatened Conrey, who seemed not to take the matter seriously.

One day Conrey started boldly to walk across the Hurley claim. Ed appeared from his cabin with rifle in hand. He fired a shot near enough to Conrey to indicate he meant business, and cursing and abusing Frank, he said that the next occasion of trespass would be Conrey's last.

Conrey went to Jerome, reported the incident and had Hurley arrested. A trial was held, but Hurley was not convicted. In those days trespass was often held to be subject to "unwritten law." Although Conrey had many friends and almost no one sympathized with Hurley, it must have been thought that he would not actually carry out his threat. Conrey did not wait long to put him to the test. This time Hurley did not miss.

A murder trial was held in Prescott and Hurley was convicted and sentenced to a life term in the prison at Florence. Conrey's widow was left with four children. Hurley's claim was not "proved up."

In 1912, I was a high school student in Phoenix. Arizona's first state governor, George W.P. Hunt, invited two of us high school students to go to Florence on a tour of the prison. This interesting and valuable experience provided me with an opportunity, which I have long remembered. The penology of the new state was just replacing some of the barbaric methods of territorial days such as treatment in a "snake pit." However, there were certain cases of problems in discipline in which a degree of harsh treatment seemed the only solution. Ed Hurley was one of such prisoners.

I took occasion to ask for and receive permission to look up Ed Hurley's record. He had at that time served eight years of his life sentence. The record told a story. Here was a man who had tolerated no infringement on what he considered his "rights." His property was his to defend. Any person who in his view, trespassed on his territory after warning, must be part of a plot to deprive him of his property. This was to him more than a piece of ground. It was a dream. There were two ways for such a dream to come true. One, of course, was to hit "pay dirt." The next best was for some speculator to show up one day after his claim had been "proved up" and title clear, offering a "considerable sum."

To give up his dream was unendurable. Hurley had never in his own mind considered his act a crime. He was sure his conviction and imprisonment were not only unjust, but were part of the plot by friends of Conrey to get his claim. Never having been submissive to orders or discipline, prison life was to him intolerable. He became a rebel. The record showed him only at his worst. "Good behavior," was not apparently ever to b entered to his credit.

Ed Hurley was still a "loner." A cemetery is one of the lesser know features of that prison in Florence. Totally unknown today is the grave of the "loner" from Little Oak Creek.

*Bill Gray's corral in May 1934 at his winter ranch near Sedona. Bill was a pioneer rancher who ran cattle at his summer ranch on Garland Prairie. His wife, Alice Gray, is a sister o the late George Jordan, who put in the first water lines and gave Sedona its first Water Company.*

Those Early Days.....

## A BRIEF HISTORY OF THE SCHNEBLY HILL ROAD
*by Ellsworth Schnebly*

When T.C. (Carl) Schnebly brought his family to Sedona in 1901, the only way to reach Flagstaff was by plodding slowly in wheeled-vehicles over the rutted, rough, rocky, and meandering wagon tracks to the south, and about six miles north of what Mrs. Virginia Finnie Webb (on Page 243 of this book) in her story "Old Roads" describes as the "Blue Grade," the first road from Camp Verde and Beaver Creek towards Flagstaff.

When Carl Schnebly, in the summer of 1902, began to haul vegetables and later fruit to Jerome and Flagstaff, he felt the need of a shorter route to Flagstaff. Others had "dreamed" about a shorter route; Dad acted.

Without any transit or other instrument, he set stakes up Schnebly Hill and asked the County Supervisors if they could build a road up that now scenic route. The supervisors then cooperated, as contrasted with the supervisors in the 1950's who for some obscure reason or foible seemed to want to close the Schnebly Hill Road forever, thereby depriving nature lovers and residents of an alternate route out of and into Oak Creek Canyon and Sedona.

Herein lies a condensed version of the prolonged controversy before the county fathers for the SECOND TIME officially recognized the fact that the Schnebly Hill Road was a "county road" and should be maintained as such, at least when feasible. The Forest Service has aided at times in maintaining this road, except when closed during the winter because storms had made it impassable or hazardous in its present condition for those who wished to travel over it to their homes or for other reasons.

While County records no longer have much information concerning the history of the Schnebly Hill Road, Ellsworth Schnebly has four paper-bound volumes (a total of 196 typed pages) as prepared, during hearings, by Beatrice Prochnow, Official Court Reporter for Coconino County while the hearings continued from December 3, 1951 until March 3, 1953, with some records up to September 5, 1904. Oddly when two young men working with the History Department at N.A.U. sought information at the Court House in Flagstaff, these two men, Bob Novak and Joe Lippert, were unable to find records. When they contacted me, I was able to loan them the 196 pages which conclude with this:

"CERTIFICATE OF REPORTER: I hereby certify that the foregoing, consisting of (the given number of pages in each volume) pages, is a true and correct record of the proceedings had in the above entitled matter the 7th day of January, 1952. Dated, January 28,1952, thru May 1,1952. (Signed) Beatrice Prochnow, Reporter."

These 196 pages contain detailed facts concerning the dispute over whether or not Schnebly Hill Road had ever been a dedicated county road, with verbatim testimony of several concerned residents: Messrs. Ed H. Sedona-Rim Rock Highway, and running thence Northeasterly on the present Schnebly Hill Road, one-half mile, to the East Line of the WV2SEV4 of Section 8, T. 17 N., R. 6 E., which is the East Line of the Patented Land in this Area. Dated at Flagstaff, Arizona, this 14th day of November 1950.

    Signed: Jane Burns
    Clerk
    Board of Supervisors
    Coconino County,
    Arizona (Official Seal)"

Two hundred people signed the petition supporting the permanent establishment of the Schnebly Hill Road as a County Road. Throughout numerous hearings, Mr. Fishback asked for the Minutes Book of 1902 (Volume B-3) but was denied the right or the privilege of having these original minutes presented at the hearings. However, T.C. Schnebly and R.W. Fishback had copied all of the minutes when they had searched records in the Court House preceding the hearings. Volume B-3 contained the original records of the status of Schnebly Hill Road and proved that the County Supervisors, in 1902, had given $1,200.00 for work on the road with additional sums later, plus donations of cash and labor by local residents.

As stated above, the controversy began, when Mr. Fishback was blocked by an obstruction across Schnebly Hill Road when going from his home on Schnebly Hill to the Post Office in Sedona. He inquired as to whom might have blocked the road and then tried unsuccessfully to have it removed until he had legal counsel. The minutes in Volume B-3 read, in part: "In 1902, there was a road extending from Flagstaff in a southerly direction thru Mund's Park, over Rattlesnake Hill, thru Dry Beaver, and into the Lower Verde. That road was known as the Old Flagstaff-Verde Valley Wagon Road. At some distance south of Flagstaff on the Old Wagon Road was Mund's Ranch and, across the Mesa toward Mund's Ranch was what was known as the Old Mund's Trail. At a point approximately 23 miles south of Flagstaff, on that Old Wagon Road the present Schnebly Hill Road had its beginning, and continued across the Mesa to a point on the Rim, and thence down the grade in a south and westerly direction to a point on Oak Creek at Sedona. From thence one could proceed across the county line into the Upper Verde and Jerome. A surveyor's map of this road was executed by W.H. Power, who was surveyor for Coconino County in 1902." (Two pages

Those Early Days.....

showing a copy of this map and a clear photograph of the encroachment in 1950 may be seen between pages 2 and 3 in Volume I of the history of the hearings in 1951 and 1952). "This road had its inception on February 24, 1902, and by referring to the County Supervisor's Minutes of their Board meeting of that date, we may read:

"SUPERVISORS' MINUTES, Volume B-3, Page 322. Flagstaff, Arizona, February 24, 1902. A petition was presented signed by 18 prominent, influential, and respected residents to "lay out and establish a public road" with a description of the route.

The Clerk was then directed to post notices in three public places as required by the Statute of August 1901. At a meeting of the Board, held on March 17, 1902, the Minutes show that the change in the Verde Road had been properly advertised and that the surveyor had been requested to make a plat of said change. At a meeting on July 1, 1902 (Page 332) the Minutes read, in part: "The following bills were approved: W.H. Power, Surveying and Plat Verde Cut-Off Road — $117.85."

Still later, at a meeting held on July 25, 1902, with the following two supervisors present: George Babbitt and T.W. Pulliam, and H.C. Hibben, Clerk, the Minutes read in part: "In consideration of the parties having charge of the funds for the completion of the Verde Cut-Off Road paying to the County Treasurer the moneys on hand supposed to be about $150.00, the Board awarded the contract to J.J. Thompson for the completion of said road, for the sum of $600.00. Said road to be completed on or before October 1, 1902. The said $600.00 to be paid to said J.J. Thompson when road is completed and accepted by the Board of Supervisors. Board adjourned."

Thus, by referring to the Minutes of the Board of Supervisors at that meeting in 1902, the obstruction on Schnebly Hill Road was ordered removed. The late Mr. Myron S. Loy of Cornville, Arizona, stated that his father, Mr. John Loy was engaged to do the first $1,200.00 worth of work on said road while the late Mr. Charley Thompson (who was postmaster in Sedona longer than any other person) said that his father, Mr. J.J. Thompson had his road camp in Bear Wallow on the north side of Schnebly Hill Road when he supervised the completion of this road.

Minutes of the Board of Supervisors dated October 6, April 27, 1903, July 2, 1903, and Sept. 5, 1904, show payments to W.H. Power and J.J. Thompson for "work on the Verde Cut-Off Road from 23-Mile Post to Schnebly's Road on Oak Creek" and "The following claims were audited and allowed:

    J.J. Thompson, Overseer, Verde Cut-Off Road    $336.00
    T.C. Schnebly, Labor on Verde Cut-Off Road    $211.00

In adding the totals of claims paid by the Supervisors for work done on the Verde Cut-Off Road, the Supervisors spent $1,800.00 in putting the road down Schnebly Hill. Donated labor and cash amounted to unknown amounts. The U.S. Forest Service was not in existence until 1905, so it had no jurisdiction over that Schnebly Hill Road whatsoever.

Those who have argued that the Schnebly Hill Road was never designated as a County Road should refer to Section 59-601 of the Arizona Code, which reads, in part: " . . . , when all of these things shall have been done, said highway shall thereafter be established, altered, or changed." Those "things" enumerated in detail had been done as required.

The Arizona Legislature has ruled in Section 59-401 of the Arizona Code on page 865: "All highways heretofore constructed, laid out, opened or established as public highways by the territory or state, or by any board of supervisors or legal subdivision of the state, and which have been used continuously by the pubic as thoroughfares for free travel and passages for two (2) years, or more, regardless of any error, defect or omission in the proceedings, and all highways which shall be hereafter established pursuant to law, are hereby declared to be public highways sixty-six (66) feet wide, unless the width thereof is otherwise specified."

A registered highway engineer's map shows Schnebly Hill Road as a Coconino County right-of-way 66 feet wide. Because of local opposition, the road has never been oiled to make it safe for travel. Inasmuch as there is no more scenic road anywhere, and since the Oak Creek Canyon Road cannot handle all of the traffic, especially during the tourist season, it would appear as if the Schnebly Hill Road should be widened, paved, and put to use as an alternate highway to Flagstaff.

The gradient on the Schnebly Hill Road of six miles does not appear to be any steeper than up the two-mile road on the switchbacks since any car can drive up both roads in high gear and each road is equally scenic.

Anyone who has to reach Flagstaff, particularly during tourist season or on weekends (when skiers flock to Flagstaff), can readily realize the necessity of having two ways of entering and leaving Sedona enroute to Flagstaff. It is to be hoped that the Arizona Highway Department will soon incorporate the Schnebly Hill Road into the state highway system. Be that as it may, it is to be hoped that the controversy as to whether this is a "county road" has been resolved and that no further road blocks or obstructions will harass anyone, except during bad weather.

*Squaw Peak School, 1890*

## THE PROSPECTOR AND HIS THREE BURROS
*by Donald B. Willard*

The time setting of this sketch was near the end of one century and another was soon to begin. Gold "fever" was dying down, but the "red metal" was coming into its day. Copper was being found by hard rock miners, and newer, bigger fortunes were to be made. Some lucky prospectors were finding ready buyers for their claims, then proceeding to "put it back in the ground" by spending all their money looking for another "sure thing." Very few were willing to give up after their first taste of even the slightest success. Ultimately, most of those fortunes mentioned were realized by the speculators and promoters, rather than the prospectors.

Over a rugged mountain wagon road a bearded man in his early thirties trudged slowly up a steep rocky canyon. Ahead of him three burros under packsaddles loaded with a miner's supplies and provisions, picked their way, often stopping to nibble grass; starting again only when prodded by their owner. The trail grew steeper and the burros moved more slowly. As evening came the climbers gained the mountain summit. Ponderosa pines spread thickly on each slope of the "rim." Far below lay a wide valley marked by a winding stretch of green cottonwoods. In the far distance the sun's last rays painted red cliffs and canyon walls with soft glowing hues. The sight was one, which unless seen, could not be dreamed, and once seen, could never be forgotten.

Our prospector "hobbled" his pack burros after removing their burdens. Thus they could not stray too far, so he would have no problem the following morning in getting them ready to continue his trip. Starting a campfire, he cooked his evening meal, then unrolled his blankets to sleep under the stars. Occasionally, his repose would be briefly disturbed by the mournful solo or chorus of prowling coyotes.

As daylight parted the shadows of night, he rolled out of his covers and made his breakfast of coffee, bacon, and some "mush" with the contents of a small can of evaporated milk. The burros were not hard to round up, and he was soon started in the direction of the new "camp," he had heard about, down the mountainside toward the valley.

Reports had drifted out into some of the early-day mining districts of Colorado, Nevada, and California about newer ore strikes in Arizona. One of those drifters, who had looked over one place after another without finding what he thought he wanted, was this man with the beard. His grubstake was the last of the proceeds from the sale of a small farm in the Midwest, which had not been a success. A restless sort of fellow, he was determined to seek what adventure and opportunity might be afforded by discovering a just-starting mining camp. His plan was to find as quickly as possible if the area had been entirely

## Those Early Days.....

"prospected." He had learned that burros were cheap, could forage for themselves, carry heavy weights, and traverse places too rough even for horses. He had stopped over night at a stage and freight wagon "station" on the road to his chosen destination. A Mexican camped near by was offering to sell three burros with their packsaddles. A trader hauling supplies to the new camp was willing to let him have a selection of merchandise, as much to lighten his load as for his profit from the sale.

It was thus equipped that he reached the newest copper camp in the West. The scene meeting his eyes as he topped the last hill was quite unexpected. Steeper than anything he had yet imagined, the road before him dropped sharply toward a smelter with its smoking stack, buildings and ore bins, and then on a nearby hillside were rows of smoking heaps of ore "roasting' over piles of burning logs to consume the excess sulphur. He found he had to pass on further down the mountain to enter the new town. It was there he met a new surprise. The "big fire" had just wiped out a large part of the "main street" section. Many of the residents had been burned out, as well as the few stores and saloons.

This disaster was to make a complete change of plans for our would-be prospector. At once he found his few supply items were in desperate demand. Knowing more supply wagons were due to arrive, he was soon "sold out," and finding a woodcutter who needed more burros to pack firewood into town from nearby canyons and hillsides, he sold them for a good profit. Meeting an arriving freight wagon he arranged a quick purchase of salable goods. In "almost no time" he was one of the town's merchants.

Years passed by and the town grew. Our merchant was the owner of a fireproof building full of merchandise, and he had invested in rental properties and mining stock. He had married a schoolteacher and they were parents of a son and daughter who finally "went away to school." A new mine was opened. Its stockowners became wealthy. A postmaster from the town became governor of the young 48th state; another man was to be a congressman and later ambassador to a great country.

Came the October '29 Crash!

But first, our merchant, who had decided to "cash in" his entire holdings, went "into the market," with the full proceeds on margin, during the prevailing spree of market speculation. Called on by his brokers as stocks plunged lower and lower, he could not meet their demands. In short order he was "sold out" for real.

The Depression!

The mines closed; there were no jobs; banks closed! A few men too proud to "go on relief," went into the hills.

Another mountain trail. Miles from town we found on the mountainside a grizzled old prospector. We stopped to talk. His story: Once he had taken a "patented claim" in payment of a debt a friend had no other way to pay. It had showed "color" in samples of rock found in a surface "vein." Our old prospector, with pick, drill steel and powder, was breaking out "high grade" and loading it in bags which he was fastening on the packs of three burros. He said he would get it down to a mill where it might bring him enough that he would be able to stay off "relief." He called the burros his Arizona canary songbirds, and said he had paid a crippled old woodcutter a few dollars for them. He said he had wanted for years to do some prospecting.

I never asked him his name.

*"Schnebly Hill Road" Submitted by Mrs. Virginia Webb of Rimrock [Soda Springs Ranch].*

Those Early Days…..

## A

Abineau, J., 50
Acker, Boss, 62
Adair, Port, 129
Allen, Charley, 86
Anddres, Arthur T., 52
Anderson place, 161, 162
Anderson,Carl, 244
Andrews, Frank, 58
Animals
    Antelope, 37, 263
    Bear, 2, 47, 61, 71, 79, 81, 104,
        109, 139, 140, 146, 147, 148,
        149, 158, 175, 227
    Bobcat, 10
    Brindle Bull, 60
    Buckskin, 210
    Burros, 80, 112, 145, 148, 149, 172,
        189, 233, 286, 287, 288
    Cattle, 15, 17, 18, 19, 38, 41, 42,
        43, 44, 45, 46, 48, 58, 59, 61, 62,
        65, 68, 69, 75, 76, 92, 103, 117,
        118, 120, 121, 125, 129, 135,
        141, 142, 143, 144, 146, 157,
        162, 171, 173, 174, 178, 185,
        186, 187, 190, 200, 203, 207,
        208, 211, 213, 214, 216, 219,
        265, 268, 280
    Chickens, 82, 86
    Cows, 41, 43, 82, 107, 109, 147,
        162, 201
    Deer, 37, 88, 120, 263
    Dogs, 79, 90, 106, 131, 147, 148,
        256, 263
    Goat, 97, 108, 127, 201
    Hogs, 65, 82, 109, 137
    Horse Herd, 126
    Horse Wrangler, 58, 62, 125
    Horseback, 21, 25, 97, 117, 144,
        147, 159, 186, 190, 193, 194,
        197, 207, 208, 213, 214, 216,
        218, 226, 237, 238, 253, 258,
        261, 265, 267
    Horses, 7, 25, 38, 39, 43, 46, 54,
        58, 61, 62, 68, 69, 83, 85, 96,
        112, 117, 125, 126, 128, 129,
        130, 132, 133, 134, 135, 136,
        141, 142, 143, 144, 145, 150,
        161, 162, 166, 171, 179, 188,
        190, 192, 193, 194, 196, 197,
        204, 207, 209, 214, 216, 217,
        218, 221, 224, 226, 229, 244,
        246, 259, 261, 262, 264, 267,
        268, 271, 287
    Mountain Lion, 248
    Mules, 41, 42, 100, 130, 207, 209,
        228, 235, 251, 262, 264, 266
    Old Wall Eye, 200, 205
    Oxen, 161, 198, 208, 209, 211
    Pack, 37, 38, 42, 54, 61, 89, 104,
        109, 111, 133, 148, 149, 163,
        170, 172, 174, 176, 194, 264,
        265, 286, 287
    Pinto, 192
    Plow, 82, 96, 217, 233
    Quail, 121, 203, 218, 222
    Range, 17, 39, 43, 45, 58, 59, 65,
        69, 75, 112, 122, 126, 128, 129,
        135, 142, 143, 145, 171, 175,
        195, 199, 200, 201, 203, 208,
        211, 219, 224, 259, 268
    Saddle, 45, 61, 83, 97, 122, 125,
        128, 129, 131, 132, 133, 134,
        158, 170, 174, 175, 176, 179,
        186, 188, 193, 200, 202, 207,
        210, 214, 216, 218, 223, 235,
        260, 267
    Sheep, 10, 19, 25, 65, 102, 109,
        150, 158, 162, 175, 258, 259
    Snake, 252, 262, 274, 279
    Squirrel, 1, 274
    Team, 58, 68, 69, 72, 75, 84, 86,
        89, 110, 114, 132, 144, 161, 165,
        174, 175, 178, 192, 193, 207,
        209, 210, 211, 217, 229, 244,
        247, 256, 261, 264
    Team Horses, 69, 72, 75, 86, 174
    Toad, 163
    Turkey, 44, 90, 218
    Wild, 37, 59, 60, 79, 91, 103, 107,
        109, 128, 137, 145, 146, 153,
        166, 188, 194, 199, 201, 212,
        213, 237, 264, 276
Aqua Fria, 199, 275
Arizona

Historical Society, 37
Postal History, xv, 21
Power Company, 252
Public Service Company, 253
Ramah, 129
State Fair, 175, 203
State University, 120, 144
Statehood, 22
Statehood, 115
Statehood, 269
Water Company, 243
Armijo
  Juan, 19, 72, 189, 195
Army Posts
  Fort Apache, 175, 226, 227, 258, 260
  Fort Lincoln, 101
  Fort Verde, 175, 185, 189, 225, 229
  Fort Whipple, 101, 142, 226, 258, 261
  Fort Wingate, 228, 258
Arnold, Wales, 58, 226, 259
Ash Creek, 84, 199, 228, 261, 263, 276
Ash Fork, Arizona, 72, 95, 165, 199, 254, 275
Ashurst, Senator, 137
Automobiles, 75, 119, 120, 170, 176, 203, 204, 224, 244, 249, 250, 252, 253, 260, 263, 266
  Baby Grand, 244, 245, 248, 249
  Chevrolet, 240, 244, 245, 248, 249
  Essex, 269
  Ford, 85, 121, 213, 238
  Hudson Touring Car, 240
  Hupmobile, 249
  Maxwell, 203, 205
  Model T, 85, 213, 238
  St. Clair, 261
  Velie, 204
  Willis, 19, 46
Aztlan Lodge, 164

## B

Babbitt, 8, 41, 52, 53, 194, 216
  David, 52
  George Sr., 8, 51, 53, 283
Back O'Beyond, 20
Back, Bill, 62
Bacon Rind Park (Indian Gardens), 3, 4, 11, 12, 15, 21, 37, 39, 40, 53, 54, 55, 56, 57, 68, 74, 75, 79, 80, 81, 82, 83, 87, 88, 100, 102, 103, 105, 139, 143, 145, 146, 147, 149, 169, 173, 174, 176, 180, 192, 197
Baillie, John, 45
Baker, Bob, 229
Baldwin
  Andrew E., 17, 97, 99
  Mrs., 232
Banjo Bill, 9, 55, 110
Banjo Bill Springs, 9
Barney
  Ben, 162
  Jim, 43, 162
  Ollie, 43
  Ralph, 49
Barney Old Field, 120
Barney Pasture, 43, 49, 112, 162, 169
Barney Spring, 162
Beal, E. F., Lt., 47
Beasly, A.H., 50
Beaver Creek, 2, 4, 58, 106, 119, 129, 166, 171, 175, 207, 226, 229, 231, 258, 259, 260, 265, 267, 281
Beaver Head, xvi, 3, 41, 47, 48, 53, 62, 96, 100, 101, 144, 165, 175, 226, 227, 228, 258, 259, 260
Beinke, Heinrich, 164
Bell
  Don, xv, 90
  L. B., 262
Benedict
  Getha, 144
  Lewis E., 170
  O. A., 233
Bernalillo County, 133
Bicycle, 224
Big Park Area, 3, 4, 37, 41, 47, 62, 67, 100, 165, 171, 194, 207
Bigham, Charley, 62
Bishop, Hilda, 40
Bismeyer, Mrs., 165
Black
  Claude, 14, 16, 240
  G.W., 52
  George, 3, 5, 13, 16, 85, 143, 144, 173, 178, 186, 240, 241, 279

Those Early Days…..

Jim, 18
Miss (teacher), 230
Mr., 178
Stella, 173
Black Hills, 201, 203, 278
Blackmore, Andrew, 19
Blue Grade, 260, 261, 281
Bonelli, Daniel, 68
Bootlegger Flat, 110
Boutwell Family, 11
Bradshaw Mountains, 269
Brands (Livestock), 43, 58, 62, 65, 171
Brennen, Dr., 42
Brewer Road, 6, 70, 85
Bridgeport, 56, 118, 119, 142, 161, 178, 269
Brinkmeyer, Heinrich, 165
Bristow
   Allen L., ix, xvi, 198, 275
   Calista A. (Aunt Dit) (Woods), 199, 275, 276, 277
   Conway, 161, 203
   Ella, 277
   Grandma/Grandpa, 200
   J.C. (Parson), 198
   John, 205, 277
   John D., 205
   John W., 203
   Kenneth G., 205
   Mary, 161
   Pleasant, 198
   Ross, 277
   Stella, 206
   Tom, 16, 44
   Will, 110
Brollier, Dave, 128
Brooks
   Frank, 102
Brown
   Carl E., 18, 45
Brown Springs, 58
Bryan, William Jennings, 119
Buggy, 119, 159, 167, 197, 223
Burch, Mitch, 259
Burrus, Charles, 144
Bushnell, Jessie, 5, 239
Butcher, Charley, 45

## C

C O Bar Outfit, 216
Calloway, Mrs. C.C., 202, 265
Cameron, Arizona, 216
Cameron, B.A., 50
Camp Verde, 3, 4, 43, 47, 69, 70, 79, 80, 88, 95, 97, 100, 101, 106, 115, 117, 118, 119, 137, 144, 145, 159, 165, 169, 171, 172, 175, 185, 189, 199, 200, 202, 204, 209, 210, 224, 225, 227, 228, 229, 251, 258, 259, 260, 262, 263, 265, 276, 277, 281
Campbell
   Hugh E., 50
   J.M., 159
   Tom, 120
CampbellMid, 144
Camps
   Beaverhead, 59
   Mining, 68, 118, 199, 225, 237, 278, 286
   Mormon, 39, 60, 70, 88
   Roundup, 171, 216
   Sedona, 61
   Summer, 3, 70, 247
   Verde, 3, 4, 43, 47, 69, 70, 79, 80, 88, 95, 97, 100, 101, 106, 115, 117, 118, 119, 137, 144, 145, 159, 165, 169, 171, 172, 175, 185, 189, 199, 200, 202, 204, 209, 210, 224, 225, 227, 228, 229, 251, 258, 259, 260, 262, 263, 265, 276, 277, 281
   Wagon, 118
Cancellations
   Postal, 22
Canyons
   Bear Wallow, 49, 71
   Carrol, 71
   Casner, 61
   Clear Creek, 151
   Copper, 199, 261, 262, 263, 276
   Diablo, 151
   Fry, 54
   Glen, 216
   Grand, 2, 74, 178, 214, 232
   James, 15
   Kinsey, 245, 249

Loy, 162
Mormon, 70, 243
Munds, 13, 143, 157
Oak Creek, xvii, 4, 11, 13, 37, 39, 40, 54, 56, 57, 61, 79, 80, 85, 86, 87, 88, 117, 123, 173, 206, 232, 234, 244, 261, 269, 281, 284
Pump House, 61, 193, 232
Red, 121
Sycamore, 2, 114, 174, 267
Verde River, 264, 267
Wilson, 54, 56, 57, 61, 70, 71, 79, 102, 147, 148, 192
Woods, 171
Carlson, Dr., 267
Carpenter, Captain, 137
Carrier, 143, 144
    Dr M.S., 71
    Dr., 71, 144, 156, 158, 159
    Eleanor, 157
    Ethel, 157
    Iva, 145
    Jane Lindsay, 157
    Melvina, 142, 143, 156, 157
    Myron A. Dr, xv, 42, 156, 157
    Myron A. Dr., 143, 156
    Myron Dr., 167
Cedar Ridge, 216
Central Arizona Light and Power Co., 252
Chain-pull, king, fifth, 264
Chavez
    Ambrosio, xvi, 16, 19, 20, 22, 71, 173, 189, 190, 191, 271
    Andrew, 191
    Apolonia, 190
    Dora, 190
    Jose, 18
    Manuel, 19, 189, 190
    Pass, 227, 271
    Tommy, 173, 190
    Tony, 18
Cherry Creek, 47, 58, 83, 118, 119, 165, 174, 228, 237, 263, 264, 266
Childs Power Plant, 251, 264
Chimney Flat, 14, 176
Chino Valley, 198, 209, 224, 254
Chloride, Arizona, 68
Christmas Party & Program, 182
Clark, E.S., 50

Clarkdale Area, 7, 49, 58, 85, 118, 172, 178, 198, 232, 233, 237, 241, 251, 252, 254, 255, 266, 267, 269
Clay Park (FoxBoro), 4, 62, 186, 187, 224, 245
Clay, Ben, 17, 62
Clear Creek, 95, 96, 151, 153, 199, 200, 202, 268, 276
Clemenceau Area, 44, 45, 85, 86, 145, 232, 251, 255, 266
Coconino Cattle Co., 44, 216, 217
Coconino County, xv, 4, 5, 10, 44, 52, 55, 56, 57, 146, 150, 151, 170, 171, 175, 178, 216, 217, 232, 238, 281, 282, 284
Coconino Sheriff's Posse, 238
Coffin, George H., 50
Colter, T.J., 50, 52
Congress Junction, Arizona, 203
Conner, Daniel Ellis, 169
Conrey Family, 279
Cook
    Bessie, 256
    Effie, 256
    Fred, 256
    Henry Elmer, 256
    J.M., 14
    Jay, 77
    Jim, 83, 84
    Martha, 10
Copper, 99, 199, 261, 262, 263, 276, 286
Copper Basin, 99
Copper Canyon, 199, 261, 262, 263, 276
    Wagon Road, 262
Cordes Junction, 229
Cordes, Arizona, 203, 229, 258
Cornish, A. T., 50
Cornville, Arizona, 21, 43, 59, 87, 144, 174, 179, 185, 187, 188, 229, 230, 257, 283
Cottonwood Cemetery, 168
Counties
    Bernalillo, N.M., 133
    Coconino, xv, 4, 5, 10, 44, 52, 55, 56, 57, 146, 150, 151, 170, 171, 175, 178, 216, 217, 232, 238, 281, 282, 284
    Mohave, 117, 119

Those Early Days…..

Payson, 150, 251
Yavapai, 16, 22, 52, 56, 69, 91,
    144, 146, 150, 193, 210, 260,
    263, 266
Yuma, 47, 226
Cow Flat, 174
Cowboy, iii, vii, xv, 198
Cox, Bill, 60
Crook Trail, 260
Crook, General George, 260
Croxen
    Edith Lamport, xvi, 176, 177, 180,
        183
    Fred W., xvi, 170
Cummings, Homer, 204

## D

Daggs, J.T., 50
Dallas, Tex, vii, ix
Davis, B.V., 9
Dawson, Henrietta, 194
Dayton, 20
Dead Man Flat, 217
Debs, Eugene V., 119
Del Rio, 237
Dentist, 84
    First in Area, 157, 158
Derrick, Frank, 11, 173, 177, 229
Dewey, Arizona, 84, 201, 237, 263,
    275
Dickinson, 198
    A.G. (Dutch), 45
    Alf, 171
    Bill (Biscuit Bill), 170
    Charlie, 171, 226
    Ed, 60
    Grandma, 230
    Sammie, 230
    W.G., 52
Dietrich, Karl A., 18
Dolan Springs, 117, 119
Doyel, Allen, 50
Drake, Arizona, 178, 267
Drum, Tom, 106
Dry Beaver Creek, 47, 226, 258, 259
Dry Creek, 43, 45, 47, 60, 85, 173,
    189, 240, 260
Dude Ranches, 267

Duff Flat, 114
Duff, Jack, 114
Dugas, 264, 265
Dumas
    D. E., 17, 159
    Dad, 210, 211
    David, 210
    Lenore Francis, xv, xvi, 150, 208
    Mack Oliver, Dr., xv, xvi, 17, 58,
        64, 68, 70, 97, 105, 125, 127,
        128, 141, 160, 188, 211, 219,
        220
    Margaret (Maggie), 82
    Mother, 82, 210, 211
    Mrs. D. E. (Maggie), 67
Dumas Ranch, 84, 188, 210, 211
Duncan, Nick, 17
Durfey, Wes, 97
Dutch Oven Poem, 153
Dutch Ovens, 151, 152, 252
Dutton, A. A., 52
Dwyer, Bill, 9

## E

Eamons, 199
Earmarks, xv, 65
Eastern Star, Chapter No. 1, 164
Edwards
    Dorothy (Owenby), 46
    Willis, 46
Ellison Post Office, 38
Elmer, Jay, 45
Erosion, 1, 37

## F

Fagerberg, Dixon, Jr., ix
Fain
    Albert, 62
    Crossing, 59
    Dan, 62, 128
    John, 62
Fairchild
    Fletcher, xv, xvi, 150, 244
Faltin, William, 120
Farley
    Henry, 186

Jim, 242
John, 237
Joseph, 14, 171, 176, 237
Lum, 186
Mary, 183
Minnie, xvi, 182, 237
Mrs., 173
Farming, 7, 8, 11, 17, 19, 39, 81, 109, 116, 117, 142, 161, 185, 204, 229, 232
  Dry, 39, 121
Farrish, Thomas, 47
Fenstermaker, J. A., 5, 15, 184
Ferry, 142, 214, 215
  Bonneli, 117
Feud
  Tewkesbury-Graham, 117
Finnie, Robert, 258
Fire, Big, 104, 159, 287
Fish
  Bony Tail, 97
  Hump Back Suckers, 103
  Trout, 37, 70, 97, 100, 104, 105, 113, 139, 147
  Verde Sucker, 97
Fish Story, 103
Fishback, R. W., 49, 52, 282
Fisher
  Chas. F., 159
  Jerry, 5
Fisher Stage Lines, 228
Flagstaff, 9, 10, 40, 41, 42, 44, 48, 49, 50, 52, 53, 54, 55, 56, 57, 59, 62, 72, 73, 74, 82, 84, 85, 87, 102, 103, 105, 107, 108, 112, 113, 120, 142, 143, 145, 150, 151, 152, 166, 170, 172, 178, 179, 180, 186, 189, 190, 193, 197, 199, 204, 205, 211, 214, 216, 217, 218, 224, 229, 231, 232, 233, 238, 239, 240, 241, 242, 244, 245, 246, 247, 260, 261, 270, 275, 281, 282, 283, 284
Florence, Arizona, 120, 279, 280
Food Prices, 241, 271
Foods
  Bacon, 210, 222, 278, 286
  Beans, 39, 79, 82, 193, 202, 257, 278
  Bear Meet, 109
  Beef, 62, 109, 137, 214
  Berries, 40
  Biscuits (biskits), 151, 200, 210
  Bread, 195, 214, 219, 222, 223
  Butter, 162, 222, 223
  Cabbage, 109
  Carrots, 109
  Chicken, 107, 223
  Coffee, 109, 114, 137, 151, 163, 171, 173, 177, 210, 214, 219, 222, 223, 278, 286
    Arbuckle Bros, 219
    green, 109, 137, 219
  Corn, 79, 81, 82, 110, 119, 137, 163, 185, 222, 271, 275
  Cottage Cheese, 222
  Cream, 103, 222
  Eggs, 129, 163, 195, 210, 222, 223
  Flour, 82, 109, 111, 194, 195, 214, 219, 223, 278
  Fruit, 8, 10, 11, 72, 82, 86, 87, 97, 109, 111, 121, 166, 167, 173, 178, 210, 223, 230, 238, 240, 241, 242, 243, 247, 256, 257, 260, 267, 271, 281
  Grapes, 166
  Hogs, 65, 82, 109, 137
  Ice Cream, 223
  Jams & Jellies, 223
  Lettuce, 109
  Milk, 41, 86, 103, 108, 112, 121, 147, 222, 286
  Peas, 86, 109
  Pink Lemonade, 106
  Potatoes, 61, 79, 80, 81, 82, 109, 148, 149, 192
  Pumpkin, 82, 110
  Quail, 121, 203, 218, 222
  Salt Pork, 109
  Sheep, 10, 19, 25, 65, 102, 109, 150, 158, 162, 175, 258, 259
  Soda Pop, 106
  Squash, 79, 110
  Sugar, 82, 109, 137, 163, 223
  Tomatoes, 82, 241, 257
  Watermelon, 85, 256
Forest
  National, xii, 5, 37, 67, 195
    Apache, 175
    Coconino, 170, 171, 175
    Sitgraves, 175

Forts
    Apache, 175, 226, 227, 258, 260
    Lincoln, 101
    Verde, 175, 185, 189, 225, 229
    Whipple, 101, 142, 226, 258, 261
    Wingate, 228, 258
Fossil Creek, 58, 200, 251, 252, 264, 265
Foxboro (Clay Park), 187, 224
Francis
    Dan M., 150
    John W., 50, 150
    Lenore, xv, 150, 178
Franks
    Jerry, 18, 43, 45
Fredricks, Con, 62, 128
Freight Teams, 37, 38
Fry Park, 44, 49, 112
Frye, Helen Varner, 18
Fulton Spring, 84
Fenstermaker, Addie C., 229
Funston, CM., 52

## G

Gardens, 11, 39, 56, 76, 102, 146
Gardner
    Gail, xv, 91, 97, 102, 260
    J.I. (Mercantile Co.), 102
Garrett, Stella, 205
Garrison
    Ersel, 121
    Jennie, 121
Gasoline, 5, 270
Geronimo, 137
Ghosts of Cleopatra, 115, 254
Gibson
    Bessie (Cook), 256
    Billie Rae, 257
    Darlene, 256
    Frank, 256
    Lucille (Newton), 257
    Paul, 257
    Peggy (Dickison), 256
    Wade, 257
Giddings, James (Ole' Rimmy Jim), xv, 127, 216
Gilbert
    Jim, 200, 205
    Nettie, 205
Gilmore, E. A., 159
Glasgow Pitch, 244, 246, 249
Glispee, Charley, 129
Globe, Arizona, 38, 39
Gold, F. M., 9, 49, 50
Goodfellow, Mr., 265
Goodwin
    John, Judge, 147
Gosney
    E. S., 52, 158
    Mrs. E.S., 261
Goswick
    George, 175
    Giles, 265
Gowan, Mr., 265
Granite Dells, 269
Grant, Fred, 170
Grasshopper Flat Area, 37, 48, 70, 77, 96, 171, 205, 256
Graves, xvi, 101
Gray, Alice, 280
Gray, Bill, pioneer rancher's old corral, 241, 280
Grey
    Zane, 71, 120
Grief Hill, 58, 100, 101, 175, 259
Grief Hill Massacre Grounds, 101
Gristmills, 95, 119, 163, 222
Grives, Ed, 230
Groom Creek, 142

## H

Hackberry Wash, 83, 263
Hall
    Marion, 129
    Mr., 209
Hall of Golden Rule, 164
Hallermund, O. P., 18
Hamblin, Jacob, 189
Hance
    George W. (Judge), 43, 58
    Josie, 43
Hancock, Alice, 121
Harbeson
    Charles, 202
    Edna, 199
    Lulu, 199, 276

Harding, O. P., Col., 8
Harlan, Lucille (Schnebly), 74
Harrington, J. O. (Jack), 10
Hart
  Dave, 8, 15
  Delia, 77, 233, 256
  Ed, 15, 173, 245, 247
  Elmer, 43
  Frank, 79
  Fred, 3, 15, 69, 146, 212, 232
  L. E. (Dad), 5, 6, 13, 19, 186, 232, 241, 245
  Les, 43
  Lute, 43, 188
  Mrs. L. E., 186
  Sarah, 246, 247, 248
  Will, 8
Hatch, John Porter, Captain, 25
Hatz, Dan, 164, 165
Hawkins
  Charles T., 18
  Ethel, 157
  L. A., Dr., 158
  Tom, 62
Hearst, Johnny, 179
Heath, Frank, 128, 129
Heckethorn, (Old Man), 105
Heckle, Bob, 91
Hendee, Arthur, 204
Hennesey, John, 50
Hibben, H. C., 51, 53, 283
Hildebrandt, Grandma, 275
History Dept. N.A.U., 281
Hock, B., 50
Holbrook, 19, 38, 39, 44, 89, 129, 242
Hollingshead, Charley, 128
Homesteaders
  Allen, Charles, 9, 86
  Chavez, Ambrosio, xvi, 16, 19, 20, 22, 71, 173, 189, 190, 191, 271
  Chavez, Manuel, 19, 189, 190
  Cook, Henry Elmer, 256
  Farley, Joseph T., 14, 237
  Franks, Jerry, 18, 43, 45
  Gibson, Frank, 256
  Harding, O.P., Col., 8
  Howard, Jesse, 9, 55
  Huckaby, Richard, 18
  Lay, Elijah, 5, 15, 41, 185, 193
  Lee, John, 62

M. A. Carrier, Dr., xv, 42, 156, 157
Munds, Jim, 48, 71, 143, 144, 157
Nuanez, Juan, 189, 190
Nuanez, L. G., 20
Owenby, Frank, 3, 5, 13, 14, 18, 41, 42, 43, 44, 48, 60
Owenby, Ira, 16
Owenby, Roy, xv, 18, 41, 45, 46, 48, 50, 60, 212, 235
Purtymun, Frank, 3, 5, 10, 11, 12, 13, 14, 15, 18, 37, 38, 40, 41, 42, 43, 44, 48, 55, 58, 60, 62, 69, 79, 80, 81, 84, 85, 95, 102, 120, 128, 129, 149, 157, 173, 177, 180, 192, 193, 194, 195, 201, 202, 203, 229, 232, 254, 256, 257, 261, 277, 279
Schnebly, D.E., 10
Schuerman, Erwin, 17, 167, 190
Schuerman, Fritz, 19, 171
Schuerman, Henry, Jr., 168
Schuerman, Henry, Sr., 71
Thomas, John, 9, 69, 70
Thomas, Lou, 8, 55, 83
Thompson, Albert, xvi, 117, 173, 176, 177, 182, 183, 195, 210, 258
Thompson, Charley, 180, 283
Thompson, Frank, 5, 10, 15, 37, 40, 149, 192, 195
Thompson, Jim, 11, 12, 43, 47, 51, 55, 61, 68, 79, 81, 88, 117, 148, 173, 174, 195, 235
Thompson, John, 3, 21, 22
Homesteaders Armijo, Juan, 17, 19, 82, 106, 189, 194
Hopkins
  James, 265
  Mine, 83
Hopper, Maud, 202
Horn Saloon, 276
Horse Thief Stories, 145, 150, 174
HorseBack, 21, 25, 97, 117, 144, 147, 159, 186, 190, 193, 194, 197, 207, 208, 213, 214, 216, 218, 226, 237, 238, 253, 258, 261, 265, 267
Hosier
  Martha (Guthrie), 252
  Odyth, 252
  Sam, 251, 252

Those Early Days.....

Sylvia, 252
Hospitals
  Flagstaff, 37
  Jerome, 168, 267
  Prescott, 168
House Rock Valley, Arizona, 214
Houses
  Adobe, xvi
  Brick, 118
  Bunk, 72, 74
  Cabins, 3, 14, 15, 17, 121, 140
  Dugout, 9
  Log Barn, 84
  Log Cabins, 5, 10, 17, 41, 61, 80, 146, 157, 166, 194, 270
  Log House, 9, 230, 232
  Rock, 168, 233
  Tent, 10, 84
Howard
  C. S. (Bear), 9, 70, 108, 109
  General, 137
  Johnny, 108
Hoxworth, George, 50
Hubbell, Don Lorenzo, 252
Huckaby, 17, 18
  Richard, 18
Humboldt, Arizona, 83, 275
Hunt, George W.P., 279
Hurley
  Ed (The Loner), 278, 279, 280
  Pat, 60
Hutch Mountain, 258, 259

## I

Indian Gardens, 3, 4, 11, 12, 15, 21, 37, 39, 40, 53, 54, 55, 56, 57, 68, 74, 75, 79, 80, 81, 82, 83, 87, 88, 100, 102, 103, 105, 139, 143, 145, 146, 147, 149, 169, 173, 174, 176, 180, 192, 197
Indian Scouts, 101, 138
Indians, 77, 79, 88, 108, 116, 137, 166, 169, 174, 202, 209, 213, 221, 227, 228, 235, 259, 275
  Apache, 11, 260, 263
  Utes, 213
Iron King Mine, 237, 238
Irrigation, 166

Irven
  Frank (Irving), 193
  Jessie, 193
  Willie, 193
Irving, 193, 251, 252, 264, 265
Irving Power Plant, 265

## J

Jackass Flat, 45
Jackson, Stonewall, 208
Jacobs, G. Thomas, 267
James, Abraham, 3, 15, 67, 68, 69, 79
Jefferson, Thomas, 115
Jerk line, 264
Jerome
  Fire of, 159
  Hospital, 168
Jerome Junction, 12, 72, 216, 224, 266, 267
Jerome, Arizona, 1, 2, 12, 21, 22, 37, 42, 43, 49, 50, 52, 53, 60, 61, 62, 70, 72, 74, 75, 78, 79, 80, 95, 114, 115, 120, 121, 139, 140, 145, 147, 148, 149, 156, 157, 158, 159, 164, 165, 166, 168, 172, 192, 193, 210, 216, 220, 223, 224, 229, 231, 232, 237, 238, 241, 251, 254, 255, 265, 266, 267, 269, 278, 279, 281, 282
Johnson, Sol, 62
Jones, J. E., 50
Jordan
  Frank, 95
  George W., 240, 241
  Helen, xvi, 240
  Walter, 5, 10, 15, 38, 70, 85, 180
  water pump, 241, 242
Jordan Road, 39, 240

## K

Keller, C. A., 50
Ketchum, Blackjack, 145
Kidd, Robert J., 52
King
  Blan, 129
  Brothers., 128, 134, 135
  Charles, Captain, 225

John, 129, 135
Sam, 128, 132, 133, 134
Kislinbury, Harry, 50

## L

Lake
  Clear, 95, 96, 116, 151, 153, 199, 200, 202, 268, 276
  Hay, 129
  Mead, 117
  Mormon, 5, 39, 60, 70, 88, 117, 229, 230, 242, 243
  Rogers, 216, 217
  Roosevelt, 39, 119, 138, 252
  Stoneman, 85, 227, 258, 260
Lamport
  Edith, xvi, 173, 177, 231
  James A., 8, 178
Lay
  Alice, 183
  America, 185
  Dave, 13, 173, 185, 186, 237
  Elijah, 5, 15, 41, 185, 193
  Inez, xv, xvi, 156, 161, 173, 185, 187, 237
  Jack, 231
  Jane, 237
  Jennie, 185
  Joe, 45, 68, 105, 141, 160, 171, 185, 186, 187, 207, 231
  Johnny, 173
  Mary, 185
Lee, John H., 15, 17
Lewis & Clark Expedition, 116, 117
Lightening Delivery Co., 84
Lime Kiln Hill, 114
Lindahl, L. K., 18, 45
Lindsay, Jane, 157
Little Daisy Mine, 95
Little Oak Creek, 278, 280
Lonesome Valley, 83, 123, 261
Lower Oak Creek, 43, 47, 53, 69, 180, 209, 223, 238
Lower Verde Area, 47, 185, 200, 201, 259, 282
Loy
  Edward, 186
  Family, xvi
  Hattie, 142, 161
  Inez, xv, 185
  James, 50
  Jane Sennette, 161
  John, 43, 48, 49, 50, 51, 52, 144, 170, 245, 283
  Lindsay, 186
  Mary, 161
  Mrs. William, 71
  Myron, 18, 49
  Samuel, 161, 162, 163
  William, 144, 157, 161, 185, 186, 187
Luke, Frank, 120
Lyle, Martha (Mattie), 267
Lynx Creek, 261, 263
Lyons Grocery, 172

## M

Mackey, A. J., 198
Mail, 21, 62, 226, 228
Marr
  Brothers, 58, 62
  Dan, 58
  Joe, 58
Marshall, Mrs. Eva, 150
Martin
  Gideon, 208
  Hudson, 208
  Jane, 208
  Jennie, 208
  Mahallay, 208
  Margaret Ann, 208
  Nancy (Thorpe), 208
Martinez
  Alejandro, 19
  Pedro, 17
Mason
  Dick, 171
  Lodge, 8
Masonic Lodge, 210
Maxwell
  Bert, 62
  Len, 202
  Minnie, 80
McCullough, Thomas, 174
McDowell, Sylvester, 239
McGeimis, Dr., 97

Those Early Days.....

McGuireville, Arizona, 47, 226, 259
McNeil, R. W., 151, 152, 153, 154, 155
Meeker, Nathan, 213
Meredith
  Charley, 217
  Vela, 217
Mesquite, 121, 202, 222, 230
Miami, Arizona, 39
Middle Verde Arizona Area, 58, 95, 119, 163, 194, 198, 200, 211
Middle Verde cemetery, 163
Midgley Bridge, 2, 54, 56, 57, 147
Miller, 59, 76, 184
  Cecil, 60
  Frances (Bristow), 110
  Phillip, 77
  Ruth, 182, 183
  Thelma, 182
  Walter, 60
Mingus Mountain, 2, 80, 83, 144, 203, 225, 237, 266, 278
Mining
  Jerome, 95, 118, 254
  Upper Oak Creek, 11
Mission Rancho, 10, 16, 40, 55, 83
Mohave County, 117, 119
Montezuma Castle, 74, 259, 273
Montezuma Well, 2, 74, 106, 259
Mooney Trail, 112
Moore, George, 45
Mormon Camp, 39, 60, 70, 88
Mormon Camp Wash, 39, 60, 88
Motorcycle, 157
Mountains
  Black, 13, 16, 18, 41, 48, 59, 92, 94, 99, 101, 118, 143, 144, 145, 170, 172, 178, 184, 188, 201, 203, 259, 260, 262, 278
  Casner, 59, 61, 128, 161, 175
  Gray, xiii, 70
  Horse Mesa, 62
  House, 2, 59, 62, 67, 83, 93, 97, 106, 160, 170, 194, 209, 214, 281, 282
  Lee, xvi, 4, 13, 16, 17, 19, 39, 42, 44, 62, 105, 157, 171, 173, 174, 186, 214, 215, 232, 236
  Mingus, 2, 80, 83, 144, 203, 225, 237, 266, 278

Schuerman, xvi, 17, 18, 19, 43, 45, 48, 67, 71, 72, 80, 100, 145, 164, 165, 166, 167, 168, 170, 173, 210, 212, 246
Secret, 162
Sierra Ancha, 39
Sierra Prieta, 91
Sugar Loaf, 78
Table, 67, 75, 256
White Hills, 59, 178
Wilson, 2, 11, 54, 56, 57, 61, 70, 71, 79, 80, 102, 146, 147, 148, 149, 192, 243, 277
Woodie, 162
Mrs. Butler, 175
Munds, 69, 142, 143, 145
  Fern, 277
  Frances, 145
  Fred, 277
  Hattie, 144
  J. L., 69
  Jennie (Wingfield), xv, 142, 144, 145
  Jim, 48, 71, 143, 144, 157
  John, 143, 144, 145, 193
  Lena, 277
  Melvina, 143, 157
  Mrs. Jim, 48, 144
  Neal, 143
  Sally (Williams), xv, 142, 145
  Sophia, 277
  William, 48, 68, 142, 143, 145, 156, 157, 159, 193
Munds Canyon, 13, 143, 157
Munds Creek, 81
Munds Fence, 69
Munds Ferry, 209
Munds Mountain, 142, 173, 270
Munds Park, 5, 41, 42, 48, 71, 90, 118, 142, 143, 144, 145, 157, 158, 170, 173, 175, 176, 211, 224, 245, 260
Munds Trail, 43, 48, 52, 53, 143, 158, 166
Murray
  J. H., 52, 230
  Mae, 11
Museums
  Camp Verde, 100

## N

Nail
  Ben, 38
  Frank, 12, 254
National Forest
  Apache, 11, 129, 136, 138, 175, 189, 260, 263
  Coconino, xv, 4, 5, 10, 44, 52, 55, 56, 57, 146, 150, 151, 170, 171, 175, 178, 216, 217, 232, 238, 281, 282, 284
  Sitgraves, 175
Nelson Shopping Center, 3, 5, 70
New River, Arizona, 203, 229
Newman Tank, 245
Nuanez, Juan, 189, 190

## O

O'Dell, E. F., 150, 151
Oak Creek Canyon, xvii, 4, 11, 13, 37, 39, 40, 54, 56, 57, 61, 79, 80, 85, 86, 87, 88, 117, 123, 173, 206, 232, 234, 244, 261, 269, 281, 284
Old Brind, vii
Old Corral, The (poem), 122
Old Jay (J. I. Gardner), 102
Orchards, 240
Our Canyon (poem), 124
Overland Telephone Co., 172
Owenby
  Birdie, 41, 42, 44, 119
  Dorothy (Edwards), 46
  Frank, Jr., 5, 42, 43, 186
  Frank, Sr., 3, 13, 14, 41, 42, 48, 68, 72, 173
  Gail (Gayley), 43
  Getha (Michael), 46
  Ira, 43
  Lena (Schuerman), 44, 45, 46
  Nancy, 14, 42, 43
  Roy, xv, 18, 41, 42, 43, 44, 45, 46, 48, 50, 60, 212, 235, 262
Owenby Ranch, 5
Ox Yoke Spring, 225

## P

Page
  Ed, 45
  Jim, 230
Page Springs, 3, 69, 113, 223, 231
Palmer, E. Payne, Dr., 17
Palmer, Ray, 97
Pardee, Cecil W. (Doc), 216
Park
  Clay (Foxboro), 4, 62, 186, 187, 224, 245
Payson County, 150, 251
Peach, Nettie Goddard, 265
Pen cancellation, 22
Peralta, Apolonia, 190
Perkins, S. J., 159
Perkinsville, Arizona, 2, 118, 255, 266, 267
Pest House, 158
Pfau Mine, 237
Phelan, J. C., 53
Pinal, Arizona, 108
Pine Springs, Arizona, 226, 227, 228, 260
Pioneer Cattle Company, 203
Pioneer Stories of Arizona's Verde Valley, 115, 226
Pleasant Valley, 38, 39, 117, 210, 276
Pollack, T. E., 50
Post, 21, 22, 25, 38, 72, 174, 175, 198, 227, 230, 242, 282, 283
Post Office
  Schnebly, 21
Postal History, xv, 21
Postmasters
  Charley Thompson, 283
  Dickinson, Sam, 230
  Gardner, Gail, 91
  Schnebly, Dorsey E., 21
  Schnebly, Mary L., 21
  Schnebly, Theodore C., 21, 73
  Thompson, John J., 22
  Willard, George M., 22, 118
  Young, Ola, 39
Power Company, 252
Prescott, Arizona Area, 17, 46, 47, 58, 68, 69, 79, 84, 85, 89, 90, 91, 92, 95, 99, 102, 118, 119, 142, 144,

Those Early Days.....

146, 148, 149, 161, 164, 165, 168, 169, 185, 188, 199, 203, 204, 209, 216, 217, 224, 225, 226, 227, 228, 235, 237, 242, 251, 252, 254, 258, 261, 262, 264, 266, 267, 269, ☐275, 276, 277, 279
Prospector, xvi
Prosser, Jimmy, 139, 140
Pull chain, 264
Pulliam, T. E., 50, 53
Pump House, 61, 80, 83, 109, 193, 224, 232, 245
Purtymun, xv, 4, 9, 16, 37, 39, 55, 56, 80, 82, 83, 110, 111, 112, 169, 173, 177, 194, 197
   Albert, 9, 10, 11, 39, 55, 82, 193
   Albert (son), 85
   Charley, 80, 85, 112
   Clara, xv, 79, 197
   Dan, xv, 113, 169, 197
   Elsie, 85
   Emory, 108, 110
   Erma, 83
   Frank, 81
   George, 43, 192, 195
   Grandma, 108
   Grandpa, 108
   Ida, 110
   Jess, 10, 11, 16, 40, 44, 55, 56, 85, 108, 110, 173, 196
   Laura (Mcbride), xv, xvi, 84, 108, 192
   Pearl, 82
   Steven, 9
   Viola, 113
   Violet, 85
   Virgie, 83, 86
   Zola (daughter), 87
Pyle, Howard (Governor), 101

## Q

Quail, Eva (Ebbie), 202
Quinlan, L. W., 52

## R

Railroads
   Atlantic, 150, 167, 227, 244
   First Class Train, 95
   Immigrant Train, 95, 185
   Narrow Gauge, xvi, 254, 255, 267
   Pacific, 116, 150, 167, 201, 205, 227
   Pacific Electric Railway, 205
   Pea Vine, 21, 224, 254
   Prescott to Ashfork, 266
   Santa Fe, 21, 47, 72, 178, 199
   United Verde and Pacific Railway, 254
   United Verde Extension, 121, 255
   Verde Mix, 267
   Verde Tunnel and Smelter Line, 255
Ralston, 203
   Aunt Teedie, 200
   Jim, 203
   John, 45, 198, 203
Ramah, Arizona, 129
Ranches
   Ambrosio Chavez, 16, 270
   Apache Maid, 129, 136
   Bar-Z, 214, 216
   Bean House, 142
   Bullard, 19, 20, 189
   Casner, 175
   Clay Park, 186
   Cloverleaf, 198
   Crescent Moon, 15, 16, 84, 211
   Cross-L, 213, 216
   Doodlebug, 16, 43
   Double O, 213
   Dude, 267
   Dumas, 84, 173, 188, 210, 211
   Durfee goat, 262
   Farley, 5
   Flying V, 38
   George Black, 3
   Giddings, James, 216
   Hart, Ed, 245, 247
   Hart, Fred, 3, 69, 146, 212
   Hash Knife, 129
   Hearst, Johnny, 179
   Hidden Valley, 233
   Indian Gardens, 3, 68, 80, 146
   Jordan, George, 43, 61, 146
   Jordan, Walter, 10, 85
   Junipine Resort, 55, 83, 86, 169,

197
Lay, Elijah and Dave, 173
Lays, Joe and Inez, 187
Lincoln, C., 69
Long H outfit, 44
Loy, John, 170, 245
Mission Rancho, 10, 16, 40, 55, 83
Munds, 143, 158
Nunez, 19
Oak Creek, 210
OK, 17
Owenby, 18
Page Springs, 69
Pendley, 10
Pendley (Falls), 55
Purtymun, 4, 112, 197
Red Canyon, 121
Red Rock, 43
Schnebly, 89
Schneblys, 18
Schuerman, 18, 43, 71, 100, 145, 170, 210, 212, 246
Scissorilla, John, 263
Soda Springs, 288
Thomas, 55
Thompson, 4, 149
Van Deren, 5
Windmill, 37, 59, 188, 216, 217
Woods, 41, 260
XL, 18
Ranger Station
  Beaver Creek, 229
  Sedona, 170, 171
Rangers
  Baily, James, 5
  Benedict, Lewis E., 170
  Croxen, Fred W., xvi, 170
  Fisher, Jerry, 5
  McLean, 5
  Thomas, John L., 5, 67
  Thompson, Claude, 4, 5, 170, 186
  Wallace, Bill, 5
Rattlesnake Hill, 282
Rattlesnake Tanks, 41, 53, 229, 259, 260
Raymond, R. O., Dr., 44
Resorts
  Brook Haven, 88
  Call of the Canyon, 8
  Chipmunk, 8

Don Hoel's Cabin, 8
Glenwood, 9
Head Hotel, 102
Junipine Resort, 55
King's Ransom Motor Hotel, 41, 69, 79
Lolomai Lodge, 90, 113, 261
Mayhews (Oak Creek Lodge), 8, 54, 57, 70, 83, 109, 111, 261
Oak Creek Lodge (Mayhews), 8, 54, 57, 70, 83, 109, 111, 261
Pioneer Hotel, 164
Red Rock Motel, 88
Schnebly Hotel, 186
Sedona Hotel, 171, 173, 178
Sherman House, 165
Tacaloma Lodge, 4
Richards
  Bowers, 137
  Carl (, xvi, 213
  Vela, 217
Rickel, Thomas A., 52
Riordan, T. A., 52
Rivers
  Colorado, 41, 47, 68, 76, 86, 89, 108, 117, 120, 142, 208, 213, 214, 216, 227, 286
  Little Colorado, 47, 129, 151, 227, 228, 258, 260
  Salt, 39, 157, 209
  Verde, ix, xi, 2, 8, 16, 37, 41, 47, 48, 49, 50, 52, 53, 54, 56, 57, 58, 59, 88, 95, 97, 101, 105, 106, 114, 115, 117, 118, 119, 142, 144, 145, 156, 158, 159, 161, 162, 164, 167, 169, 170, 174, 178, 180, 185, 188, 198, 199, 200, 205, 209, 211, 217, 222, 226, 228, 229, 237, 251, 254, 255, 258, 259, 260, 264, 266, 267, 270, 271, 276, 277, 282, 283, 284
  Zuni, 25, 129
Roads
  Beaver Creek, 2, 4, 58, 106, 119, 129, 166, 171, 175, 207, 226, 229, 231, 258, 259, 260, 265, 267, 281
  Beaver Head, xvi, 3, 41, 47, 48, 53, 62, 96, 100, 101, 144, 165, 175,

226, 227, 228, 258, 259, 260
Big Park, 3, 4, 37, 41, 47, 62, 67, 100, 165, 171, 194, 207
Black Canyon Highway, 41, 48, 101, 118, 145, 259, 260, 262
Highway No. 179, 70, 226, 245
Highway No. 89A, 3, 54, 70, 88, 114, 147, 256, 262
Jordan, 39, 240
Munds, 53, 57, 143
Oak Creek Canyon, 88, 261, 284
Old by Virginia Finnie Webb, xvi, 281
Old Flagstaff Lower Verde Road, 48
Old Verde, 41
Rim Rock, 3, 4, 94, 282
Route 66, 47
Schnebly Hill, xvi, 2, 4, 42, 43, 48, 49, 50, 51, 53, 57, 71, 73, 89, 90, 102, 142, 143, 166, 217, 224, 244, 247, 250, 261, 281, 282, 283, 284
Van Deren, 105
Verde Cut-Off, 50, 53, 56, 283, 284
Robinson
 Jack, 16
 Johnny, 16
Rock Formations
 Bell Rock, 2, 67, 97, 100, 207, 288
 Camel Head, 91, 102
 Cathedral Rock, xiii, 67
 Church Rock, xiii, 67
 Coffee Pot Rock, 96
 Court House Butte, 67
 Court House Rock, xiii, 67, 97, 100, 166, 210
 King Herod & The Three Wise Men, 78
 Merry Go Round, 50
 Queen Victoria, 77
 Red Rock Crossing, 2, 67
 Schuerman Rock, 166
 Slide Rock, 2, 110, 266
 Steamboat Rock, 2, 54, 67, 88, 180, 240
 The Squaw & The Papooses, 77
 Thumb Butte, 92, 269
 Tiger Head, 91
Rock Springs, Arizona, 203

Rodin, Billy, 103
Rogers
 Frank, 120
 Mack, 145
Roundups, 45, 46, 125, 170, 171, 187, 212, 214, 216
Ruffner, George, 216
Rutledge, Charley (, 192

## S

Sanders, Dave, 129, 134
Schell Spring, 259
Schnebly
 Carl, 13, 96, 281
 Clara, 77
 D. E., 4, 13, 17, 43, 52
 Ellsworth, ix, xvi, 67, 72, 80, 95, 96, 229, 281
 Family, 53
 Genevieve, 74, 75, 76
 Henry, 77
 Lucille, 74
 Margaret, 77
 Pearl, 72, 74
 Sedona, 3, 73
 Theodore C., 72, 73, 273, 282, 283
Schools
 American Union Sunday, 240
 Aqua Fria, 199, 275
 Camp Verde, 277
 Clear Creek, 199, 202, 268
 Cottonwood, 232
 Country, 37
 House, 109, 111, 275
 Indian, 225
 N.A.U., 281
 Normal, 150, 199, 204, 275
 Phoenix High, 120
 Red Rock, 167, 173, 189
 Sedona, 70, 72, 173, 174, 176, 182, 196, 238
 Squaw Peak, 199, 276, 285
 Summer, 4, 109, 111, 196
 Winter, 109, 111
Schuerman
 Dorette, 168
 Erwin, 17, 167, 190
 Fred E., 17

Frieda, xvi, 164
Fritz, 19, 171
George, 164, 165
Helene, 167, 168
Henry, Jr., 168
Henry, Sr., 71
House, 165
Lena (Munds), 46, 277
Scissorilla, John, 263
Scott
  David, 119, 159, 222
  John, 128
Scouts, 269
Sedona
  Art Barn, 242
  Country, xvi
  Founded, 3
  Westerners, ii, vii, ix, xi, xii, xiii, xv, xvi, 67, 117, 142, 169, 213, 226, 251, 269, 272
Seiber, Al, 137
Seligman, Arizona, 235
Sennette, Jane, 161
Seven Springs, Arizona, 129
Sharp, John, 129, 132
Shaw, Iva Carrier, 145
Sheriff
  Dickinson, Bill, 176
  Francis, John W., 150, 151, 152
  Harrington, J.O., 10
  Hubbell, Don L., 252
  McDowell, Sylvester, 239
  Mulvenon, 150
  Munds, John, 69, 144, 145, 193
  Ruffner, George, 144, 216
  Steele, W.C., 239
  Steele, Will J., 239
Shumway, Andrew, 9, 84
Sisson
  Bill, 90
  Family, 90
  Mrs., 113, 261
Smelters
  Clarkdale, 121, 251, 255
  Clemenceau, 44, 45, 85, 251, 265
  Cottonwood, 251
  Humboldt, 83
  Jerome, 118, 255
  Miami, AZ, 39
  United Verde Copper Company, 121, 266
  UVX, 232
Smily, Captain (Major), 137
Smith, 184
  'Old Jack', 104
  Abraham L. (Link), 10, 229
  Addie (Fenstermaker), 229
  Bill, 45
  Charles Albert, xvi, 229, 232, 234
  Charley, 40
  Delia, 13, 77, 83, 84, 86, 231, 233, 256
  Ella, 231
  Grant, 229
  Ira, 10
  Jack, 104
  Jimmy, 229
  Marvin, 232
  Myrtle, 106, 254
  Nellie, 229, 230
  Roerick (Roe), 229, 230, 231, 232
  Tom, 198
Snakebite
  Medicine, 114
  Remedy, 97
Soldier Point, 171, 173
Soldiers, 70, 79, 101, 108, 169, 171, 174, 190, 208, 235, 258, 259
Spear, Frank, 14, 44, 84
Spencer Place, 55
Spring Creek, 59, 114, 142, 144, 157, 162, 220, 240
Springerville, Arizona, 44
Squaw Peak, 199, 200, 202, 203, 259, 276, 285
St. Johns, Arizona, 189, 190
Stable
  Marg's, 68, 69
  Morg's, 68, 69
Stage Station, xvi
State Fair, 175, 203
State Senator, 145
State University, 120, 144
Statehood, 22, 115, 269
Station
  Beaver Creek, 226
  Beaver Head, 41, 47, 48, 258, 259
Steele
  Minnie Farley, xvi, 237
  Ray, 238

Those Early Days.....

W.C. Steele (Will), 15, 238, 239
Will J., 239
Steele Place, 14
Stemmer, Charles C., 13
Sterling Springs, 113
Sterzing, Vic, The Old Adobe, ix, 274
Stevens, Billie, 202
Strawberry, 265
Stuinkle, Henry (Hank), 212
Summerhayes, Martha, Mrs., 260

## T

Tarr, Elwin F., 158
Taylor
  Ben, 173
  Russell, 39
Teachers
  Black, Miss, 230
  Croxen, Edith Lamport, xvi, 176, 177, 180, 183
  Dawson, Henrietta, 194
  Francis, John W., 150
  Franks, Jerry, 18, 43, 45
  Georgia Tomlinson, 186
  Hance, Josie, 43
  Maxwell, Minnie, 80
  Miller, Frances, 110
  Owenby, Birdie, 41, 42, 44, 119
  Rheubottom, Mrs., 162
  Schnebly, D. E., 10
  Schnebly, Ellsworth, ix, xvi, 67, 72, 80, 95, 96, 229, 281
  Stemmer, Charley, 186
  Thompson, Olga, 186
  Weatherford, Miss (Calloway), 202
  Wyncoop, Mrs., 234
Tempe Normal School, 120, 144
Tetzlaff, Teddy, 120
Tewkesbury-Graham Feud, 117
The Sage of Sedona (poem), 236
Thomas
  Bessie, 4, 37
  Doodie, 16
  Grandpa, 8
  Ivy (Smith), 232, 233
  John L., 8
  John L. V., 8, 9, 69, 70
  Louis H., 8
  Mrs., 261
  Ralph, 16
  Rosa, 8
Thompson
  (Jim), J. J., 11, 12, 43, 47, 51, 55, 61, 68, 79, 81, 88, 117, 148, 173, 174, 195, 235
  Albert E., ix, xv, xvi, 3, 8, 41, 46, 47, 65, 67, 88, 114, 117, 139, 140, 141, 146, 149, 160, 169, 173, 176, 177, 180, 182, 183, 188, 189, 192, 195, 207, 210, 212, 226, 235, 258
  Charles S., 180, 256, 283
  Clara, 195
  Claude, 4, 5, 170, 186
  Ed, 10
  Family, 37, 61, 74, 111, 147, 148
  Frank, 5, 10, 15, 37, 40, 149, 192, 195
  Fred, 195
  Greene, 182, 183, 192, 193, 196
  Jim, Jr., 55
  John J., 3, 21, 22
  Lewis, 186
  Margaret, 12
  Morgan, 5
  Olga, 186
  Wes, 206
Thompson's Ladder, 82, 193, 196, 197
Thorbecke, Mrs. August, 164
Thorpe, Nancy, 208
Thumb Butte, 92, 269
Thurston
  Ed, 43, 49
  Harvey, 45
Todd, F. A., 10
Tonto Basin, 39
Tonto Natural Bridge, 265
Tonto Rim, 47, 260
Trailer Park, Mac's, 87
Trails
  Crook, 260
Trees
  alders, 1
  cedar, 60, 130, 259
  cottonwood, 198, 263
  Fruit Trees, 8, 10, 11, 121, 230, 238, 257, 267, 271
  Juniper, 1

Manzanita, 4, 80, 86, 87, 111
oaks, 1
Peach, 163
pine, 162, 172, 176, 195, 229
Plum, 231
spruce, 173, 177
Sycamore, 1
Tying A Knot In The Devil's Tail (song), 91

## U

United Verde Mine, 166

## V

Vail, J. A., 50
Van Deren
　Dolly, 182, 183
　Iva, 105, 182, 183, 186
　Jimmie, 60
　Lee, 4, 13, 16, 39, 42, 44, 105, 173, 174, 186
　Lloyd, 179
　Walt, 171, 173
Vanished Arizona, 226, 260
Verde
　Hot Springs, 251
Verde Valley
　Local Option Social Club, 106
　Pioneers (book), 100
　Pioneers Association, 115
Villa
　Juan, 199
　Poncho, 199

## W

Wagner
　George O., 159
　Jim, 49
Walker
　Ed, 62
　Joe, 62
　Party of, 169
Walker, Bessie Hopkins, 265
Wallace
　Bill, 5
　Frank, 44
　Mrs. W. F., 78
Washington, George, 208
Water Company, 280
Water System
　Cottonwood, 121
　Sedona, 243
Weatherford
　Flora, 261
　J. W., 50
　Miss, 202
　Virginia, 265
Webb, Virginia Finnie, Old Roads, xvi, 258, 281
Webber
　Jake, 204
Wentworth, Mrs. M. P., 18
West Fork, 8, 54
Wet Beaver Creek, 229, 258, 260
Wheeler, 113
Whipple, Lt. A.W., 47
White
　Cecil, 18
White Flat, 178
Willard
　Alexander Hamilton, 115, 116
　Bea (Birdie), 236
　Charles D., 117, 121
　Dolph, 223
　Don, ix, xv, xvi, 1, 22, 95, 105, 115, 222, 236, 254, 278
　Donald B., The Loner, The Prospector and His Three Burros, xvi, 286
　Donna, 120
　Ellen, 118
　Frances (Munds), 143, 145
　George Mack, 22
　Jim, 62
　Joel, 117
　Jonathan, Lt., 116
　Lewis, 117, 119
　Mary, 119
　Meredyth, 120
　Minnie (Steele), 239
　Ruth, 120
　Wallace, 62, 174, 179, 180
Willard Spring, 118, 143, 144, 145, 173

Williams, Arizona, xv, 2, 142, 145, 227, 242
Williamson Valley, Arizona, 142
Wilson
   C. B., 186
   Jimmy, 145
   Richard, 71, 79, 146
Wingfield
   Clint, 145
   Frank, 202
   Hattie (Munds), 144
   Howard, xv
   Jennie (Munds), xv, 142, 145
   Minnie, 277
Wingfield Commercial Company, 137
Wingfield Saloon, 106
Wingfield Store, 263
Wingfield wagon, 58
Winslow, 47, 151, 190, 242, 252
Woman Suffrage, 145
Woodcock, Dr. Lee B., xvi, 236
Woods
   Calista A., 199, 275
   Lola, 275
Woods Spring, 48
Woolfolk, Charlie, 102, 103
Woolsy, Jim, 146

## Y

Yates
   Amos, 120
   Ruth, 120
Yavapai County, 16, 22, 52, 56, 69, 91, 144, 146, 150, 193, 210, 260, 263, 266
Yew, 60
Young, H. V., 115, 254
Yuma County, 47, 226

## Z

Zane Grey, 71, 120
Zane Grey Wash., 71

www.ingramcontent.com/pod-product-compliance
Lightning Source LLC
Chambersburg PA
CBHW070720160426
43192CB00009B/1262